£35 —

D1196362

Information
and the Arab Cause

LIBRARY
ALMA COLLEGE
ALMA, MICHIGAN

The author (*right*) with President Sadat

Information
and the Arab Cause

M. Abdel-Kader Hatem
Deputy Prime Minister of Egypt

LONGMAN GROUP LTD
London

Associated companies, branches and representatives throughout the world

© Longman Group Ltd 1974

All rights reserved. No part of this publication may be reproduced, stored in a retrieval system, or transmitted in any form or by any means, electronic, mechanical, photocopying, recording or otherwise, without the prior permission of the Copyright owner.

First published 1974

ISBN 0 582 78040 3

Printed in Great Britain by
W & J Mackay Limited, Chatham

Dedication
To all seekers after truth everywhere

Acknowledgements

I should like to acknowledge the great assistance that I have received from my publishers, Longman Group Limited.

My particular thanks are due to Mr Roger Stacey, managing director of the Longman Arab World Division; to Mr Alan Gilchrist, who has added valuable and detailed comment; and, above all, to Mr Robert Coombs, who has worked so hard and capably on the editing of the book.

To those gentlemen, and to all their colleagues, I am deeply indebted.

The Author

Contents

Contents

Foreword

by John Bulloch

The first news of the outbreak of the 1973 war in the Middle East was given to a startled world in terse communiqués broadcast by Cairo and Damascus radios a few minutes after hostilities had actually begun. In unemotional tones, the announcers described the Egyptian crossings of the Suez Canal, and the beginnings of the Syrian drive into the occupied Golan Heights, then immediately went on to warn their listeners of possible air raids on Egyptian and Syrian cities, and to detail precautions to be taken.

Those first broadcasts of the war set the pattern for all that followed, and were clear examples of some of the lessons set out by Dr Hatem in these pages—the need for swift and accurate information coupled with preparation for the future. They also did much to help the Arab side win "the information war" in 1973 as decisively as they had lost it in 1967.

For it was clear within hours of the outbreak of fighting that this time the communiqués issued in Cairo were telling the truth, and in their factual simplicity were in marked contrast to the rather hysterical commentaries being broadcast from Israel, where commentators threatened "to turn (the Arabs') nights into days", or "to crush their bones". An early indication of the new Egyptian approach was given when Cairo radio reported "eleven Israeli aircraft shot down for the loss of ten of our own". That is something which would never have been said in 1967.

There were, of course, lapses from total accuracy, and at times certain details had to be suppressed in the interests of military security. But censorship of correspondents' dispatches from Cairo was kept to a minimum, and as soon as practicable, journalists were permitted visits to the battle fronts. All these things represented a considerable change from 1967.

It is clear from Dr Hatem's book that, as the Minister responsible for Information in the Egyptian Cabinet, the vast improvement noted resulted from a deliberate policy which he had laid down. After more than twenty years' experience of the organization and running of Information Services, he had formed his own theories, based on a practical grasp of the different factors involved, and ensured that they were put into effect in Egypt.

Dr Hatem drew on the mistakes of the past to ensure the successes of 1973. As he notes, the Egyptian Government imposed little censorship in 1956, but by 1967 seemed to have lost its touch, so that "irresponsible bombast did duty for calculated information responses to Israeli provocation." He has also grasped the essential point that the public "does not react to the world as it is, but as it is convincingly reported to be." In 1973 the lessons had been learnt by those engaged in the Egyptian Information Service; and the view taken by some about there having been one major failure—to grasp the seriousness of the Israeli crossing to the West bank of the canal—concerned a failure of military appreciation, not of dissemination of facts.

While Dr Hatem's book is primarily for specialists by a specialist, it will be of wider interest to all students of Middle East affairs, as he has been at the centre of affairs in Egypt for so long, and has fortunately included accounts of some of the major events since the Free Officers' movement in 1952 set a feudal, decadent and poverty-stricken country on the path to dignity, self-sufficiency and a leading role in world affairs.

Information and the Arab Cause shows how Egypt learnt the lessons not only of the 1967 conflict, but also of the periods of truce between the Middle East wars, when Israel was winning friends all over the world by its skilful manipulation of the information media. As the man largely responsible for countering that campaign, Dr Hatem was in a unique position to draw up a blue-print for the use of other countries, not only Arab, who find themselves in a similar position. He has done so extremely effectively.

John Bulloch
Middle East Correspondent
The Daily Telegraph

Preface

Industrial man's insatiable appetite for fuel energy has focused attention on the wealth of the Arab World. Notwithstanding this source of revenue enjoyed by a number of Arab states, the region as a whole has till very recently suffered from a prolonged lack of understanding of its true character and its reasonable interests. In this sense the Arab World was perhaps not exceptional, though it is fair to say that it bore more than its share of misconceptions until the outside world became generally aware of its key position both as a provider of oil, and, in the context of Palestine, as an element indispensable to international peace. It has become obvious that a correlation exists between, on the one hand, knowledge of the affairs of the Arab World *per se* and, on the other hand, an appreciation of the ways in which attitudes and opinions are first created and then expressed. Proper understanding of the region presupposes some familiarity with the methods and capabilities of the modern media.

For these reasons it seemed to me that any review of the changing impact of information on Arab fortunes must be preceded by an examination of the properties of the various means of attitude formation, and by some discussion of the concept of public opinion. It is manifestly impossible to offer definite conclusions about these subjects, which are vast. For all that has been written about them, the characteristics of information and of public opinion have suffered from a dearth of understanding, which has been no less real than the misconceptions vitiating particular national and international issues. Within the pages of a single book all one can hope to do is to point to those sociological factors which have a bearing on the Arab World.

Our examination of these factors, which I have entitled *Characteristics of Information*, forms Part One of this book.

From this aspect of our subject we shall pass in Part Two—*The Arab Cause*—to an examination of the problems of the region, with particular reference to the events of the era beginning with the Egyptian revolution of 1952. We conclude our study at the opening of the peace talks in Geneva on 21 December 1973. It may be felt that I have concentrated excessively on the part played by Egypt. In justification I would point out that developments over the past generation have underlined the key role played by my country in shaping the characteristics of the present situation. Also, that for much of the period I have had the privilege of being closely associated with Egypt's Information Services, and that I can therefore perhaps claim to write at first hand about this aspect of the subject in ways in which it would be impossible for me to do about its other facets. I can only hope that, in conjunction with similar books written from the viewpoints of other countries in the region, this work may contribute to a genuine international understanding of the totality of a problem now widely regarded as critical in terms of world peace.

PART ONE
Characteristics of Information

I
Introductory

To go back no further, each generation this century has had cause to believe that at a global level it faced problems of unprecedented magnitude. Few would deny that the world today is passing through one of the most critical phases of its history. Its technological achievement continues to expand at a rate apparently far in excess of the adaptive capacity of governments, let alone of individuals. In this book we have to bear in mind, on the one hand, the advances of the means of war and destruction, and, on the other hand, those of material well-being and comfort. Among all these means we are primarily concerned with what are generally termed *communications*, in regard both to transport and more particularly to the dissemination and exchange of *information*, in other words with the so-called *mass media*.

With sophisticated instruments to call on, man possesses the capability for a measure of stability, security and peace, with their attendant prosperity and progress; he also has the capability for upheavals, suspicion, and war, with their attendant misery, backwardness and death. For all that is said about the increasing tendency of machines to rule men's lives, these instruments are in the final analysis neutral. The use to which they are put depends on man, his understanding of them, his willingness or otherwise to employ them for good or ill. Human response to the challenge must more than ever before depend on an ability and an inclination rapidly to modify instinctive and traditional reactions to events and situations. Moreover, increasingly the human response has to be reached by, or at any rate acquiesced in by, large masses of people, even though the detailed formulation of the response may be assigned to officials and experts. The day is long past, if indeed it ever existed, when governments or a privileged few were free to take major domestic or international decisions untroubled by considerations of the reaction of their peoples. Now more than ever before the course of events depends upon the collective reactions of large publics, which to an ever greater extent have come to transcend the frontiers of the sovereign state.

The development of mass publics, as we know them today, originated in the decline of the relatively static society of mediaeval times and the rise of national consciousness. Paradoxically, this resulted simultaneously in both a widening and a contracting of psychological horizons. On the one hand, the new nationalisms of Western Europe tended to reject the wider unities of a common religion, a common system of land tenure and, among a section of their populations, a common language, which had prevailed under feudalism. On the other hand, they gradually imposed a consciousness of belonging to a unit greater than that of the old seigniorial domain or province. In other words, the group basis of collective opinion tended to become bigger, but as it grew it found itself aligned against equivalent though often hostile groups elsewhere in the form of other sovereign states. At this stage there was nothing democratic about the formulation of a public reaction to events. The creation of the national state was accompanied by an immense strengthening of the central government, and often of the person of the monarch himself, an inevitable process because the reversal of the centrifugal tendencies of feudalism could only be achieved by a strong and united government, which in the conditions of the time implied a concentration of power in the hands of a single individual, a Henry VIII of England or a Louis XIV of France. As the basis of the nation solidified, and especially with the rise of industrialism, the dominance of the monarch was challenged, eventually to be replaced by the dominance of a class. Government, though, remained restricted in membership, and mass participation in its processes was still far off. Public opinion was moulded by the dominant socio-political group, and tended to manifest itself in the context of issues susceptible to mass comprehension, not to say over-simplification. It could hardly have been otherwise in an age of overwhelming illiteracy. As a result, mass

4

opinion often expressed itself in demonstrations of hostility towards other countries, and was formed on the basis of such information as the government of the day, with its limited communications media, was willing and able to disseminate.

For most of the world it was not until the present century that the situation changed. The introduction of compulsory education in some countries and the increase of literacy in most, coupled with the revolutionary technical advances in the transmission of information, ideas and comment, mean that it is no longer possible to confine the expression of public opinion to the rare occasion of some especially emotive issue. Public opinion has become more obviously continuous, and the number of topics on which the public may have an opinion has greatly increased. One has only to reflect on the widespread topicality of the concept of *the quality of life*, and on the common currency of words such as *ecology* and *pollution*—concepts which would have been regarded as recondite even a decade ago—to appreciate just how far we have come.

In parallel there is another development of momentous consequence. To a degree it works against the circumscription of public opinion within a purely national context, which as we saw was one of the consequences of the passing of feudalism. Over roughly the past two hundred years movements have arisen in support of an identity of interest transcending national frontiers. Early examples were the liberal and even democratic ideals which stemmed from the American and French Revolutions, though admittedly their implementation often went hand in hand with a growing and sometimes belligerent nationalism, as in the cases of Germany and Italy. Next, and originating in the conditions of industrial change, the various forms of socialism displayed an international character, which to a greater or lesser extent the socialist parties in different countries retained until the outbreak of the First World War, at which point most social democrats placed their patriotic loyalties above their internationalism. Although the latter ideal survived somewhat longer in Russia, it was in the twenties and thirties largely eroded by Stalin's policy of "socialism in one country", and during the Second World War became submerged by the imperatives of the patriotic struggle against Nazi Germany. Since 1945 it has been

transmuted in a different sort of supra-national grouping, and has found
expression in organizations such as Comecon and the Warsaw Pact.
In response to or in parallel with this, we now see a number of other
regional groupings: the military organizations of NATO and
SEATO, the Common Market, the RCD of Turkey, Iran and
Pakistan, the Organization of African Unity, and the various concepts of the "Arab World", the "Third World", and the "West".
The units of loyalty and hence of an important facet of public opinion
are becoming larger, though still less than global. While causes of
possible hostility between one sovereign state and another are thereby
reduced, the possibility of inter-group friction remains and in some
cases may even increase. The sheer size of the units, coupled with the
immense growth of the destructive power of the weapons of war
and with the administrative and financial capabilities of governments
and regional group organizations in mobilizing these resources,
imposes on all a duty of greater vigilance over the control of possible
causes of hostility between the regional and other blocs involved.

Short of the attainment of an effective system of world government, the vital responsibility for removing these potentially destructive factors, or at any rate for keeping them in check, must rest with
individual national governments. In this connection public opinion
can be a key factor for good or ill. In any case, as we have already
indicated, public opinion today is involved in such a comprehensive
range of matters, affecting the life and well-being of both the state
and the individual, that it is manifestly impossible for a government
totally to ignore it. But to what extent is public opinion a free agent?
We shall have more to say of the constituents of public opinion in the
chapters that follow. For the moment suffice it to say that public
opinion can be only as good, or as bad, a guide to governmental
action as the reliability of the material which goes into its making.
Essentially the material may be termed *information*.

Ideally the perfect public opinion would be one based on a society
endowed with the highest analytical qualities, possessed of and
capable of assimilating all the relevant data on a given issue, and
capable of accurately forecasting eventual consequences, not only
on the immediate issue, but also on related issues both at home and
abroad. But publics are not like that, and, as far as one may foresee,

they never will be. However intelligent, and however well and honestly instructed, they will remain susceptible to illogical emotions based on personal, family or group experience, and on the manner in which information is presented, including the personality of the presenter and a host of possible nuances and emphases intentional or not. Nor is it humanly possible for the presenter to know and hand on every last item of possible information with a bearing on a particular issue. However dedicated and honest they may be, and however they may abhor the deliberate falsification of news or fact, the controllers of the information media, whether a government or some other group of individuals, can never hope to present all the relevant data. To the extent that failure to tell the whole truth represents some falsification of the entire body of fact, and that the item unwittingly omitted could with hindsight be seen as crucial, all information is inadequate, and in consequence all opinion based on it is bound to be imperfect.

Unintentional omission is one thing, deliberate falsification, in the generally accepted sense of the word, is quite another and incalculably more serious, not to say sinister. Much news and information disseminated for the purpose of moulding opinion has in the past been, and probably continues to be, in an intermediate position between these two extremes. The presenter, whether acting on behalf of a government or other public body, or on behalf of a private undertaking, as for example a professional advertising executive, may well be concerned with persuasion. The organization which he represents may be honestly convinced on the basis of available facts that a particular course of action, or a particular product, is in the best interests of the the public. From its point of view, therefore, no question of misrepresentation arises from the dissemination of the facts and arguments in support of its case and from the omission of the countervailing arguments, of which indeed it could well be ignorant. This is probably the case with much propaganda, which, in its over-simplification and excessive enthusiasm, may be faulted on the score of insufficient research into particular issues, rather than on that of an intention to defraud or mislead. The solution is not easy. It lies in the creation of a climate of opinion which will demand full information on important matters, and which, while stopping short of obstruction when urgent action is clearly called for, will nevertheless exercise its critical faculties. Such a climate cannot depend exclusively on governmental media, and must increasingly rely on international information services, which in time may come to complement the national. The development is bound to be slow, conflicting as it does with deeply entrenched habits and attitudes. But it is essential in this contracting world, where individual countries and supra-national blocs are evermore dependent on one another, and where a truly international habit of thought may be the only means of avoiding an acceleration of the crises in inter-state relations with which this generation is already too familiar.

If an incentive towards international attitudes is needed in the case of publics exposed to inadequate though not deliberately dishonest information from their governments, how much more vital is it for those living under régimes which are in no way inhibited about the falsification of fact or interpretation? The present century provides many examples of the evils of which such régimes are capable, and it is probably true to say that the current connotation of the word *propaganda* derives from the particular use made of this instrument by Josef Goebbels in Nazi Germany. Before condemning out of hand all governments which have occasionally been less than truthful, however, it is as well to remember the pressures to which they are sometimes exposed. The prevailing patriotic, not to say overtly nationalistic, sentiments among the publics of many countries over the past hundred years or so can hardly have disposed them to a careful study of the facts of any dispute with their neighbours. Until the last few decades war was habitually regarded as "glorious", publics were quick to detect slights on the national honour, and in the absence of overwhelming evidence to the contrary—and not always even then—the popular reaction to a difference with another sovereign state was one of "my country right or wrong". In an earlier age, when the monarch and his immediate advisers possessed exclusive power, this might not have mattered. But with the growing importance of public opinion, governments, even in non-democratic states, could no longer afford to flout prevailing popular sentiments. In the case of true democracies, the dilemma could be resolved by the

8

normal democratic procedures involving the press, open discussion, and the deliberations of the national assembly or parliament, processes which helped to ensure against the taking of precipitate and irreparable measures towards a foreign country. Elsewhere, however, members of the ruling class or party needed to retain popular support but were unwilling to admit the public to democratic participation in government. This inclined them towards spectacular actions not susceptible to the sort of minute examination likely to result from prolonged public discussion. The advantage from their point of view was that they could represent themselves as the embodiment of the public will, especially of its more belligerently patriotic aspects, and thus endow their intrinsically undemocratic power base with the semblance of popular support. In seeking to entrench their position by this genre of populism, they were attracted to any instrument which demagogy and xenophobia could provide. Furthermore, in some cases the prospect of a spectacular foreign policy, even at the risk of war, was alluring as a means of diverting public attention from the régime's domestic shortcomings; the activities of the Nazi government in Germany between 1933 and 1939 provide ample evidence of this sort of motivation.

The existence of public opinion, therefore, is a fact with which increasingly over at least the past two hundred years governments have had to learn to live. The future security of mankind demands that, recognizing this fact, governments accept a responsibility to divert national opinion away from attitudes inimical to good international relations, and further so to educate opinion that in its turn the public becomes capable of exerting sufficient pressure against any succeeding government inclined to espouse policies contrary to the interests of world peace and harmony.

The need for a deliberate and urgent policy of education in internationalism becomes starkly apparent when we realize that the expenditure for war and destruction exceeds by far that earmarked for peace and development. The world spends more on weapons alone than on education or public health. For instance, in 1968 the countries of the world together spent $153,498 million on armaments, a sum greater by 40 per cent than the total sums spent by all the nations together on education and more than three times the total expenditure on public health.[1] This means that the world devotes 7–8 per cent of its total income to the cause of war, an amount corresponding to the total income of one billion people in, say, Latin America, South-East Asia and the Middle East. This state of affairs is bound to prevail so long as the world does not succeed in removing the ever-present threat of upheavals and war.

During the whole of last century and the first forty years of this one, the efforts to attain peace were largely negative. That is because, following in the wake of wars, they were not preventive but merely attempted disarmament without grappling with the roots and causes of the problem.

Hence, attempted solutions served as palliatives only. Despite the creation of the League of Nations in 1919, this negative approach underwent no real change until after the Second World War, when the nations which had suffered the anguish of war began to think of means of banishing its very concept from the minds of people. This thinking crystallized far enough to be included in the preamble of UNESCO's constitution, which states that: "Ignorance of each other's ways and lives has been a common cause, throughout the history of mankind, of that suspicion and mistrust between the peoples of the world through which their differences have all too often broken into war."

Thus, the nations of the world have at last realized that the ideal means of overcoming wars is to strike at the will to make war and at its psychological origins; that is, to reach out for the mind of man through information, propaganda, education and upbringing for the cause of peace.

However, this approach has not yet become positive enough, since, no matter how desirable, it still remains to a great extent a voluntary effort. Again, the world must overcome the collective root causes of war: the absence of international justice between peoples, the spread of aggression and of imperialism in its multitudinous forms, and the gross disparity between such nations as have almost everything and those that have almost nothing. The gulf between rich and poor is as decisive a factor of insecurity and instability between the nations as it is between the sons of one same

[1] Cf. *UNESCO Courier*, November 1970.

nation. Notwithstanding the decline of certain facets of conventional imperialism in the sixties, brought about by the emergence of many newly-independent nations, the residues of aggression and other forms of colonialism still survive in parts of the world.

So far the call for peace has been merely emotive and through individual choice, whereas necessity dictates that the emotive impulse become a rational conviction and the individual choice a collective commitment. Information must play a preponderant role in that respect. Security is closer to attainment when information, and propaganda as well, preach that mankind is called upon to live in peace and brotherhood, regardless of different political, economic and social systems, of customs and modes of thinking. Peace and security become more attainable when information and propaganda preach that people are accountable not only for their kin, friends and compatriots, but also for the mass of humanity everywhere, for the kinship of a shared destiny.

In order to achieve these aims, information and propaganda should strive for international understanding, and to deepen the elements which enable cultures and civilizations to broaden the spirit of comprehension, teaching men to appreciate their human worth while stressing the merit of values, aspirations and needs common to the lives of all the peoples of the world.

Information and propaganda must also seek to impress upon peoples that human knowledge is the result of a common endeavour to which all the peoples of the world have contributed, that all cultures have drawn upon other interacting cultures and will continue to do so. Culture has one boundless homeland: the world. Our own Arab civilization, for instance, gave the world eternal values and principles, inasmuch as it fused with former civilizations. Not surprisingly, therefore, it still continues to avail itself of cultures consonant with its values and traditions, while interacting with others from both East and West, satisfying its needs without losing sight of its own unique and distinct personality.

Again, information and propaganda should expound the rights of man by stressing the inherent equality of people, regardless of race, sex, colour, language, creed, ideology or social status. They must reaffirm the equality of rights between nations large and small, as well as the right of each to the full development of its spiritual and material resources.

This is in addition to lauding the efforts which consolidate international solidarity and understanding, and to projecting the necessity of solving international problems through peaceful means without exposing world peace to danger.

Similarly, information and propaganda should strive, in our present age when the scientific and technological revolution has such achievements to its credit, to impress upon peoples that our world has become infinitely smaller, because the advanced means of mass public contact have in a sense abolished geographical borders and barriers between them. Hence, all the nations of the world must open up before each other, furthering increased understanding, and thereby increased co-operation. It is the closed borders of the past that have led to the closed mentalities, laying deposits of misunderstanding which hindered world harmony, resulting in strife and crises, and often in the outbreak of war.

Information and propaganda should also point out that patriotic tendencies need not conflict with internationalism. For the independence and sovereignty of no nation will be permanently assured except under the aegis of one world, united and safe from the threat of wars. Nor can the search for wealth, prosperity and affluence be justifiably realized save only within one secure world, free of the deprivation and want which lead to senseless, destructive wars.

Indeed, information and propaganda should strive to impress upon peoples that the best way of bringing the larger nations to halt their megalomaniac tussle for world supremacy is not merely to condemn them, nor to tax them with imperialist and expansionist greed, nor even to boycott them as a passive means of protest, but rather for the nations to make a solid, united stand against imperialism and expansionism.

It follows, therefore, that information and propaganda must reflect the same idealistic philosophy which gave birth to the United Nations, and must expound the roles of the UN specialized agencies, particularly those which work for the common good in the fields of information, education, health, welfare, technical assistance, ecological preservation, youth and the protection of the rights of man. Here again, it should be stressed by these two media that the United Nations Charter may best be put into effect, not by decrying its shortcomings, but by creating a strong and well-knit public opinion striving fervently towards peace. Hence, it will be incumbent upon all nations to respect this Charter and to avoid infringing it for whatever reason.

In this way, information and propaganda can realize, by practical application, the import of the preamble to the UNESCO Constitution which states that UNESCO has been created "for the purpose of advancing, through the educational and scientific and cultural relations of the peoples of the world, the objectives of international peace and of the common welfare of mankind for which the United Nations Organization was established and which its Charter proclaims."

The aggressive tendencies that lead to war originate in the mind of man, and hence are affected by environmental and circumstantial factors that may activate it to an aggressive impetus towards war, or may sublimate it into a counterforce tending towards peace. Thus, if it were possible to strike at the psychological source of warfare—within the mind of man—it would be possible to control and deactivate it, notwithstanding the causal factors. Herein may be found the vast magic power wielded by information and propaganda for the sake of peace.

From the late eighteenth century, through the nineteenth, down to the middle of the twentieth,—from the Napoleonic Wars to the Second World War—all major conflicts were followed in time by active rearmament. Either the conquered nations sought revenge, or the victors realigned themselves into new power groupings. Excessive rearmament invariably led to another war. Hence the frequent international conferences attempting to impose limits on rearmament, to achieve disarmament, or to establish international arms control. Sadly, these efforts were in the long run abortive, in face of war propaganda and rearmament. It is these which create the will to go to war.

The task ahead calls for nothing less than the permanent repudiation by the overwhelming proportion of mankind of the prejudices and divisive attitudes of the past, attitudes which, as we have seen, were at times exploited by particular governments for their own purposes, and others of which developed from age-old distrusts to become mere automatic reflexes. The task implies a recognition, both subjective and intellectual, of the truth that peace and harmony among the nations and among the existing regional groupings and power blocs are just as much in the common interest as is the maintenance of public order among neighbours in the same village or town. In other words, the recognition of the overwhelmingly greater importance of the identity of interest of all mankind, as opposed to the social, political, economic and cultural differences, some of them relatively minor or temporary, which appear to set one group apart from another. Specifically, and in relation to the problems of today, the new attitude includes a desire to foster true international justice and the basic rights of man. Equally, it requires us to combat the evils of ignorance, prejudice, aggression, imperialism, surviving colonialism and the gross disparities of wealth between nations. It does not demand any rejection of honourable national loyalty or patriotism, but enjoins us to regard these qualities as parts of a greater loyalty to mankind as a whole, and to acknowledge our common world heritage as being enriched by the cultural diversity of the constituent parts. The development of an international consensus in favour of peace and harmony cannot take place in isolation. In practical terms the international bodies capable of disseminating effective propaganda to these ends must have the willing co-operation of all the nations and supra-national groupings. Consequently, the creation of the desired international climate must accurately reflect parallel desires and attitudes at the national and regional levels.

Within the confines of one short book, it is scarcely feasible to particularize the development of a proper international response to each of the major issues which contain perils for the future of mankind. Any attempt along those lines could all too easily produce a book of such resounding superficiality as to be useless, or, insofar as it postulated a measure of over-simplification, worse than useless. The present author, therefore, believes that he can best hope to make a positive contribution to the species of internationalism here adumbrated by confining himself to Egypt in particular and the Arab World in general, a region with whose information services he has been intimately connected over the past twenty years. Accordingly, the discussion of the character and dissemination of information needed for the encouragement of international peace and harmony will be conducted in the context of the Arab-Israeli conflict. That conflict is essentially global in its repercussions. It is therefore submitted that the discussion, albeit limited in territorial terms, will inevitably touch on most of the fundamental considerations which must feature in any assessment of global relationships in their totality. Indeed so crucial a factor is the present confrontation in the Middle East that it is hardly too much to claim that the experience which would be gained from its successful resolution would be of enormous and enduring benefit for the future of mankind as a whole.

In Part Two, therefore, we shall discuss major developments in attitudes involving the Arab World, that is to say in the attitudes of others towards the Arab World and of attitudes within the region itself. We shall consider the manner in which the mass media have been harnessed to both the Arab and the Zionist causes, especially in the crises of 1948, 1956, 1967 and 1973. Finally, we shall examine the prospects as they appear in late December 1973 for an acceptable and peaceful solution to the troubles of the region, a solution which, if attainable, will, as already indicated, confer upon mankind immeasurable advantages towards an equally beneficent solution to the other international problems of today and tomorrow. Before embarking on these subjects, we must in the remaining chapters of Part One look more closely at the conceptual characteristics of public opinion and of information, at the fundamental formative elements of public opinion, and at the means by which it is influenced for good or ill by particular species of information, notably by public relations and propaganda.

2
The Concept of Public Opinion

(a) Past attitudes to public opinion

On local, national and international planes, public opinion determines the forms of behaviour adopted by the community. Very early, man grasped the nature of public opinion and elaborated methods to influence others in order to realize his own objectives. Yet, throughout history this concept has been in a state of transformation. If we look through the definitions and concepts of public opinion elaborated by sociological theorists, political scientists and social psychologists, we find little agreement among them on the exact meaning of the term, though it has been used in various contexts by all these researchers. At one time it was used in reference to prevalent beliefs, climate of opinion, consensus, and the more settled convictions of a group. At other times, it referred to the process of developing opinions, as distinct from the end product. It was also used to denote statements which are the result of a reasoned logical process, in contrast with those which have been arrived at by illogical or emotive means.

In this chapter, however, we shall not attempt to present a historical résumé of the various meanings that commentators of differing schools of thought and of different periods have ascribed to this term. We shall rather consider only a few instances of older, unconscious attempts which have revealed a partial understanding of the concept of public opinion. These will be followed by a review of some of the more important and popular contemporary meanings and definitions.

The term *public opinion* was not used in our sense until the eighteenth century, when large *publics* came into existence due to the rapidly increasing population. However, older discussions of public opinion do not differ much from modern writings in estimating the influence which popular opinions exert upon the actions and daily life of man. The only difference which distinguishes the older discussions from the more recent writings relates to awareness of the extent of the influence which public opinion has or should have on the actions of statesmen and philosophers.[1]

In primitive societies, innovations and unusual occurrences seem to have been dealt with by the application of the customary rules, mores and beliefs, rather than by discussion and the conscious formation of opinion. The existence of communities did not necessarily mean the existence of public opinion, if by that term we mean speculative views held by the mass of the people with the aim of introducing alterations or improvements into the prevailing institutions. This is attributed to the fact that members of these communities were influenced by habits rather than by thoughts.[2] But there were large and distinct variations among primitive societies, and scholars and researchers are now more cautious about their generalizations on primitive peoples than were those of a century ago. Since 1900, ethnologists have elaborated extremely varied descriptions of social organization among primitive peoples. Margaret Mead, for instance, has illustrated three types of primitive community on the basis of opportunities available to the individual to express his opinion.[3] Although there may have been no public opinion, in any contemporarily accepted sense, there were distinctions in the range of personal opinion expression. Whatever system existed, the individual was held within the limits and restrictions of traditional expression. In any case it would be misleading to speak in terms of influencing the masses. The sort of tribal organization of which Margaret Mead wrote was small enough for a consensus of opinion to arise without external influence, and to do so within forms accepted by all. This is almost a negation of propaganda, for the influences were exerted by all on all, not by any sort of oligarchy. Research specialists and

[1] Hans Speier, *The Historical Development of Public Opinion*, American Journal of Sociology.
[2] A. V. Dicey, *Law and Public Opinion in England*, Macmillan and Co. Ltd. London, 1905.
[3] Margaret Mead, "Public Opinion Mechanics Among Primitive Peoples", *Public Opinion Quarterly*, I: 3: 5–16.

students of public opinion are unanimous in believing that primitive man must have been aware of the significance of public attitudes. Hence, he must have also used them to realize his own objectives. He elaborated such techniques as totem, taboo and magic, all of which had a powerful effect upon the particular society. This is not strange, for man in the earliest times had no individual entity, but rather derived his being from belonging to a group: his tribe, clan or extended family. This fact applies equally to the leaders of those ages as to common men. Hence arose the pressing need to learn the nature of prevalent public attitudes, and the methods necessary to orientate them into desired directions.

With the invention of writing and the rise of the first civilizations, public opinion grew in significance and, consequently, the techniques for controlling and guiding it were developed. We know, for example, that the rulers of Sumer, Babylon and Assyria, despotic as they were, heeded the public to a considerable extent. These ancient empires even elaborated effective methods to frighten their enemies and rivals by representing their rulers as superhuman heroes who mocked death and feared no power, however great. They also built up the aura of their own armies as being unflinching and invincible, and their weapons as infernal machines which would hurl forth flames and destruction. Such were the methods which would influence both friends and enemy masses, and which are portrayed on the monuments left by these empires. Ancient Egyptian remains, too, manifest a conscious and profound awareness of the significance of public opinion. These monuments also indicate that the Ancient Egyptians resorted to sophisticated methods to influence minds in desired directions. For instance, the deification of the ruling Pharaoh, the consecration of priests, the erection of massive temples, pyramids and edifices, the elaboration of religious rites and the wearing of gold crowns were meant to influence public opinion and to secure power through mastery over imaginations and thoughts, though this is not to say that the leaders themselves necessarily doubted the truth of the image which they sought to project.

Although the term *public opinion* in its modern usage was not coined before the end of the eighteenth century, its rational content and concept were exhibited in the writing of the ancient Greeks and

Romans. In this connection, it would be enough to note the existence and use of such ancient Greek words as *ossa, pheme* and *nomos*, and the Latin words *fama, fama popularis, rumores* and *vox populi*. Public opinion played a leading part in Greek civilization. The government of Greek City-States—described as *democratic*—derived its power from the approval of the ruled, albeit of the non-slave minority. Consequently, there was wide scope for the exchange of opinions and for the development of the secular, rational view, as well as for rebellion against aristocracy, despotism and esoteric cults. This was conducive to an overwhelming concern with public opinion as invested with actual sovereignty, and to the decrease of the tyranny of rulers. Attention was increasingly given to the realization of the will of the people. As Rome rose to power, public opinion went through a further stage in its development and in the recognition given to its importance, especially in matters related to the affairs of governments. New words and phrases coined by Roman thinkers and philosophers, such as *vox populi* (the voice of the people) and *res publicae* (public affairs), as well as the famous slogan *S.P.Q.R.* (the Roman Senate and the Roman People), all indicated unequivocally the growth of importance attached to public opinion. As in Ancient Greece there had been such imposing thinkers and philosophers as Socrates, Plato and Aristotle, who grasped the meaning of public opinion, so, too, in Rome there appeared orators and thinkers such as Cicero, his brother Quintus, and others including especially such satirists as Juvenal, who contributed to the formation and moulding of public opinion. Quintus wrote a whole treatise on propaganda and its techniques. Roman civilization further abounded in arts and literature which had a powerful influence upon minds, imaginations and patterns of behaviour. Hand-written pamphlets were also circulated to citizens. Ancient Rome even boasted a daily press, and for four hundred consecutive years *Acta Diurna* appeared in publication.

For over five hundred years after the fall of Rome, much of Europe lay in the Dark Ages. By contrast, with the rise of Islam, Muslim philosophers and thinkers restored to public opinion the ancient importance which it enjoyed in the East. As the Middle Ages receded, public opinion in Europe also recovered its position, though its real triumph was achieved only in the fifteenth century, when Gutenberg

invented printing. Universities multiplied, scholars set about studying human behavioural sciences, literature as well as the other arts
proceeded towards a great revival. The achievement of Martin
Luther is a tremendous example of the importance of public opinion.
The wide support which he received made it possible to question
successfully the grip of religious domination. It also made possible
the elimination of obsolete and decadent customs, conventions and
values. Machiavelli's *The Prince*, a handbook for rulers, is regarded
as an important reference work on public opinion and on the leading
role it plays in the domain of politics and government. Machiavelli
speaks of *publica voce*, the voice of the people, which is no more than
the older form of today's term *public opinion*.

The seventeenth century raged with religious wars, which were
in fact aimed at the control and domination of minds. A flood of books,
pamphlets, treatises and dissertations were written by scholars of
differing religious views. Thinkers revolted against the enslavement
of the mind and the suppression of public opinion. Milton, in the
Areopagitica, called for the liberty of unlicensed printing and publication. John Locke's *Essay Concerning Human Understanding* was written
in defence of freedom of thought. William Temple wrote his famous
Essay Upon the Origin and Nature of Government, tracing the sources of
political authority and attributing it to the prevailing "opinion" as
much as to the wisdom, goodness and valour inherent in the ruler.
The newspaper was an important development which played a major
part in the consolidation of public opinion. In 1609, the first "news-
letter" appeared in Augsburg; the first English newspaper appeared
in 1622, and the first French one in 1631. The rapid development of
commerce, the rise of the middle class, the spread of literacy, all gave
increasing power to public opinion. In 1694, the Licensing Act
expired in England, and freedom of thought and of opinion was
realized for the first time in Europe.

In his *Enquiry Concerning Human Understanding*, David Hume (1711–
1776) noted that man is a social no less than a reasonable being. But
since, in order to live, man cannot be entirely social or reasonable, he
must also be an active being. Hume then asserts that a kind of life in
which both elements blend seems most suitable for the human race.
In later sections of his work, Hume holds that nothing is more free

than the imagination of man, for, although it cannot exceed the original stock of information furnished by the senses, it has an unlimited power of mixing and playing with ideas in all the varieties of fiction and vision. The mind can feign a train of events and act upon them as if they had reality. In addition to this, Hume believes that custom is the great guide of human life.

The consequences of the removal of religious, legal and other impediments to the expression of opinion were viewed with concern by some distinguished observers of human behaviour in the late eighteenth and early nineteenth centuries. Among them were men who welcomed the ideals of liberty inherent in the American and French Revolutions, but who felt genuinely disturbed by the prospect of the spread of democracy. They regarded public opinion as malleable in the hands of agitators and demagogues with the power of shaping it for purposes divisive of society and probably incompatible with the ideal of individual liberty. The mob oratory, hysteria and resultant Terror of the French Revolution, over the period 1792 to 1794, prove these fears to have been far from groundless. A few years earlier the young American nation had, almost by definition, owed its existence to the popular appeal of a certain type of liberty, yet some of its most eminent leaders displayed genuine misgivings concerning excessively democratic interpretations of the importance of public opinion. James Madison (1751–1836) delineates a two-fold concept of public opinion in *The Federalist*, distinguishing between, on the one hand, principles of social morality from which specific rights are deduced, "including the right of the majority to act so long as it remains within the framework of justice," and, on the other hand, the need for checks and balances to prevent public opinion from violating the immutable standards of justice.[4] Madison explains quite frankly his view of human motivation.

"The latent causes of faction are thus shown in the nature of man; and we see them everywhere brought into different degrees of activity, according to the different circumstances of civil society. A

[4] Francis G. Wilson, "The Federalist on Public Opinion", *Public Opinion Quarterly*, Winter 1942; Vol. VI, No. 4, p. 574. See also Henry Steele Commager's introduction to selections from *The Federalist*, New York, Appleton Century-Crofts, 1949.

zeal for different opinions concerning religion, concerning government, and many other points, as well of speculation as of practice; an attachment to different leaders ambitiously contending for preeminence and power; or to persons of other descriptions whose fortunes have been interesting to the human passions, have, in turn, divided mankind into parties, inflamed them with mutual animosity, and rendered them much more disposed to vex and oppress each other than to co-operate for their common good. So strong is this propensity of mankind to fall into mutual animosities, that where no substantial occasion presents itself, the most frivolous and fanciful distinctions have been sufficient to kindle their unfriendly passions and excite their most violent conflicts.

But the most common and durable source of factions has been the various and unequal distribution of property. Those who hold and those who are without property have always formed distinct interests in society. Those who are creditors, and those who are debtors, fall under a like category. A landed interest, a manufacturing interest, a mercantile interest, a moneyed interest, with many lesser interests, grow up of necessity in civilized nations, and divide them into different classes, actuated by different sentiments and views. The regulation of these various and interfering interests forms the principal task of modern legislation, and involves the spirit of party and faction in the necessary and ordinary operations of government."[5]

Alexander Hamilton (1757–1804) spoke contemptuously of "the imprudence of democracy where the people seldom judge or determine right." A few years before he became the second President of the United States, John Adams said: "The people of all nations are naturally divided into two sorts: the gentlemen and the simple men." The simple men, the common men, could not be expected to harbour significant opinions.

These views were honest intellectual reservations which did not grow exclusively out of economic or political self-interest. It was a period in which popular democracy was viewed with suspicion by some of the better minds among the Founding Fathers. The attitude is perhaps most succinctly illustrated in the words of Gouverneur Morris (1752–1816) who towards the end of the eighteenth century said: "The people never act from reason alone, but are the dupes of

[5] Henry Cabot Lodge (ed.) *The Federalist*, New York, G. P. Putnam & Sons 1888.

those who have more knowledge." In 1835, Alexis de Tocqueville, (1805–1859), French traveller, politician and social philosopher, published the first edition of his *Democracy in America*. Since its publication in Paris, the book received great interest and has been revised, edited and republished in a number of editions. According to James Bryce (1838–1922) in *The American Commonwealth*, de Tocqueville held that the chief weakness of the American government and people was the tyranny of the majority. Although Bryce perhaps summarized too superficially, it is clear that de Tocqueville did fear a situation in which mass public opinion ruled without permitting sufficient individual expression.

In fact men are by their nature divided into two parties: those who fear and distrust the people and who wish to concentrate all power into the higher classes; those who identify with the people, have confidence in them, and consider them the most honest and safest, although not necessarily the wisest, repository of the public interests. In every country these two parties exist and they will declare themselves. If this is still true today, the pessimism of the first group is far easier to comprehend in the conditions of the turn of the eighteenth and nineteenth centuries, when the behavioural sciences were at an early stage of development, and when the nature of majority opinion was imperfectly understood; for example it was not appreciated that the totality of public opinion represents an amalgam of attitudes held with varying degrees of intensity, and that holders of the majority view on most matters may as individuals adhere to the minority view on others. Democracy was suspect because neither opponents nor adherents appreciated certain vital ingredients of its currently accepted form, that is to say a respect for the honestly held opinions of minorities, and the need wherever possible to ensure that individuals are free to pursue customs, doctrines and patterns of living different from those of the mass, always provided these individual activities are not injurious to the interest and well being of the community as a whole. If faction and conflict are to be avoided, restraint and tolerance are just as much properties of true democracy as is the determination that the essential aspirations and beliefs of public opinion be protected from the selfish ambitions of individuals, classes or power groups.

But this is to anticipate a concept of democracy not consciously adopted till the present century. Over the remainder of the nineteenth, many students of political science were still wary of democracy. Some postulated a distinction between valid public opinion and mass opinion; others saw public opinion as a continuum rather than as the sum of accepted decisions on specific issues; yet others considered it as operating within the context of formal society as opposed to the context of more natural groupings. These varying concepts are exemplified in the thoughts of Mackinnon, Cooley and Tonnies. A century ago, W. A. Mackinnon declared:

> "Public Opinion may be said to be that sentiment on any given subject which is entertained by the best informed, most intelligent and most moral persons in the community, which is gradually spread and adopted by nearly all persons of any education or proper feeling in a civilized state."[6]

At the same time, C. H. Cooley wrote:

> "Public opinion, if we wish to see it as it is, should be regarded as an organic process, and not merely as a state of agreement about some question of the day."[7]

In 1887, Ferdinand Tonnies, at the age of thirty-two, produced his first edition of *Gemeinschaft and Gesellschaft*. From that time until his death in 1936, he enlarged upon and revised the fundamental ideas outlined in this book.

> "There are two ways of thinking," wrote Tonnies. "The first is in terms of Gemeinschaft, not subject to exact translation but called 'community' for convenience; the second is in terms of Gesellschaft, equally difficult to translate but spoken of as 'society' for ease in handling. When the natural will predominates, association is of the 'community' type; but when the rational will leads, the form is of the 'society' type.
>
> "There are many types of 'community' and 'society' relationships. Neither is known in a pure form, but there always is a tendency towards one type or the other. In the Middle Ages, for instance, there

[6] W. Mackinnon, *On the Rise, Progress and Present State of Public Opinion*, p.15.
[7] C. H. Cooley, *Social Organisation*, Charles Scribner's Sons, New York 1909, pp. 123–124.

was simple family life, folk living, and paternalism; now, there is an atomization of the social structure, mobility and the dog-eat-dog calculations of business. 'Community' periods are characterized by concord in family life, folkways and mores, and religion; 'society' periods are noted for convention as a way of ordering personal affairs, legislation for national life, and public opinion for cosmopolitan life."[8]

Tonnies described our life today in part as follows:

"The forms of rational will set the individual as giving and receiving against the whole of nature. Man tries to control nature and to receive from it more than he himself is giving. But within nature he is confronted with another rational will which aspires to the same, i.e., with another individual who is to gain by his losses . . . In every regard the capable man of Gesellschaft, whether he considers himself free master of his wealth or master only of his labour power and other capabilities, is always ambitious and calculating, accepting opinions critically and using them to his advantage."[9]

One of the principal functions of public opinion in a 'society' organization, states Tonnies, is to reduce the morality of that form of life to rules and formulae. It is as easy for public opinion to seek despotic powers against the lower classes as to demand freedom for the upper classes. The press is the real instrument of public opinion, "weapon and tool in the hands of those who know how to use it and have it to use."[10] In community, or Gemeinschaft, there are popular beliefs, which are to be sharply distinguished from the social judgements to be referred to as public opinion. Public opinion, in this sense, deals with those topics which are controversial and discussible in the societies concerned, and not with those aspects of mind-life which are comparatively fixed.

Similarly, the end of the nineteenth century begot the thoughts of the sociologist Gustave LeBon, who was one of the first to appraise masses of people in a modern sense. He held that in the collective

[8] Ferdinand Tonnies, *Fundamental Concepts of Sociology*, New York, American Book Co., 1940, pp. 270–271. Translated and supplemented by Charles P. Loomis.
[9] *Ibid.*, pp. 161, 192–193.
[10] *Ibid.*, p. 256.

mind the intellectual aptitudes of individuals are weakened."The heterogeneous is swamped by the homogeneous, and the unconscious qualities obtain the upper hand."[11] Furthermore, crowds think in images which frequently have no logical connections.[12] In addition, crowds are cognizant of only simple and extreme sentiments; the opinions, ideas and beliefs suggested to them are accepted or rejected as a whole and are considered as absolute truths or falsehoods.[13]

LeBon, writing shortly before the turn of the twentieth century, prophesied:

> "While all our ancient beliefs are tottering and disappearing, while the old pillars of society are giving way one by one, the power of the crowd is the only force that nothing menaces, and of which the prestige is continually on the increase. The age we are about to enter will in truth be the ERA OF CROWDS."[14]

A. V. Dicey writes of public opinion as a body of convictions, beliefs, and prejudices, as well as of what he calls cross-currents due to controversy. Few have placed greater emphasis on the importance of public opinion than Dicey; and few have been more afraid of its manifestations. He lectured in 1898 on the relations between public opinion and law. These lectures were subsequently gathered in book form under the title of *Lectures on the Relation Between Law and Public Opinon in England During the Nineteenth Century*. The first lecture begins with the statment that his aim is to show the close dependence of legislation in England during the nineteenth century upon the varying currents of public opinion. A footnote to this first sentence points out that Napoleon once said that opinion rules everything. Dicey holds that slavery rested upon the opinion of the slaves themselves.

> "The blacks," he states, "obeyed the slave owner from the opinion, whether well or ill founded, that in the long run they would, in a contest with their masters, have the worst of the fight; and even more from that habit of submission which, though enforced by the

[11] Gustave LeBon, *The Crowd—A Study of the Popular Mind*, London, T. Fisher Unwin, 1896 translation, p. 32.
[12] *Ibid.*, pp. 45–46.
[13] *Ibid.*, p. 59.
[14] *Ibid.*, p. 15.

occasional punishment of rebels, was founded upon a number of complicated sentiments, such, for example, as admiration for superior ability and courage, or gratitude for kindness, which cannot by any fair analysis be reduced to a mere form of fear, but constitute a kind of prevalent moral atmosphere. The whites, in short, ruled in virtue of the opinion, entertained by their slaves no less than by themselves, that the slave owners possessed qualities which gave them the might, and even the right, to be masters."[15]

Dicey's view of the nineteenth century may be summed up in one quotation:

"Parliamentary sovereignty, in short, taught as a theory by Blackstone and treated as a reality by Bentham, was an instrument well adapted for the establishment of democratic despotism."[16]

In a revised edition published seventeen years after he first delivered his lecture, Dicey finds that:

" . . . any grand scheme of social reform, based on the real or supposed truths of socialism, ought to be carried out by slow and well-considered steps taken under the guidance of the best and most impartial experts. But the democratic idea that the people, or any large number of the people, ought to have whatever they desire simply because they desire it, and ought to have it quickly, is absolutely fatal to that slow and sure kind of progress . . . Hence, it is all but certain that great changes planned by enthusiasts will, if they seem to be popular, be carried out with haste . . . ; on the other hand that, on some occasions, a party of self-called reformers will force on the electors changes which, whether good or bad, are opposed by the genuine convictions of the people. All that it is necessary to insist upon is that either blunder is likely to cause huge loss, and it may be ruin, to England."[17]

Actually, the nineteenth century saw the practical application of the theory of public opinion. As a result of the Industrial Revolution, science and invention spread the means of communication, enormously increasing the power and importance of public opinion. Whilst

[15] A. V. Dicey, *Lectures on the Relation Between Law and Public Opinion in England during the Nineteenth Century*, revised edition; London, Macmillan & Co., 1914.
[16] *Ibid.*   [17] *Ibid.*

the Industrial Revolution led to the creation of new social relationships, new theories began to evolve in the cultural, political, economic and social domains. The telegraph and telephone, in particular, opened up new areas for the dissemination of thoughts and ideas. The spread of democratic ideas and parliamentary forms also added to the impact of public opinion.

(b) Twentieth-century attitudes to public opinion

The beginning of the twentieth century brought forward new writers on public opinion. Of those, the eminent sociologist Edward Alsworth Ross was among the first to be completely explicit as to how the mechanism operates, observing:

> "Rarely can one regard his deed as fair when others find it foul, or count himself a hero when the world sees him a wretch."

The first hold on a man by his fellows is, therefore, their power to set him against himself and to stretch him on the rack of whatever ideas of excellence he may possess.[18] The sanctions of intercourse lie next. When a person offends public opinion, he will suffer coldness and avoidance to a greater or lesser degree. The open snub, the patent slight and the glancing witticism are but polite varieties of the hoots of the mob or the hisses of an audience. From then on, public opinion expresses itself even more directly, for example in economic reprisals and positive physical violence. Public opinion in the United States, according to Ross, since it was not broken into small currents by class lines, sect, caste and so forth, has a tidal volume and sweep.

> "We, the Americans, are come to a time when ordinary men are scarcely aware of the coercion of public opinion, so used are they to follow it. They cannot dream of aught but acquiescence in an unmistakable edict of the mass. It is not so much the dread of what an angry public may do that disarms the modern American, as it is sheer inability to stand unmoved in the rush of totally hostile comment, to endure a life perpetually at variance with the conscience and feeling of those about him."[19]

[18] Edward Alsworth Ross, *Social Control*, New York, The Macmillan Co, 1901, p. 90.
[19] *Ibid.*, p. 105.

In short, Ross had defined public opinion as including public judgement, sentiment and action. This definition is based on Ross's finding that the opinion an individual has of himself is not formed by the perceptions of the senses but is moulded by suggestion.[20]

Walter Lippmann, (b.1889) the noted American journalist, in 1922 published his work *Public Opinion*, which has greatly influenced current thought on the relationship between the masses and democracy. The theme that man is somewhat less than a thinking animal is now fairly commonplace, but at the time this book was a watershed. In the publishing world, a stereotype is a plate made by taking a mould of a printing surface and making from this a cast in type metal. According to Lippmann, the minds of men are poured into moulds in a similar manner, and these same minds then reproduce the same general ideas in accordance with the pattern of the mould. Except where we deliberately keep prejudice in suspense, Lippmann says, we do not first study a man and then judge him to be bad. We see a bad man. We see a dewy morning, a blushing girl, a pious priest, a humourless Englishman or a carefree bohemian. In the daily world, this is often the basis of judgement, long in advance of the evidence, and it contains within itself the conclusion which the evidence is pretty certain to confirm. Neither justice, nor mercy, nor truth enter into such judgement, for the judgement has preceded the evidence. Lippmann then proceeds to argue that public opinion is primarily a moralized and codified version of preconceptions, since "the pattern of stereotypes at the centre of our codes largely determines what group of facts we shall see, and in what light we shall see them." Hence, public opinion, of necessity, must be based largely on mythology. A myth, as Lippmann notes, may be wholly true, partly true, or false. "What a myth never contains is the critical power to separate its truths from its errors. For that power comes only by realising that no human opinion, whatever its supposed origin, is too exalted for the test of evidence."

In 1923, a year after the appearance of Lippmann's book, A. L. Lowell (1856–1934), for many years the President of Harvard University, published what may be the model definition of public opinion

[20] *Ibid.*, p. 105.

in his book *Public Opinion in War and Peace*.[21] Typical of his vision is the following:

"Human thought, and especially collective thought, is not a problem of statistics. It is forever in process of change. The important matter is not what people think, but what they are tending to think; not so much their attitude toward a matter about to be presented to them, as what they will think after it has been presented to them; not their judgement upon an act about to be performed, but what it will be when it has been performed."[22]

To solve such problems, he explored the various types of attitudes and dispositions. He found that people could be divided into four classes: first, radicals, who are discontented with present conditions and anxious for improvement; second, liberals, who are contented and sanguine; third, conservatives, who are contented but not hopeful of improvement; and fourth, reactionaries, who are not contented with existing conditions and who, at the same time, see no prospect for better things to come. The preponderance of these dispositions, writes Lowell, indicates the nature of government: first, stable government, resulting from a preponderance of liberals and conservatives, as opposed to radicals and reactionaries; second, unstable government, resulting from a preponderance of radicals and reactionaries, as opposed to liberals and conservatives; third, progressive government, resulting from a preponderance of liberals and radicals, as opposed to conservatives and reactionaries; and fourth, unprogressive government, resulting from a preponderance of conservatives and reactionaries, as opposed to radicals and liberals.

Adolf Hitler's *Mein Kampf*, the first half published in 1925 and the second half in 1927, is "a queer mélange of semi-truth and unadulterated nonsense, combined with an almost uncanny psychological insight into the mind of the mob."[23] It is a book on the magic of mass-hypnotism and of the evil uses to which this force can be put.

"The great masses' receptive ability is only very limited, their under-

[21] Abbott Lawrence Lowell, *Public Opinion in War and Peace*, Cambridge, Harvard University Press, 1923.
[22] *Ibid.*, p. 287.
[23] Walter Phelps Hall and William Stearns Davis, *The Course of Europe Since Waterloo*, Second edition, New York, D. Appleton Century Co. 1947, p. 714.

standing is small, but their forgetfulness is great," declares Hitler.[24] "Therefore, a few simple ideas must be hammered into the heads of the people, day after day, week after week, year after year. Tell only one side of the story, for the masses are not in a position to distinguish where the wrong of the others ends and their own begins."[25]

What could be more ridiculous, asks Hitler, than for a soap producer to admit in an advertisement that any other soap was also good? Tell the same story over, over, over, for the masses "will lend their memories only to the thousand-fold repetition of the most simple ideas."[26] The great lie is, of course, more readily believed than the small lie. Hitler maintained that

"in the size of the lie there is always contained a certain factor of credibility, since the great masses of a people may be more corrupt at the bottom of their hearts than they will be consciously and intentionally bad, therefore with the primitive simplicity of their minds they will more easily fall victims to a great lie than to a small one, since they themselves perhaps also lie sometimes in little things, but would certainly still be too much ashamed of too great lies."[27]

Hitler talked to people. And when he talked, he demanded absolute attention. Never does he boast more than when he tells of how his thugs maintained order at Nazi meetings. He preferred to talk to a mass audience. For large groups, after proper preparation—lights, bands and waiting—become mobs easily controlled. Note the waiting. People, especially in the evening, become tired. As Hitler advocates:

"It seems that in the morning, and even during the day, men's will-power revolts with highest energy against an attempt at being forced under another's will and another's opinion. In the evening, however, they succumb more easily to the dominating force of a stronger will. For, truly, every such meeting presents a wrestling match between two opposed forces. The superior oratorical talent of a domineering apostolic nature will now succeed more easily in winning for the new will people who themselves have in turn experienced a weakening of their force of resistance in the most natural way, than people who still have full command of the energies of their minds and their will power."[28]

[24] Adolf Hitler, *Mein Kampf*, New York, Reynal and Hitchcock, 1940, p. 234.
[25] *Ibid.*, p. 237. [26] *Ibid.*, p. 239.
[27] *Ibid.*, p. 313. [28] *Ibid.*, pp. 710–711.

History attests to the fact that Hitler's own appraisal—"after any three-hour speech, all are with me"—was correct. Hitler attributes this to his own greatness, but he never seems to understand exactly why he, Hitler, had such great powers, unless it was an act of God. He did not fancy this last interpretation since it lessened his personal greatness.

Somewhat oversimplified, the main factor on which Hitler played was that "the mob has a fatal habit of engulfing those who come merely as passive spectators."[29] It might be suggested tentatively that Hitler, probably unknowingly, was applying certain principles of hypnotism. For those interested in the matter, Estabrooks' *Hypnotism* is suggested, for it is a work that combines both readability and accuracy. A special chapter is devoted to "This Man, Hitler". Estabrooks believes that Hitler's power, or that of most other great public figures either of our own day or as described for us in history, will be found in their abilities in hypnotism.[30] However this may be, there is a very practical supplement to *Mein Kampf* in the *Goebbels Diaries*.[31] It is an account of Goebbels' machinations to attempt to make the people, including the Nazis, believe in the incredible falsehood that was the Nazi state. It is also an account of the spell that Hitler cast over his followers. An appraisal by Goebbels, from a magazine devoted to advertising and selling, follows in its entirety:

> "In the evening I had a long talk with my mother who, to me, always represents the voice of the people. She knows their sentiments better than most experts who judge from the ivory tower. Again, I learned a lot, especially that the rank and file are usually much more primitive than we imagine. Propaganda must, therefore, always be essentially simple and repetitive. In the long run, only he will achieve basic results in influencing public opinion who is able to reduce problems to the simplest terms and who has the courage to keep forever repeating them in this simplified form despite the objections of the intellectuals."

[29] G. H. Estabrooks, *Hypnotism*, New York, E. P. Dutton & Co. Inc., 1943, p. 208.
[30] *Ibid.*, p. 214.
[31] Louis P. Lochner, *The Goebbels Diaries*, Garden City, Doubleday & Co., Inc. 1948.

By 1937, those interested in public opinion witnessed a most ambitious attempt in this field, when the study made by Floyd H. Allport, professor of social and political psychology, appeared as the first article in the first issue of *The Public Opinion Quarterly*. Since Allport's contribution has served in a very broad way as a frame of reference for the materials appearing in the Quarterly, his conclusions have had considerable importance in setting the pace for published research. He begins with a study of the fictions and blind alleys of public opinion, which he classifies as:

the personification of public opinion;
the personification of the public;
the group fallacy of the public;
the fallacy of partial inclusion in the use of the term 'public';
the fiction of an ideational entity;
the group-product or 'emergent' theory;
the eulogistic theory;
the confusion of public opinion with the public presentation of
    opinion represented in the journalistic fallacy.

He then finds that the phenomena to be studied under the term 'public opinion' are essentially instances of behaviour of which the following conditions are true:

they are behaviour of human individuals;
they involve verbalization;
they are performed by many individuals;
they are stimulated by and directed toward some universally known
    object or situation;
the object or situation they are concerned with is important to
    many;
they represent action or readiness for action in the nature of
    approval or disapproval of the common object;
they are frequently performed with an awareness that others are
    reacting in the same situation in a similar manner;
the attitudes or opinions they involve are expressed or at least
    the individuals are in a state of readiness to express them;
the individuals exhibiting such behaviour may or may not be in
    one another's presence;

they may involve verbal contents of both permanent and transitory character, constituting "genetic groundwork material" and "present alignment", respectively;

they are in the nature of present efforts to oppose or accomplish something, rather than long-standing conformities of behaviour;

being efforts toward common objectives, they frequently have the character of conflict between individuals aligned upon opposing sides;

they are sufficiently strong and numerous, as common behaviours, to give rise to the probability that they may be effective in attaining their objective.

Allport concludes with his own definition:

"The term public opinion is given its meaning with reference to a multi-individual situation in which individuals are expressing themselves, or can be called upon to express themselves, as favouring or supporting (or else disfavouring and opposing) some definite condition, person or proposal of widespread importance, in such a proportion of number, intensity and constancy, as to give rise to the probability of affecting action, directly or indirectly, toward the object concerned."[32]

While Allport defined the above concept of public opinion, others arrived at similar or varying conclusions. In regard to public opinion polling, David Krech, a noted psychologist says:

"If we continue to define 'public opinion' in terms of verbal reactions of people without having a clear understanding of what a belief, or opinion, or attitude, or judgement is, many of our public opinion pollsters will find themselves in the position of a blind man, equipped with a high-powered microscope, in a dark cellar, looking for a black cat which is not there, and regularly issuing 'trend reports' of the 'cat's progress' ."[33]

According to another definition: "public opinion refers to people's attitudes on an issue when they are members of the same social

[32] Floyd H. Allport, "Toward a Science of Public Opinion", *The Public Opinion Quarterly*, January, 1937, Vol. 1 No. 1, p. 23.
[33] David Krech, *Concepts of Public Opinion and Psychological Theory*, International Journal of Opinion and Attitude Research, Spring 1948, Vol. 2.

group."[34] This probably represents something approaching a consensus of the experts.

It is reasonable to conclude that:

"Public opinion is any collection of individual opinions, regardless of the degree of agreement or uniformity. The degree of uniformity is a matter to be investigated, not something to be arbitrarily set up as a condition for the existence of public opinion."[35]

Setting aside for the time being the underlying reasons for the importance of public opinion, Earl L. Vance, another researcher on the subject, states that news not only influences our thinking but is our thinking.[36] Thus, what we call our "thinking" about most of the events and issues international, national and even local that make up so large a part of our lives, is largely merely a function of the news. The thinking of millions becomes the work of a handful of strategically placed persons—a man at a radio microphone, another at a news desk, a third at a typewriter a hundred or a thousand or ten thousand miles away. Irrespective of the keenness of the individual mind, here is where its "thinking" is done, its "opinions" are formed. For an opinion is, in essence, but a summary of one's information, and we do not react to the world as it is, but to the world as it has been convincingly reported to be. The primitive delivered up his human sacrifice to appease his gods, whether they were there to receive it or not. However the gods may have felt about it, the victim was dead. Man today enacts the exact counterpart, measuring the results with a factor of millions. Scientists who gave us an atomic bomb and politicians who determine its use, no less than the primitive, are responding to such information as has been vouchsafed them. If the end be disaster, they—again like the primitive—mercifully cannot know it. They can act only upon what they have been led to believe at this moment to be the relevant conditions respecting their deeds. If later it should turn out that the facts were other, or that there were other relevant facts not yet known, God help us. Vance makes the further point that "the so-called 'educated' person

[34] Leonard W. Doob, *Public Opinion and Propaganda*, New York, Henry Holt & Co. 1948, p. 35.
[35] H. Childs, *An Introduction to Public Opinion*, New York, John Wiley & Sons.
[36] Earl Vance, *The News: Fourth Dimension of Education*.

in America typically gets his current information from much the same sources as the barely literate."[37]

An exhaustive study of the American soldier during World War II revealed the reliance of the fighting man upon group opinion in stress situations:

> "Compared with the feeling that one must not lose face in the eyes of one's fellows or let them down, patriotism, hatred of the enemy and other stereotyped explanations of what keeps a person going in combat seem to have been negligible factors."[38]

(c) Guidelines for defining public opinion

For all our advances in psychology and the behavioural sciences, our knowledge is very far from complete. It is therefore inevitable that the manifestations of public opinion should give rise to a variety of interpretations, some contradictory, and none admitting of definitive description in any classic sense. The intensive study which the subject has attracted during the present century, and which it continues to receive, does however suggest fruitful lines of future enquiry. Additionally, it seems at least to have provided us with certain rules, or perhaps more accurately guidelines, for adding to our understanding. In concluding our examination of the concept of public opinion, we believe we can probably do no better than to define these guidelines as follows:

Public opinion must be voluntary. In this respect, it reflects all genuine opinion, whether individual or group opinion. The uniform expression of opinion imposed *from above*, following strong pressures such as fear or outright coercion as in oligarchies or despotisms, cannot be public opinion.

Public opinion differs from community opinion. The community, in this specialized connotation, is smaller than the public. To generate public opinion, all communities should be incorporated within a single public. Otherwise there will be more than one public, and consequently more than one public opinion, within one people.

Public opinion takes account of minority opinion. Extending our re-

---

[37] Earl Vance, *The News: Fourth Dimension of Education*, p. 560.
[38] Samuel A. Stouffer, "A Study of Attitudes", *Scientific American*, May 1945, Vol. 180, No. 5, p. 14.

marks on the relationship of community and public, we submit that public opinion is the expression of the attitude of all those of its members who show interest in any given subject. Public opinion then includes the simultaneous expression of majority opinion, assuming there is one, and of minority opinion or opinions. Where differences are so wide as to prevent the minority from freely modifying their outlook in ways necessary to their working with the majority, then there is no longer one public but several. According to the democratic definition, a public cannot be so called unless all its members act together. Within such a public, the process of exchanging influences and reactions can occur, while at the same time many different attitudes can be maintained and minority points of view tolerated. This respect for minority positions entrenches the notion that coercion should have nothing to do with public opinion, except in the negative sense of stimulating a reaction against repressive activities, whether that coercion stems from the administrative acts of despotism, or from the contrived mass pressures of demagogues.

Public opinion implies controversy over identifiable issues. Public opinion is the outcome of free choice. To find expression it needs an issue capable of arousing controversy. Thus it differs from deep-rooted values, convictions and customs. As a product of influences interacting among a group of people, public opinion is the sum of opinions which are actually attitudes adopted by individuals towards a given controversial issue, in other words, a free generalization of individual opinion, provided the latter is the result of free choice and conviction.

Public opinion is of limited duration. Once the controversial issue is acceptably resolved, the particular public opinion called forth by it withers away. Public opinion that has been more or less artificially stimulated through deliberate incitement or provocation, as for example by the oratory of agitators, is least likely to persist for long. But in any case it is difficult to visualize a permanent public opinion, short of a permanently active stimulus, for it appears to be a condition of its existence that public opinion should be the product of dynamic movement. Without this, what might appear as constant public opinion becomes rather conviction, valuation or habit.

Public opinion may be active or passive. Just as there is an implied free choice between contrasting alternatives, so can there be free rejection of all the alternatives positively presented. As there is an active *assenting* public opinion, so there may be a passive *rejecting* public opinion.

Public opinion must not be confused with the media. We must beware of the common mistake of describing press, radio and television as public opinion. Theoretically, it is obvious enough that they are not public opinion but the media informing it and illustrating it. In practice, the inter-relationship is often so close as to blur nice distinctions, because practically speaking opinion is the sum of individual knowledge, knowledge which in the modern world is supplied on a massive scale by the media. What is clear is that the more profound and free this knowledge, the more profound and free will be individual opinion, and hence in turn public opinion. It is therefore vital to ensure that the media shall not be manipulated to coerce opinion, in ways such as *brainwashing*, whether intentional or not.

Public opinion must be conspicuous. A prime condition of the existence of public opinion is its *expression*. Concealed views may be strongly held, but it is only through exposure to the influences of public discussion, and through their relationship with corresponding or conflicting views, that they are converted into ingredients of public opinion. That their expression increasingly depends on the capabilities of mass communications is further evidence of the interlocking relationship of public opinion and the media.

Our review of these guidelines reminds us that, just as the opinion factor is dynamic, so the concept of the public is susceptible to change and expansion. We have tried to draw a distinction between the public and the community in the narrow sense of the word. In our introductory chapter, we saw how for practical purposes the public tended to be regarded as coterminous with the citizens of the national sovereign state, though to some extent this view is being modified by the rise of an inter-regional or even international consciousness, in gradual recognition of mankind's ultimate dependence on the development of a strong and enlightened world public opinion.

Whether on the national or the international plane, this elusive concept of public opinion is created and nourished in certain identifiable ways. Very simply stated its raw material is *information*. Without information, however rudimentary, primitive man would have remained in ignorance of the traditional and habitual responses to extraneous stimuli of his tribal society; indeed, without information any sort of social arrangement is inconceivable. In the next chapter then we shall endeavour to trace how the concept of information has developed and expanded. We shall study special types of what may be termed *highly motivated information*, such as *public relations* and *propaganda*, where there must inevitably be an element of selectivity on the part of the presenter, who in these instances has as a major or important purpose the building of a case in favour of one particular course of action, or one group of people, or one body of philosophy, rather than of another.

From a conceptual treatment of our subject, we pass on to its practical application. To do so we need to study the formative elements of public opinion, first (in Chapter 4) in terms of their underlying components—cultural heritage, common values, habit and the like—and then (in Chapter 5) in terms of the recognized information media. We shall observe the grave responsibility resting on the controllers of the media, in whose hands lie the alternatives of preparing public opinion either for a course of action conducive to peace, progress and happiness, or else for one leading to war, conflict and misery. And mindful of the overriding current importance of the nurturing of international habits of thought, as mentioned in our first chapter, we shall not ignore those media which are particularly suitable for the proper inculcation of such attitudes.

3
Information: the Raw Material of Public Opinion

(a) The concept of information

Although information in its present and self-conscious form represents a phenomenon of the twentieth century, its roots go deep into the remote past.

Primitive tribes knew three types of information: that given by the look-out who was employed by his tribe to study the state of the weather, to learn if it would allow work or not, or if any natural catastrophe was imminent; that offered by the sage, or wise man, who was consulted on matters relating to the life and interests of the tribe, and who furnished it with sound views and practical solutions for its problems; and that provided by the teacher, who undertook to bring up the children and make of them good individuals capable of preserving the customs and values of their tribes.

The ages of the dawn of history also knew information in some form or other. Historians explain how the kings and priests gave considerable attention to influencing their followers by providing them with such information and news as would endear them to the people. The Ancient Egyptian kings recorded laws concerning taxation, irrigation, judicial procedures and penalties. Papyri left by the Pharaohs, as well as the inscriptions on the walls of their temples, teem with significant references and items which could be qualified as relatively advanced forms of information. For example, a papyrus document contains instructions to the people on the conduct which should govern relations between them and senior state officials commissioned by the Pharaoh to inspect their conditions and the work of state functionaries. These functionaries, too, were ordered to relay to their superiors all the information and news which they could gather. Another papyrus instructs and warns people against the danger of prostitution and immorality, and lays down the punishment to be inflicted upon those who violated these edicts. It also explains such methods as were then believed adequate to eliminate these serious social ailments.

The arts of information were practised on a large scale in the Islamic ages. The Caliph used to co-opt on to his council wise and experienced men for their advice and opinions. He also sent to his Viceroys in the various regions such messages as would furnish them with news, advice and directives on the best methods of gaining the confidence of the people. The Caliph enjoined his Viceroys to provide him with news and information relating to the regions which they ruled. Besides, the Islamic Caliph used to brief the people on the course of events and to bring the laws within the grasp of the people's knowledge by promulgating them at public meeting-places and in the mosques. The Fatimids, especially, mastered the arts of information, and employed advanced methods. Their Caliphs used to distribute to leading personalities information and important decisions written on pieces of paper. They also made use of a public crier who would roam the town and villages to inform the people of what the rulers wanted them to know.

Coming down to more recent times we note that, with the invention of printing, information began to assume a form that we should recognize today. Later still, in the New World, the founders of the American state were greatly concerned with information, as a result of their interest in sounding public opinion. George Washington wrote once that, in respect of a government which relies largely in its initial phase on public opinion, there was a pressing and imperative need for the existence of a great measure of complete and careful understanding on the part of those who undertake administrative posts. Washington also used to arrange for those of his friends who lived in various parts of the United States, and who held no government posts, to provide him with information about the areas where they lived. On 26 July 1789, Washington wrote to David Stewart, in Virginia, saying that he wanted a good medium of information to keep him aware of the public opinion prevailing, as well as of the public views of the laws and of his own person and conduct.

In modern times information has become part of the daily life of people all over the world. Governments are fully aware that it is incumbent upon them to provide news, information and facts which will help the peoples to participate in government affairs. Thus, government information all over the world plays a major role in the dissemination of news and facts.

Concern with public opinion is no longer limited to the local public opinion of each state, but has grown to encompass world public opinion. Hence, information has begun to receive world-wide attention. This is due perhaps to the fact that serious studies undertaken by leading researchers have established that efficient and disinterested information could largely contribute to the spread of world peace and security. The United Nations has grasped this fact, and the UN Economic and Social Council consequently recommended that UNESCO should discuss efforts exerted by the developing countries to consolidate and strengthen their information media.

A state's economic, social and political structure necessitates the employment of the various information media and methods. These include relaying information by one person to another, the exchange of information among organized groups, or mass information media represented by the press, publications, broadcasting, television, cinema and the other arts. In this respect, as in many others, the realization of the hopes pinned on information depends on the will, integrity and objectivity of the people, all of which can be achieved only through information. There is nothing new about this assertion, for Aristotle believed that friendly action was necessary to achieve adequate communication with the people. He also believed that people could not coexist in peace, unless each of them respected the interests of the other.

We turn now to the forms of *highly motivated information* mentioned in the previous chapter. Although the term *public relations* was not in general use until after the First World War, many aspects of the basic activities of public relations have their origins in the past.

(b) The concept of public relations

Primitive sorcerers and witch-doctors undertook public relations activities in the names of their tribes, when they developed such myths and legends as justified the elimination of certain habits which were considered harmful to the tribe and its safety.

In the fifth century B.C., Simonides placed his poetry at the service of public relations, when he offered to write eulogies for those prepared to pay for them; but it seems that this initiative was distasteful at the time. Pindar, fastidious as he was, received the price of glorification from those who were the subjects of his poems of praise. Among his clients were the merchant princes of the Aegean Sea. The Rosetta Stone presents another example of public relations activity undertaken by the priests of Ancient Egypt. Inscriptions on the stone, which was hewn at the behest of the Egyptian priests in 196 B.C., informed the reader that the young King Ptolemy V was intelligent and just, and that his policies would lead to prosperity. In the year 60 B.C., after Julius Caesar was elected Consul of Rome, he gave instructions for the publication of the Acts of the Roman Senate. A bulletin called *Acta Diurna* was then issued. The bulletin announced that the crown was offered three times to Caesar, but that he declined to accept it on each occasion.

The history of changing attitudes to economic matters is immensely significant to an understanding of the modern world. For example, over a great part of the Middle Ages in Western Europe, the Catholic Church prescribed excommunication for transgressors against a principle of Saint John, which was regarded as condemning the purchase of an article for resale at a profit, irrespective of whether the article remained in its existing form or was transformed in any way. Later Thomas Aquinas modified the principle to allow for "just" profit, not exceeding a small proportion of the price. But the profit motive remained suspect. Thus in the early sixteenth century the commercial and banking interests of the Fugger family of Augsburg, which extended to various countries, suffered both from the many restrictive laws and from a generally hostile climate of opinion. Jacob Fugger complained to Conrad Bettinger about this problem. Bettinger, a counsellor to the Holy Roman Emperor Charles V and a humanist researcher in his own right, wrote a series of essays on the moral and legal aspects of commerce. He said that merchants often sold their commodities at a price which involved loss, and that, accordingly, a merchant should be free to demand a higher price for his commodity.

He also criticized the restrictions on monopolies. As a result of Bettinger's activities, the council of Augsburg voted away the restrictions imposed upon trade at the time. In a very real sense, therefore, Bettinger had successfully performed a public relations exercise.

George Washington practised various methods of influencing public opinion. For example on 16 January 1792 through his Secretary of Defence he issued a statement on the Indian War, in the course of which he stated that, when a society is called upon to contribute to the alleviation of the pain of those who suffer as a result of enemy conduct, it is desirable for the holders of administrative posts to avoid committing evil and vice. Later both Washington and his State Secretary, Thomas Pickering, distributed ten thousand copies of the *American Teachings* in support of their policy against revolutionary France in 1798.

Napoleon Bonaparte was no stranger to public relations techniques. In 1793, as an officer in the regiment assigned to suppress a rebellion against the French revolutionary government, he wrote a note to the effect that the violence of the revolution was much less than the revenge which the previous régime would have exacted had the rebellion succeeded. The note effectively drew the government's attention to young Bonaparte. Later, on his return to France as a famous general, his reputation made in his Italian campaign, Napoleon wore simple clothes, visited minor government officials whom he regarded as hostile, and made sure that his modesty would be mentioned in the official gazette.

In Britain, as in the US, the appointment of public relations executives in government departments during the Second World War heralded the development of public relations as a profession. *Persuasion*, the British Public Relations Journal, published an article in its Winter 1949 issue, saying that the war had brought about a gap between local authorities and their publics. With the advent of peace, the atmosphere was propitious for the creation of public relations of an official nature.

Mass communications in today's society have developed to such a degree of sophistication as to become a widespread, complex industry. In one sense they have come to constitute a serious challenge to both rulers and ruled. Nevertheless a sincere democratic ruler must use up-to-date methods of mass communication to secure the comprehension of the masses for government actions.[1] Moreover, a society in which government affairs are smoothly run is a society which consists of homogeneous and harmonious individuals, groups and organizations.

It is common knowledge that the process of government is not easy. James Forrestal, the US Defence Secretary in President Truman's government, once told a friend that the difficulty of the exercise of government lies in the fact that it is not enough that this should be done well, but that the people should be convinced that it was being done well. In other words, there is a need for competence and for publicizing the facts pertaining to it. Hence, an official's duty before the public is continually to explain his efforts and analyse his reactions to these efforts, especially since administrative bodies exist in unstable environments in which the tides of mass support are in a continual state of flux. Effective balance lies at the heart of mass support. Indeed, modern society with all its complications requires that the masses should discern and comprehend the problems of the age. If citizens have to make intelligent statements on problems of general policy, there should be some bridge of understanding between them and the government.[2] Scott M. Cutlip warns that, if public undertakings do not accept the social responsibility inherent in them today, the masses will find ways and means to impose this responsibility in a more flexible and mobilized manner than ever before in history.[3]

Human understanding has come to constitute one of the fundamental requirements observed by rulers in all affairs of state. The rulers attain this understanding by providing themselves with an adequate machinery for mass communication, which helps continually to inform the public, and also to make the government more aware of the needs of the public. The science of public relations was developed as a necessary tool to meet the demand for modern, responsible administration by the public and the private sector alike.

[1] Bernard Rubin, *Public Relations and the Empire State*, New Brunswick, New Jersey, Rutgers University Press, 1958, p. 30.
[2] Curtis Fuller, "A Statewide Information Bureau", *State Government* Vol. XIV, April 1941, p. 77.
[3] Scott M. Cutlip, "A Reconsideration of Public Opinion Platitudes", *Public Opinion Journal* 1963, p. 13.

Many specialists consider that public relations were the outcome of the appearance of technology, and especially of the development of the mass communications media. They also believe public relations to have been the fruit of the growth of industry in the twentieth century. Scott Cutlip says that public relations represent a necessary response to the needs of a society which has attained a high degree of industrialization, urbanization and inter-dependence.[4] Curtis MacDougall, an authority on public opinion, says that public relations as a profession, though still in a stage of trial and error, are an inevitable outcome of any complex industrial society, for the masses have multiplied in number and become so diffused that communicating with them requires the help of experts.[5]

Charles S. Steinberg isolates five important factors which have contributed to making public relations an important and specialized process. These are: first, the increasingly complicated framework of industry and its further removal from direct contact with the masses; second, the appearance of a wide and complex network of mass-communication media; third, the emergence of the interests of larger establishments and the attendant consequences; fourth, the appearance of increasingly acute competition, which dictates respect for public opinion and the need for mass support; fifth, the growth of public demand for facts and information, as a result of the spread of education and knowledge.[6]

It is now clear that the emergence of public relations was in keeping with the recent attempts to investigate public opinion and mass communication in modern society. For administration cannot be effective unless it is based on accurate knowledge of public opinion, and unless it takes into consideration the desires of the ruled. We may subscribe to Thomas A. Bailey's view that public opinion is "the queen of the world". We may also affirm that governments derive their power from the satisfaction of the ruler, or else conceive of public opinion as a whimsical, ignorant giant, but a giant which

[4] Cutlip, *op. cit.*, p. 13.
[5] Curtis D. MacDougall, *Understanding Public Opinion*, New York, Macmillan Co., 1952, p. 560.
[6] Charles S. Steinberg, *Public Relations, Public Opinion and Mass Media*, New York, Harper & Brothers, Publishers, 1958, p. 16.

still has the power and may one day use it in a manner that may entail serious consequences.[7]

It is abundantly clear that the authority of mass will is evidently associated with the modern definition and assessment of democracy. Democracy cannot succeed unless the citizens entertain genuine interest in the government.[8]

Harold Lasswell says that open interaction between opinion and politics is the distinct feature of popular government.[9] In the same manner, Aristotle affirms the role of the citizen in government when he says that the citizen is the person who takes part in government, thus becoming both ruler and ruled.[10]

In the democratic state, a healthy society depends upon the continuous and effective political participation of the people. Aristotle has distinguished this fact as evidence of the fitness of the masses for politics. He stipulates the principle that the public should be sovereign. He says that a majority makes better judges than one person in music and poetry, for some persons would understand one part while another understands other parts, and thus all of them would understand the whole. Hence, the inhabitants of a house are in a better position to judge it than the mason who built it, the sailor can better judge the rudder than the carpenter who made it, a guest can better judge the meal than the cook.[11]

Needless to say, government by the people means government characterized by a high degree of the people's participation; for the people are the most important element, not only in politics but in the development of resources as well. Although the true purpose of social development is the realization of the individual's happiness and prosperity, the highest welfare and happiness will be achieved when individuals use their intelligence, energies and spirit to realize

[7] Thomas A. Bailey, *The Man in the Street*, New York, Macmillan 1948, p. 1.
[8] Bertrand R. Canfield, *Public Relations: Principles, Cases and Problems*, Homewood, Illinois, Richard & Irwin, Inc. 1960, p. 306.
[9] Harold Lasswell, *Democracy Through Public Opinion*, Menasha Wisconsin, Bantam 1941, p. 41.
[10] Aristotle, *Politika* (Jowett transl.) Book III, Ch. 13 in Richard McKeon, ed., *The Basic Wonderful Aristotle*, New York, 1941, p. 1195.
[11] Bernard Berelson & Morris Janowitz (eds.) *Reader in Public Opinion and Communication*, New York, the Free Press of Glencoe, 1953, p. 3.

this development. For man wants to feel that he is important, that he has a responsibility, that he has a part in decision-making, and that he is needed and useful for the realization of something which is bigger than himself. Democracy is actually founded on faith in the basic dignity and importance of the individual.[12]

Democracy, then, requires the participation of persons who have their own views on various matters and situations. As we said, it operates through the satisfaction and participation of the people, and the governing authority of the masses in a democratic society cannot live without the understanding and acceptance of the governed. This fact was further elaborated by Leonard D. White, an authority on public administration. He says, in effect, that public relations, to a great extent, is that subject which enhances dignity or loses it in the course of public service. The nature of the existing relations of any administrative body may assume thousands of aspects, from the aggressive and destructive to the positive and constructive. Hence, it is clear that effective administration rests upon winning over the masses through good public relations.[13]

Public relations, then, is the new science in democratic societies, and it aims at conviction. John Marston says that the very nature of democracy involves the chance of convincing the masses through reason.[14] Public relations, too, can help promote the understanding of the masses and their true desires. In this respect, Harold Levy says that the responsibility of public relations in a government organization consists largely of the responsibility of fulfilling twin obligations: the information of the public and the reinforcement of cordial relations between the public and the establishment.[15]

James McCamy also said in his *Government Publicity* that a programme of public relations should be used to avoid inappropriate

[12] James McGregor Burns and Jack Walter Peltason, *Government by the People: the Dynamics of the American National State and Local Government*, Englewood Cliffs, New Jersey, Prentice-Hall Inc. 1960, p. 18.
[13] Leonard D. White, *Introduction to the Study of Public Administration*, New York, Macmillan & Co. 1949, p. 224.
[14] John E. Marston, *The Nature of Public Relations*, New York, McGraw Hill Book Company Inc. 1963, p. 347.
[15] Harold Levy, *A Study in Public Relations*, New York, Russel Sage Foundation, 1943, p. 47.

information, and to promote mass comprehension in order to repel unjust and unjustified criticism of mass organizations.[16]

However, a close analysis of what has been written on public relations may help in understanding their functions, which are as yet a partly-understood field.[17] Future research on the scope and nature of public relations could add new vistas which may help the elaboration of philosophical grounds for this new science.

Although most available definitions are based on specific action undertaken by various government units under study, there are some recognized factors in public relations. J. A. R. Pimlott, for example, points out that there are two main premises on government public relations: the documentary premise by which democratic administrations apprise the public of their action; and the administrative premise according to which certain policies cannot effectively be carried out except by the active and conscious participation of the public or sectors of it. It should be necessary, in this respect, to ensure the awareness of the public and its co-operation.[18]

Edward L. Bernays, a forerunner of research in the field of public relations, has deduced three major functions for public relations. These are: information, conviction, and correlation. Hence, he defined public relations as:[19] first, information which is given to the public; second, conviction aimed at the public to alter its emotions and conduct; third, efforts to create a complete correlation between the emotions and actions of one body and those of its public.

According to Steinberg, public relations include the clever use of communication and information and the swaying of public opinion. He says that those who make use of them seek to convince the public of their objectives and of their economic, cultural and social needs.[20] This definition also emphasizes the action.

Another definition is advocated by Rex F. Harlow. He considers

[16] James McCamy, *Government Publicity*, Chicago, The University of Chicago Press, 1939, pp. 31–34.
[17] Rubin, *op. cit.*
[18] J. A. R. Pimlott, *Public Relations and American Democracy*, Princeton University Press, 1951, p. 76.
[19] Edward L. Bernays, *Your Future in Public Relations*, New York, Richard Rosen Press Inc. 1961, p. 21.
[20] Steinberg, *op. cit.* p. 10.

that public relations is a science through which the establishment can consciously attempt the fulfilment of its social responsibility and the realization of mass awareness and consent, all of which are pre-requisites for success. Elsewhere, he describes public relations as a process which is used by the establishment to analyse the needs and desires of those concerned in order to adopt a harmonious action.[21]

Other researchers describe the function of public relations as a planned effort at influencing, with the aim of attaining a suitable opinion, through an acceptable achievement honestly presented. This is essentially a dual effort, since a planned action must depend on accepted and agreed data, as well as reflect the executive principles of the corporation, organization, or community. In this sense, public relations are principles of execution, or a philosophy of company policy.[22]

Each organization has its particular problems, environment, objectives, purposes and clientele, and each is also a continuous function. Considering that public confidence is the outcome of sound public relations—a frail treasure easily lost—it is imperative that public relations should be honest, true, frank, authoritative and responsible; as also that they should be fair and realistic, acting in the public interest.

Thus it is clear that public relations have come at present to encompass mass information, orientation, research, advertising and public opinion analysis.

Although the objectives of public relations and *publicity* are about the same their means are markedly different. Public relations aim at honest conviction, that is influencing public opinion for the genuine interest of the public. On the other hand, publicity sometimes aims at subjecting minds, distorting facts, and interfering with the freedom of choice.

Thus public relations represents an important process which consists of providing the public with continuous facts on a given topic, enabling the public to form rational and sound views on disputed matters; for the most knowledgeable people are the most able

[21] Rex F. Harlow, *Public Opinions in War and Peace*, New York, Harper & Brothers, 1942, pp. x and 130.
[22] Edwin Emery, Philips H. Hult and Warner K. Agee, *Introduction to Mass Communications*, New York, Dodd, Mead & Co., 1960, p. 330.

to form intelligent opinions and choices based on rational thinking. In fact, formal education and the spread of knowledge through modern communications have furnished people with valuable data on disputed matters.

The function of public relations is not confined to the dissemination of facts on disputed matters only. It also includes arousing more interest in the matters faced by the public. An indifferent public should be persuaded to express its opinion and to participate in the formation of the group opinion. In other words, public relations undertake the responsibility of transforming the passive emotions of many persons into positive views on disputed matters. Passive emotions never lead to the creation of the public opinion required for the democratic process; for the formation of public opinion in the democratic state depends largely on the flow of facts and information as the fundamental objective of public relations. Therefore, public relations encourage the masses to form independent responsible decisions which would realize the true and genuine fulfilment of their needs. Disinterested data made accessible to the public through public relations furnish the necessary facts for the realization of the function of the progressive democratic society. Democracy lives and flourishes through the dissemination of truth and fact made available through public relations. Thus, public relations and democracy attempt to realize the common objectives of freedom and right, for each of them wants to make of the mass communication media their own tools and not their masters.

An extensive and proliferating literature on the subject stands as eloquent testimony to the difficulty of attempting comprehensive definition. From the historical examples given we sense from early times a recognition of the uses of public relations, both on the part of individuals desirous of good standing among their fellows, and on the part of rulers desirous of public acclaim. With the enlargement of the governing circle, and ultimately the advent of democracy, a proper co-ordination of interest as between government and people became ever more important. It did so in comparable ratio to the ever-expanding range of topics relevant to national well-being, concomitantly with the development of an industrialized society. For their efficient functioning governments today need more than ever to be aware of the views, aspirations and predictable reactions of the people; in other words to gauge public opinion, in relation to an escalating multiplicity of subjects, some highly specialized and technical, and in relation to a growing demand for democratic participation. On the basis of such awareness, the government must equip itself to project its policies in terms of public expectation, more or less coherently expressed. Furthermore, on occasion there rests on government the duty of preparing the public for novel modes of thought in response to the emergence of new factors and anticipated developments, whether on the national or the international level, factors and developments which the mass, lacking requisite specialized knowledge, could not reasonably be expected to assimilate without some instruction and guidance. We thus come face to face with a dilemma of democracy. In an age of dynamic change, including technological advances which increasingly and without warning proffer to man opportunities for good or evil according to his choice, and when instant action may be called for to avoid the latter, how can governments hope to carry with them the approval, albeit implied, of the mass? As far as one may judge in the present state of our knowledge, the answer seems to be contained in more sophisticated communications, a technological remedy to a technological disease, always provided that sight is not lost of the character of good public relations as a *two-way operation*, intrinsically educative, in which government and people in turn influence one another with a view to establishing that harmony of interest characteristic of any efficient and beneficent régime, particularly that of a democracy.

Similar imperatives are increasingly apparent in the conglomerates which feature so prominently in the modern industrialized state, whether in the public or the private sector. For example *market research*, a species of public relations, has developed in response to the dependence of the economics of mass production on the assurance that its products will be acceptable to the demands of a mass consumer. It goes hand in hand with *publicity*, which seeks to stimulate those demands. However, in some of its forms, publicity differs from public relations. Inasmuch as publicity may aim at subjecting minds, distorting facts, and interfering with freedom of choice, it has more in common with certain types of propaganda which we shall discuss later in this chapter. Modern conglomerates maintain on their staffs, or have access to the services of, professional public relations experts, whose functions include the maintenance of *communications* between the workers and the administration, in a situation where feelings of depersonalization and of remoteness conflict with that contemporary desire for participation which manifests itself at the industrial no less than at the national level. The importance of ever more sophisticated and efficient public relations links cannot be denied in an age which constantly affords examples of industrial unrest, including strikes, sometimes attributable less to grievances resulting from low wages and poor conditions than to feelings of remoteness from "the men at the top", whose very identity may be unknown to the mass of workers.

In the multiplicity of its facets the science of public relations mirrors the ever developing complexity and specialization of the modern world. In such circumstances where the science constantly assumes new aspects and responsibilities, and bearing in mind its essential research function, it inevitably defies exact definition. We must therefore content ourselves with the observation that it has become an indispensable tool in the hands of any organization, including governments, charged with the responsibility of making policy, enunciating legislation, and devising executive measures affecting large groups of people.

At the widest level, public relations are vital for the fostering of those international attitudes which we regard as inseparable from the proper formulation and projection of information for peace. In Part Two—*The Arab Cause*—we shall examine the workings of public relations in terms of the Arab-Israeli confrontation, and shall observe the ways in which the world's response to the successive phases of that crisis has been conditioned by the extent and manner in which the participating states and organizations have employed the public relations and propaganda media at their disposal. Before doing so it is necessary, among other things, to turn our attention to the particular characteristics of propaganda itself.

(c) The concept of propaganda

Like information in general and like public relations, propaganda has been with us in one form or another throughout recorded time. The hieroglyphics of Ancient Egypt recorded detailed accounts of every feat of arms, of every peace treaty, of every economic transaction or expedition sponsored by the Pharaoh, often proclaiming glories which could have been more correctly ascribed to some predecessor. Ancient Hindu manuscripts contain advice on propaganda; for example in Kautilya's *Arthasastra* we find:

> "The King's astrologers and other followers must rouse the fervour of the army, and his secret agents must spread rumours between the ranks of the enemy that they must assuredly be overcome."

According to Driencourt, Aristotle's book on *Rhetoric* provided

> " . . . the first surviving handbook of its kind of propaganda: the propaganda of persuasion by speech and oratory. The book remains a classic of spoken propaganda as technique."[23]

Although it seems fair to assert that propaganda has always existed, the present century has, in this field no less than in that of public relations, witnessed such a transformation in the incidence of propaganda as to suggest changes of kind rather than mere changes of degree. The progress of education in making the average person accessible to propaganda efforts, coupled with the proliferation of the media rendered possible by technology, has enormously spread the catchment area. A world wide audience, reared on a diet of information, public relations and propaganda, has become increasingly hungry for this fare. The propaganda statements of one group stimulate counter-propaganda from its opponents, which in turn gives rise to a propaganda rebuttal from the first group, and so on. More propaganda breeds still more propaganda. The same technological advances in this, as in other areas of progress, have been accompanied by improving expertise and professionalism. Like public relations, propaganda and its twin publicity have as never before been researched by academic and practitioner alike. While the motivation of the former may lie in the realm of pure knowledge for its own sake, the latter has predictably drawn from the findings of those more or

[23] Driencourt, *La Propagande, Nouvelle Force Politique*, p. 27.

less disinterested studies lessons and techniques which he has been only too inclined to put to work on purely materialistic tasks. In such circumstances it was only to be expected that propaganda should become more self-conscious and sophisticated. Moreover, given the ill-repute attaching to it following its widespread use by the Nazis, its practitioners have been at pains to disguise it as pure information as far as possible. Notwithstanding some successes, these tactics of concealment have done nothing to diminish the present and comparatively recent public awareness of the existence of propaganda as such.

Propaganda is a favourite tool of political oppositionists, since it is comparatively cheap and its sources may be left concealed. The unification of Italy, Germany and most modern states was preceded and accompanied by the active promotion of nationalistic emotions, spread in the main by vocal minorities. Social revolutionary propaganda has laid down the groundwork of maximum arousal techniques by way of political organisms and their affiliates. Non-political movements also use propaganda to induce unsympathetic authorities to refrain from interfering with them. A movement is non-political when its pronounced aim does not call for changes to the institutions of power. All movements have consequences, however, which in some degree affect the internal and external balance of power, regardless of the intended purpose. Sensing the degree to which all social processes are linked together, the wielders of power often resort to the persecution of minority movements, or try to manipulate them for political purposes. Nevertheless, propaganda has sometimes been effective in staving off political intervention, especially when the propaganda appeal is made in the name of divine or natural law. It is small surprise, then, to discover that the incentives to engage in propaganda diminish when hopes are frustrated. Labour movements have gone through periods of revulsion against *mere talk* in favour of strictly economic measures or even violence.

Possibly the greatest incentives for propaganda in our age have been economic and connected with the growth of industrialism. Advertising media resulted from the speculation which fed the coffers of capital upon which the expansion of commerce and industry depended. As we noted earlier in our discussion on the market research function of public relations, the advantages of large-scale production could be achieved by the successful stimulation of consumer demand. For publicity purposes, therefore, the advertising media trained millions of buyers to change their taste in clothes, interior decoration, personal habits and dress, eating and amusement. The use of mass-persuasion was accelerated by the spread of literacy and education generally, and by the enormous growth of mass media.

Conceptually organic, propaganda is no more susceptible to the processes of codification than other forms of organized information. The problems of definition adduced in respect of public relations apply equally to the case of propaganda. In some ways a derivative of public relations, propaganda used in the widest context, or as social psychologists have sometimes defined it, simply means any attempt to influence minds and opinions. But this would encompass almost all forms of communication, education and information. A somewhat narrower concept of propaganda is the dissemination of information from concealed sources or with concealed objectives. Motives are difficult to designate and record, and can be reported only indirectly since they are subjective states, and the discussion of motives usually involves evaluation. Yet a motive of devious manipulation, and its evaluation, must enter into what most social scientists (as well as the common man) have defined as propaganda.

F. Tonnies has characterized propaganda as "the agitation of public opinion on a large scale for the purpose of spreading an idea without regard to its truth or accuracy." Propaganda, therefore, refers to "any organized or cohesive group effort to spread a particular doctrine or series of doctrines." Thus, in its simplest and most inclusive context, the propaganda process is an attempt to convince. There is a conscious and definite interest in the inculcation of a particular content into the attitudes and opinions of as yet unconvinced individuals and groups, rather than an attempt to convince through objectivity and discussion.

The scope of this concept may be confined by noting that propaganda is developed within the process of communication, as opposed to the control of opinion by coercion or other forms of behaviour. It may be defined as:

"a technique of social control, or as a species of social movement. As technique, it is the manipulation of collective attitudes by the use of significant symbols (words, pictures, tunes) rather than violence, bribes or boycott."[24]

We may further delimit our scope by noting that propaganda is material which is consciously disseminated, with a preconceived intent on the part of the propagandist: "Propaganda refers to the conscious attempt to manage the minds of other, and usually more numerous, publics."[25]

Again, propaganda is usually characterized by the selection of material favourable to the interest of the propagandist, and the suppression of unfavourable information, for there is no attempt to present the facts objectively. There may be deliberate distortion by selection, for the objective of the propagandist is to achieve public acceptance of the conclusions, not to argue the logical analysis of the relative merits of the case.

The most general conclusion about propaganda is that it increases whenever the general equilibrium of society is threatened or upset, and decreases with the restoration of the imperilled equilibrium or with the emergence of a new level of adjustment. This view needs to be more specific in order to account for the use of propaganda, rather than coercion, when social equilibrium is endangered. In addition, the likelihood of propaganda is increased whenever there are traditional institutions of freedom, whether free government, free market, free education or free activity.

In short, it can be said that during any given period the volume of propaganda activity depends upon such factors as: (a) the introduction or discouragement of new acts; (b) the availability of mass media and the prevailing level of literacy and general education; (c) the degree of discontent with the old; (d) the number of persons performing or refraining from performing a new act; and (e) the depth of devotion to persuasion in place of coercion.

Whatever arouses controversy is likely to foster propaganda until

[24] H. D. Lasswell, *The Person: Subject and Object of Propaganda*, Ann. Am. Acad. Pol. Soc. Sci., pp. 179–89.
[25] H. L. Childs, *The American Political Scene* (E. B. Logan, ed.) Harper & Brothers, New York, 1936, p. 226.

the incentives which sustain the use of mass persuasion are reduced, or discontent is dissipated fruitlessly, or a new positive adjustment is made in prevailing social practice.

As an act of advocacy, propaganda differs from such parallel methods of communication as instruction, information and orientation; for it selects the contents of communication in such a way as to influence attitudes on controversial issues. When the government publishes a booklet on the care and feeding of babies, this act is informative and instructive, not propagandist in nature, unless there is doubt about the content of the booklet. Similarly, to analyse controversial ideologies for the sake of sharing enlightenment is inquiry, not propaganda. Private arguments between friends cannot be termed propaganda unless they are part of an organized campaign to disseminate certain views. Thus propaganda involves psychology, participation and controversy. Since any political act may influence mass opinion, regardless of the means employed, an important part of total policy is the calculating and managing of psychological effects. When aimed at an enemy during wartime, this is *psychological warfare*.

The volume of propaganda is affected by whatever discredits the old or reduces the difficulty of behaving in new ways. What is particularly significant to propaganda is the volume or heterogeneity of a public. Even in totalitarian states, a massive effort of internal persuasion is necessary in order to overcome the links of old associations, or fear, or hostility, or perplexity at the prospect of a new way of life. In Soviet Russia (after 1921) for instance, the full force of radio, lectures and pamphlets was mobilized in a crescendo of massive campaigns on behalf of literacy, the care of tractors, and the raising of hygienic standards. Inborn resistance was overcome by a broadside of symbols and slogans assisted by every other influence.

According to Hitler, propaganda is a means to an end and is complementary to the aims of information. Propaganda, therefore, must have a definite plan for communication with the masses, with a strategic purpose in view; otherwise, it would be simply playing with the thoughts and emotions of the masses. Josef Goebbels defined political propaganda in his famous speech in Nuremberg on 6 September 1934. He said:

"Political propaganda is designed to establish the state's beliefs in the minds of the masses and make them committed to these beliefs. Propaganda could no longer be simply a means to seize power; it had to become a means for consolidating this power. Political propaganda is the most effective weapon for seizing power and for serving the state if we intend to stay in power."[26]

In Socialist countries, the political propagandist is regarded as a man who serves the interests of the state. Lenin viewed this kind of propaganda as the political education which should be undertaken by every communist. Hence, the name of "agitator", which denotes one who acts to spread communism in bourgeois countries.[27]

Short of tidy definition we can identify the major characteristics of propaganda. Dealing in the persuasion of mass opinion rather than in its physical coercion, flourishing in conditions of controversy, such as the alienation of a large segment of the public from the views or interests of the dominant group, propaganda is primarily concerned with the promotion of predetermined doctrines. To this end, it is bound to be selective in its use of information, normally disseminating only those facts most likely to suit its purpose. That is not to say that propaganda is necessarily dishonest or harmful, though the present century provides examples enough of its calamitous results in the hands of a group prepared to distort truth through oversimplification or deliberate falsehood, on the grounds that conviction of the rightness of the doctrines propagated justified any means conducive to acceptance. Notwithstanding the stigma attaching to propaganda following the activities of such groups, it seems only fair to point out that the selectivity in terms of material need not operate against the public interest, always provided it is employed not to stifle essential facts however injurious to its case, but rather to bring to light truths which might otherwise remain hidden. For example a party in opposition may justifiably concentrate its propaganda effort on publicising information which the dominant group has been at pains to conceal.

[26] Driencourt, *La Propagande, Nouvelle Force Politique*, Paris, 1950, p. 80.
[27] Lenin, *Que Faire?* Moscow, 1954, p. 197.

(d) Information, public relations and propaganda compared and contrasted

Strictly speaking, information, even in largely unprocessed form, is never motiveless, for every action implies the consequence of some stimulus, conscious or not. For example, the purely instructional functions of formal education must have originated in the needs of social groups, however small, for types of expertise essential to existence in face of rudimentary problems, whether natural or man-made. Instruction of this sort has long since become formalized and the original motivation is forgotten. When, however, we turn from mere instruction to other functions of education in its fullest sense, we find motive in the inculcation of socially desirable modes of thought, with at the highest level of education proper guidance on the skill of thinking. This generates a critical faculty on the part of individual and group alike, and is mankind's guarantee against the consequences of the distortion inherent in propaganda in its corrupt form. Yet, while pure information can never be without motive, the motivational aspect of the acquisition of pure information figures relatively small by comparison with motivational contributions to the spread of public relations and propaganda which for this reason we have designated as *highly motivated*.

In addition to their high motivation, public relations and propaganda display other shared characteristics, setting them apart from pure information. Both address themselves to masses of people rather than to individuals or small homogeneous groups. Both deal in persuasion rather than coercion. Both employ selection by habitually presenting only those facts and truths relevant to the task in hand. Both are affected by the modern phenomenon of proliferating audiences, which educational and technological progress, in the shape of growing literacy and ever more accessible communications, daily render more receptive to novel ideas, good and bad. And both employ the same media, which we shall discuss more fully in the fifth chapter.

Public relations and propaganda part company in the objectives to whose attainment they direct their capacities for persuasion, selectivity and use of the media. As we saw earlier, public relations are or should be constantly concerned with harmony, that is the spreading of awareness of an identity of interest as between government and governed, administrators and the people, employer and employee, the fulfilment of the democratic ideal of participation and the eradication of its antithesis: alienation. Public relations are successful in proportion to their efficacy not only in creating but also in maintaining the conditions of this harmony. Their job is never done. By contrast, propaganda thrives in an atmosphere of disharmony, of conflict and of disenchantment on the part of a particular group with the dominant ethics, ideals or policy within a given society, irrespective of whether those ethics, ideals and policy are consciously embraced by the majority, or, as is often the case, are merely acquiesced in through the ignorance or apathy of the mass, or even forcibly imposed by the governing group.

Again, public relations and propaganda differ in the formulation of doctrine, and, assuming the propaganda to be successful, in the manner of the acceptance of the doctrine by public opinion. For with public relations the doctrine and resulting policy are expounded only after careful study of public attitudes and expectations. Public relations are a two-way affair, entailing diligent research on the part of their practitioners, followed by the education in its fullest sense of the public and its representatives. With propaganda on the other hand the process is essentially one of the imposition by persuasion of predetermined doctrines. This is not to deny that in their initiation the doctrines may not have passed through a phase of active discussion and independent thought, have enjoyed the benefits of public opinion research in the quest for the truth and all relevant data, and have been exposed to public relations techniques. But those were the preliminaries to the propagating phase and will probably have been largely confined to the circle of the future propagators. The real propaganda starts only after a body of doctrine, a *party line*, has been hammered out. At that stage it is not easily susceptible to modification except in its more peripheral aspects. To this extent, and while recognizing that there are areas in which the frontiers of public relations and propaganda become blurred, we can as a working distinction say that public relations differ from propaganda, in so far as the former tend to encourage independent thought and the free exchange of opinion between the ruling group and the mass, whereas propaganda at its most characteristic discourages these activities. Moreover, while the job of public relations is never done, that of propaganda has a more limited objective. Once the propagandists have succeeded, their task is by definition complete. In a political context, for example, a party which has used propaganda to achieve democratic power is likely thereafter to direct its persuasive energies into public relations channels. If it does resort to propaganda, this will really be new propaganda, or more properly counter-propaganda, directed to the maintenance of the party in power through combating the propaganda of its rivals, who may include the former government party as well as other newly disaffected groups.

Finally and importantly we come to an aspect of the formation of public opinion where public relations and propaganda merge. The collective capabilities of the mass are not sufficient, at any rate up to the present time, for public opinion always to comprehend the logic of untried or unpopular lines of action. For example, public opinion may vaguely appreciate the existence of a national financial crisis while not being prepared to accept the necessity for increased taxation, or it may theoretically recognize the value of anti-pollution measures while resisting the application of consequent regulations. In the present condition of democracy it is important for the electorate to be convinced of the national advantages of unpalatable measures; otherwise they are open to persuasion by specious arguments and propaganda from the opposition party. Moreover, government measures increasingly entail a degree of urgency for their effective promulgation. But a sense of haste is not characteristic of the normal workings of public relations, based as they are on extensive research and discussion. In such circumstances, governments are sometimes justified in employing propaganda to bring before the public the salient truths of an issue, truths which the mass could not otherwise be expected to grasp quickly, if at all, particularly if they are of a specialized or technical nature.

The compulsions towards honest propaganda of this sort are especially strong in the realm of international affairs, where timing is often critical, where many key facts are available as classified information known only at the highest level, where the consequences of a wrong decision are incalculable, and where in any case the pre-existence of propaganda-conditioned reflexes properly calls for counter-propaganda to supply world opinion with the means of effecting a balanced judgement, in other words to bring to light an adequate selection of facts and essential considerations which would otherwise remain hidden. The Arab–Israeli confrontation, with which we shall concern ourselves later in this book, admirably illustrates this function, in a situation in which the Zionist party to the conflict has for decades exploited its greater access to the mass media to mould much of world opinion in a manner favourable to its cause. The interests of truth and objectivity demand the presentation of the facts in their totality, and consequently demand the most effective and widest publication of the Arab case. It is in circumstances like these that public relations, in alliance with honest propaganda, exercise their most valuable function by bringing before world public opinion the truth in its most complete yet assimilable form. This is the essence of information for justice and peace.

4
Formative Elements of Public Opinion: Components

(a) Main and auxiliary elements

We pass now from the conceptual facet of our study to the means by which public opinion is shaped. In its conscious formation it results from the use of the media, which we shall describe and attempt to evaluate in the next chapter. First of all something must be said about less apparent, even elusive, formative influences. To distinguish them from information, we refer to these formative elements as the components of public opinion. Upon the presence, to a greater or less extent, at any time, of these components, and upon their interaction one with another, depend the effectiveness and proper use of the various information media.

Scholars may define public opinion in different ways; yet they unanimously agree about its formative elements. Where they differ concerns the factor of priority: which element precedes the other. The main components then may be summarized thus:

first: the *people* from whom the group or public is formed;

second: the *physical environment* in which these people live;

third: the *challenges*, needs and potentialities which control their lives;

fourth: characteristics of their *behavioural patterns*.

Each of these main components embodies other auxiliary ones from which, directly or indirectly, it emanates. These are: the importance of the individual; cultural heritage and upbringing; events; customary beliefs, common values and nationalism; habit, attitude and knowledge; family, school and religion; myths and legends; leadership.

(b) The importance of people

Man has always striven to understand himself and the forces affecting him, so as to obtain better control over his own circumstances and destiny. The physical environment is now fairly well understood. The understanding and control of man himself, however, have not been nearly so successful.

For various reasons, it is not possible to know the totality of one particular person; nor, consequently, is it possible to know all about several people, however lengthy or comprehensive the research. What little knowledge man possesses is not too well unified, and so only segments can be grasped at a given moment. What is known systematically about the individual in psychology has been learned from observing him carefully under clinical conditions. An inferential understanding of his behaviour may be acquired by studying lower animal organisms whose lives can be controlled more easily and efficiently. Unfortunately, psychologists are not in agreement concerning principles of human behaviour. In a real sense there are schools of psychology, as well as concepts and theories, which vary as a function of the particular psychologist's training, bias and interests. Most of the differences are verbal, but a few are quite fundamental. Some psychologists, for instance, contend that an explanation of an individual's behaviour in a given situation is not adequate until it can be related to the basic, innate drives within all organisms, such as the need for sex or food. In short, the application of psychological principles or laws to social situations involving many people is no easy matter, because so often it is next to impossible to control or specify the other conditions which are supposed to be equal and which certainly, in the realm of man's social life, almost never are.

At any event, mutual misunderstanding between people is a necessary and important matter, if only because it is these very people who constitute the formative elements of public opinion. They are the ones whose real interest determines the social behaviour which realizes their aspirations, whether for war or for peace.

(c) Cultural heritage and upbringing

Cultural heritage is one of the main constituents of public opinion. It plays an important part in the adaptability of individuals or groups, and prepares them for certain responses or reactions that influence their social behavioural patterns. The more that is known concerning the particular social-class status of the family in which the child is born and will be reared, the more specific can the predictions become. For instance, should the child be raised in a staunchly Republican rural area of the United States, and should his family be also traditionally Republican, the odds are in favour of his voting the straight Republican ticket at the age of eighteen. Should the family be Catholic, it is likely that he will adhere to the Catholic viewpoint on political, social, economic and international issues. If he is to be educated in upper-class surroundings, it is probable that he will never be an active supporter of a revolutionary movement. It is safe to say, too, that he will absorb the racial prejudices, if any, of his parents and his immediate milieu. The future role of an embryo in the public opinion of his time, in short, is not completely unpredictable.

There is nothing mysterious about what the anthropologists call culture; it is a system of habits which all adults share in varying degrees, habits which help them in making adjustments to their environment and to one another, and which children acquire from their parents and from contact with their society. To state that a country has a tradition of obedience or of recklessness is to imply that its people are obedient or reckless and that the habits associated with those traits are reinforced in the young. The various social institutions, especially the family, the church and the immediate community, have as their most important functions the perpetuation of culture or a segment thereof.

It must be recognized, however, that forecasts concerning very specific habits or attitudes which are based exclusively on the knowledge of cultural traditions can often go astray. In the first place, traditions are frequently perpetuated only after undergoing some change. Historical events leave their mark upon a society, which means that for some time their effects continue to be transmitted from generation to generation. The loss of the American Civil War by the South, for example, led to the establishment of certain traditions which thereafter have been influencing Southern public opinion on many crucial issues. The contemporary importance of these traditions as factors determining public opinion cannot be discovered from a detailed analysis of the Civil War, its aftermath, and even conditions in the South during the first seven decades of this century: the social heritage in this respect has changed with the passage of time. Some Southerners, for example, are still hostile towards the North, but their hostility has grown less intense and is invoked less frequently. The forms and the strength of any tradition among the people whose public opinion is being analysed must be ascertained. Culture changes because the people who embody it respond to varying circumstances in their society.

Public opinion on issues that are definitely related to the cultural heritage may be called *enduring public opinion*, whereas that which appears to be unrelated to solutions and decisions already agreed upon in the culture may be termed *momentary public opinion*. For instance, the aversion of the Arab people from imperialism and foreign domination may be called enduring public opinion, since this aversion stems from a cultural tradition going back to our forefathers. On the other hand, a local disaster such as a fire or an earthquake will form a momentary public opinion, for, in spite of the impact of such events, the response does not emanate from any deep-rooted cultural tradition.

Not every member of a society indiscriminately acquires all of that society's cultural traditions. The specific customs he learns are those of the various groups to which he may belong. Individuals in our society, for instance, are sex-typed. As a function of their sex, they are trained in different ways and are expected to assume different social roles. Dolls versus engines, daintiness versus toughness, sewing versus arithmetic, restraint versus freedom, marriage versus career—it is almost automatically possible to associate the first of each of these five pairs with girls and women and the second with boys and men. At the same time, the two sexes are also socialized somewhat similarly in respect to many issues such as religious beliefs and standards of living. Social groups frequently follow cultural traditions which present greater contrasts. Therefore, when the public opinion of a group is being related to culture, the particular segment of the culture for that specific group must be specified.

Before culture can determine behaviour, moreover, the individual's skill must be adequate to permit more or less normal learning.

The behaviour of a blind or moronic infant will be markedly affected by the physical disability or by the low intelligence. In certain aspects, he is constitutionally incapable of absorbing what his contemporaries can learn. Normal skill of this kind, however, can be assumed for public opinion in general, although occasionally an abnormal or out-standing individual such as a leader may have to be surveyed in all his uniqueness.

Studies have been made of identical twins who, for fortuitous reasons, have been reared apart in contrasting social environments. When examined later in life, they are found to differ in respect of personality traits and in intelligence as measured by tests. The differences cannot be ascribed to the factor of skill. To a certain extent they must be attributed to variations in the cultural surroundings, but they must also result from divergent methods of socialization. It would seem that behaviour in general is influenced by the content of culture as well as by the ways in which culture is learned.

Many of the socializing influences are themselves culturally deter-mined. Thus, in respect of *upbringing*, parents employ traditional ways of caring for the infant. Some parents, however, are not able to follow the dictates of the culture. If they are neurotic, their neurosis may find expression especially at the points where tradition is vague. They may over or under-punish a child because they, as well as less disturbed people, honestly do not know in what circumstances and how often to encourage or discourage certain types of behaviour in the young. Such treatment—whether good or bad—will very likely have permanent effects upon the children's adult personality, and hence will influence them in their role as carriers or representatives of public opinion. This is simply another application of the principle that *present behaviour results from past experiences*.

Each generation, apparently, is doomed to face and experience its own difficult problems as it is being socialized. During the childhood of various generations there are booms or depressions, wars in progress or repercussions from wars, slow or rapid social changes, a dominating spirit of optimism or of fatalism. Each crisis, the peculiar condition of a given society at a given period, has an impact on children. Youngsters during wartime have to learn about short-ages, rationing, sacrifices, death, battles and hatred. What effect these lessons have upon them later depends upon the kind of world they find at hand when they begin to function as independent adults.

If the basis for enduring public opinion is established during socialization, then this type of public opinion is changed when the methods of socialization are altered; yet they cannot be easily altered, because they are part of the culture. Here, then, is an important reason why basic social changes occur so slowly. The interaction, however, can be affected when either youth in the process of socialization or adults in the process of socializing are changed.

Much of public opinion emanates from *enduring public opinion* which has been moulded in varying degrees in the course of an upbringing. A glance through history shows that both the historian and the average man tend to vacillate between two viewpoints: sometimes it seems as if history were determined by social or economic forces, and sometimes as if by great men or leaders.

(d) Events

Psychologists define an event as a collection of complicated stimuli which produce responses within people. Culture affects people by producing an event such as the celebration of a national holiday, or the activities of the police force. The process of socialization is a serial one, like weaning, or like a conversation at the dinner table which deliberately focuses upon etiquette, or which inadvertently reveals to a child the prejudices of the parents. Leaders create events such as a speech at a mass meeting, or an administrative ruling. These have an impact upon people.

Each event is an outgrowth of forces within the society, whether it be part of the cultural tradition, a consequence of socialization, or an expression of leadership. The relation of the event to society, however, is not always easy to determine and, therefore, it is often pragmatically convenient to refer to the event itself as the determinant.

During a period of inflation, for instance, there are many factors at work. Some of these arise from social and economic strains having a long history of their own, others spring from momentary interactions between numerous peoples. These factors need not be determined to point out the concrete stimuli accompanying the inflation which influences people and public opinion.

Natural events are sometimes of crucial importance in the determination of human responses. A hurricane sweeps through a community, and people's behaviour towards one another is changed:
they become more friendly and mutually helpful and co-operative in
a manner which departs from their normal custom. At such a moment, they will tolerate or encourage actions which ordinarily are
taboo. But, natural events of this type being of limited duration,
public opinion is affected by them only for a while. As a matter of
fact, almost all human reactions to natural events also contain a
cultural element. It is misleading to believe that the natural in
Nature necessarily brings out the natural in Man. During and after
a hurricane, people may be terrified and behave atypically, but even
then their cultural background will affect a segment of their behaviour. Most men in our society, for instance, will allow women to be
rescued first from a sinking ship or a burning building. Actual public
opinion during a catastrophe, therefore, is not entirely dependent
on the event and its consequence: more enduring elements may be at
work too.

External public opinion is itself an event which affects not only
leaders but also the people themselves who are expressing their attitudes. What they think and do in the future is largely dependent upon
the extent to which their present behaviour proves rewarding or
punishing. If, for instance, actual public opinion approves of
drinking, and drinking is not proscribed by law, then the chances of
future indulgence in drink are increased. Repetition may involve
both the participants and their neighbours who have learned that
such behaviour is tolerated. In no less mysterious a fashion does
drinking become a cultural tradition and part of enduring public
opinion in an area.

(e) Customary beliefs, common values and nationalism

Clyde Kluckhohn and Dorothea Leighton point out that a stable
social structure prevails only so long as the majority of individuals in
a society find enough satisfaction in the attainment of socially
approved goals to compensate for the constraint which a stable social
life imposes. The means and ends of the culture of an ordered society
make sense to the participants. Synthesis is achieved partly through

the overt statement of dominant conceptions and aspirations of the group in its codes, fostered through the family, religious and other institutions, and partly through unconscious apperceptive habits, habitual ways of looking at events.[1] The ways in which the group expects its participants to view things become identified with an immutable human nature.

> "To most people most of the time the habitual ways of speaking, acting, feeling and reacting to which they have been accustomed from childhood, become as much a part of the inevitables of life as the air they breathe, and they tend unconsciously to feel that all 'normal' human beings ought to feel and behave only within the range of variation permitted by their own way of life. Then, however, when they have to deal with other groups who have been brought up with a somewhat different set of unquestioned and habitual assumptions about the nature of things, they all too often label the other group as 'ignorant' or superstitious, 'stupid' or stubborn."[2]

The physical scientists were not exceptional in their attitude that facts and social policy do not mix. For example, certain ideas expressed by Ralph Linton in 1936 were looked upon at least as mildly unusual. He said:

> "None of the problems involved in the present situation are really insoluble, and, if our culture and society collapse, they will not fall from lack of intelligence to meet this situation, but from lack of any united will to put the requisite changes into effect. What the modern world needs far more than improved production methods or even more equitable distribution of their results, is a series of mutually consistent ideas and values in which all its members can participate.
>
> Perhaps something of the sort can be developed in time to prevent the collapse which otherwise seems inevitable."[3]

Since the time that Linton wrote these words, his position has been accepted widely. Of course, Linton had struck upon nothing new. He was merely re-shaping ideas as old as the history of thought.

[1] Clyde Kluckhohn and Dorothea Leighton, *The Navaho*, Cambridge, Harvard University Press, 1946, p. 217.
[2] *Ibid.*, p. 232.
[3] Ralph Linton, *The Study of Man*, New York, D. Appleton-Century Co., 1936, p. 287.

Plato viewed a person isolated from a state as no person at all; an arm separated from the body, although looking like an arm, can have no function. Coming down to modern times, we find John Dewey saying that for a number of persons to form a community "there must be values prized in common."[4]

In *The Making of the Modern Mind*, John Herman Randall says:

"Whatever its origin and its ultimate value, patriotism is beyond doubt the most widespread social idea of the day; it is the modern religion, far stronger than mere Christianity in any of its forms, and for the tribal gods of which masses of men will still die. Commercial and industrial expansion afford it large scope, but it is in war, in devotion to military glory and heroism, that it finds its chief rituals. Nationalism has been taught . . . until to fail to feel the sweeping force of its appeal is to fail to belong to the modern world, to be an outlaw and a wanderer upon the face of the earth—that dreadful thing, a man without a country . . . "[5]

Harold J. Laski notes that in our political thinking we tend

"to adopt a sort of mystic monism as the true path of thought. We represent a State as a vast series of concentric circles, each one enveloping the other as we move from individual to family, from family to village, from village to city, to county, then to the all-embracing State . . . Trade-unionists and capitalists alike must surrender the interest of their smaller and antithetic group persons to the larger demands of that all-embracing One, the State. Of that One, it is first that you are part; only in secondary fashion do you belong to church, or class, or race . . . "[6]

Aldous Huxley has summarized nationalism as the theory that the state to which a person is subject is the only true god, and that all other states are false gods.[7]

(f) Habit, attitude and knowledge

The outstanding characteristic of human beings, it has been said and

[4] John Dewey, *Freedom and Culture*, New York, G. P. Putnam's Sons, 1939, p. 12.
[5] John Herman Randall Jr., *The Making of the Modern Mind*, revised edition, Boston, Houghton Mifflin Co., 1940, pp. 668–669.
[6] Harold J. Laski, *Studies in the Problem of Sovereignty*, New Haven, Yale University Press, 1917, pp. 3–5.
[7] Aldous Huxley, *Ape and Essence*, New York, Harper and Brothers, 1948, p. 126.

should be said again and again, is their ability to learn. The progress of the infant to maturity is measured by what he learns. Some of this depends upon his physiological development and capacity, but the rest depends upon the experiences he has in his environment and subsequently upon the effects these experiences have on his personality. Learning refers to behaviour, which becomes different as a result of past experience. The differences can be roughly described as a change in the stimuli to which approximately the same response is made, or as a change in the response to approximately the same stimuli. All learning, including the simplest type of conditioning, requires that a drive be active within the individual and that some kind of reward be attained. Those famous dogs of Pavlov, for instance, which salivated after hearing the sound of a tuning fork when that sound had previously occurred before the unconditioned stimulus of food, exhibited this learning only under certain conditions: they had to be hungry; an optimum time interval had to separate the two stimuli; they had to be undistracted by other sounds; and occasionally the conditioned response of salivating to the bell had to be reinforced by actually offering them food.

A learned connection between any stimulus and any response is defined as a *habit*. A habit, however, is not a mechanical bond between any one stimulus and any one response, functioning automatically when the stimulus is perceived. Again, a drive must be active, or else the stimulus is not perceived, or no response occurs: habits serve drives. The stimulus, moreover, may be complex and patterned, such as the face of a person which habitually provokes an unfriendly response. It may be an internal response, like a thought after seeing a sign, which acts also as a stimulus to evoke a drive—this type of response is called a drive-producing response, or a response with drive value. The response components of the habit, in addition, need not be identical: a man who wants to smoke may habitually reach for a cigarette with his right or his left hand, he may smoke one of his own on one occasion, or borrow one from a friend on another, or he may be content with any form of tobacco. The concept of habit, therefore, is being employed most broadly to include behaviour as diverse as swimming or race prejudice. Learning can then be viewed as the process of establishing, weakening, strengthening or eliminating habits. Certain aspects of personality are so important that they must be singled out for special treatment. They are responses which are habitually evoked, but they also possess relatively singular characteristics. Here, they will be termed attitude and knowledge.

An individual has *attitudes* toward other people and toward objects in his environment. Usually an emotional or evaluative reaction is involved: the attitude is friendly or unfriendly, favourable or unfavourable, positive or negative, respectful or disrespectful, etc. When it is said that a person has an attitude toward his country, other nations, democracy, communism, his friends, his enemies, Negroes, Jews, meat, oranges, contraception or helicopters, the implication is that he always has either a specific or a general feeling regarding these concrete or symbolic stimuli, and that his behaviour is more or less governed accordingly.

Actually, as employed by laymen and social scientists, *attitude* is a somewhat vague term which frequently merely calls attention to a psychological problem without contributing to a coherent solution. It is, however, a convenient concept when a detailed analysis of individual behaviour is not feasible—as is almost always the case in studying public opinion and propaganda—provided that its psychological attributes are specified.

An attitude is an internal response which the individual has learned as a result of past rewards and punishment. Attitudes are acquired and are not inborn; and a considerable part of human behaviour depends upon the social environment rather than upon the germ plasm. The attitudes behind race prejudice, for example, are the culmination of previous experiences, and they therefore are inevitable only because such experiences are likely to occur and recur in a particular society. Similarly, political attitudes develop as the individual matures.

Before an attitude can be aroused, some kind of stimulus has had to be present. The stimuli may be varied—the colour of a face, the shape of a nose, the curl of the hair, the nature of the surname, the type of clothing, alleged forms of conduct, and the sound of a particular word are some of the stimuli evoking race prejudice—but almost always they are part of a pattern, or are arranged in what has been called a *gradient*.

Attitudes, moreover, are a distinctive kind of internal response. When they are aroused, they predispose the individual to make certain overt responses. The attitude, consequently, has become an *anticipatory response*, which is one occurring earlier in a response sequence than it did originally, just as a child who has been burned by touching a radiator soon learns to keep clear of all objects looking like radiators *before* he touches them.

The complicated character of an attitude becomes more evident when its drive property is examined in relation to the entire personality of the individual. Some stimulus, for example, makes the individual aware of the fact that he is hungry. Such a drive, however does not function by itself: he almost never has a generalized craving for food, but seeks a particular kind more or less in accordance with the customs of his everyday existence.

Almost every internal response, therefore, involves an attitude. However, some differentiation between an attitudinal response and other internal responses must be clarified. Internal responses with stimulus and drive value may be called attitudes only when the external responses to which they give rise are considered significant in society.

Innumerable habitual responses occur within the individual which have no drive value, or at least a minimal drive value. The response to the stimulus: "What comes after three?" is of course: "Four". Such a response is called knowledge. *Knowledge* is ordinarily considered to be, very simply, that which is known about any kind of phenomenon. The implication is always that the knowledge either resides directly within an individual, or is in a form (like a book) that can be readily learned by somebody. Knowledge is thus another residue of past experience which can affect present and future behaviour. The concept of knowledge, then, refers not only to schooling or technical competence, but also to experience. Knowledge as an habitual response is related to drive and hence to attitude. Some stimulus must arouse a response involving knowledge, and almost always a drive has been previously aroused.

Apparently related to knowledge, but basically different from it, is *skill,* which can be said to represent a person's more or less innate capacity to perceive stimuli and adopt or modify habitual connections between stimuli and responses. Similarly, individuals differ in respect of overall skill called *intelligence*, a term most generally referring to the ability to learn, or at least to that part of the ability which is unaffected by previous experience.

(g) Family, school and religion

Perhaps the most important institutional basis of public opinion is in the *family*. Fundamental attitudes about love, motherhood, individualism, conformity, social status, competition and goals, doubtless find their origin in the family. Early in life, the child learns the stock answers to his endless questions, leading him to realize that probing any matter in depth leads to puzzlement and confusion.

Later on, it becomes clear that most of the answers are built on hearsay, or "this is what people say", or "I may be wrong, but this is my view", or "I heard it on the radio", or "this is the case as far as I know", and so on. . . . By the age of four or five, most children have been conditioned to heed their parents' command by saying stock expressions in a stock manner, based on their past experience.

Formal education—the *school*—takes up the task of preparing children to face life from here. The prime factor of education as an institution forming public opinion is that it does not change opinion to conform to facts, but tends to justify any form of opinion that is part of the existing culture. It is the tool most frequently used to reinforce existing beliefs. Therefore, education must aim at realizing the following goals:

> It must build up character by emphasizing the great and noble deeds of forebears, and the heroism of folklore.
> It must inspire patriotism and love of the motherland.
> It must build up self-respect and stress the merits of endeavour and success.

The influence of *religion* on public opinion is difficult to appraise because of the problems associated with intensity of belief, particularly in matters of family and sex. All major religions tend toward the attitude that sex is to produce offspring and that all sexual activities outside of marriage are sinful. The Kinsey report contains this significant statement:

"The differences in sexual activity between religiously devout persons and religiously inactive persons of the same faith are much greater than the differences between two equally devout groups of different faiths. In regard to total sexual outlet, the religiously inactive groups may have frequencies that are 25 to 75 per cent higher than the frequencies of religiously devout groups. Among religiously inactive males there are definitely higher frequencies of masturbation, pre-marital intercourse, marital intercourse, and the homosexual."

Religion, however, exerts a wide influence on even non-devout individuals, by way of the influence which it has had throughout the centuries. In an older day, when churches and church courts had authority over the life and death of each and every individual, departures from the expressed sexual codes made the culprit painfully aware of the sources of the sexual mores. In the present day, the influence of the church is more indirect; but the ancient religious codes are still the prime source of the attitudes, the ideas, the ideals and the rationalizations by which most individuals pattern their sexual lives. Another tendency is the circular definition process. For example: God is good; good is God. Ask what God is and the answer is "good". Ask what good is and the answer is "God". Undoubtedly, such attitudes influence the sources as well as the formation of public opinion.

(h) Myths and legends

Legends are modified accounts of past events and historic figures, whereas myths are imaginative accounts of the meaning of life. Coming down to us from the past as a part of our cultural heritage, myths and legends are adult extensions of the infantile world of fantasy and make-believe. Whether the birth of a legend is deliberate or not, the fact remains that masses of mankind live in these images. During the latter half of the nineteenth century, various social theorists became increasingly preoccupied with the phenomena. Students of religious ideas and institutions, taking up the cudgels for rationalism, discussed the mythology of the various religions. Evolutionists studied myths and legends as an early development in cultural history. Historians pieced out the historic record with mythological evidence. And finally, by the close of the century and the opening decades of the present one, certain modern beliefs were discussed in terms of mythology and legendry by Sorel, Pareto, Delaisi and others.[8]

Among primitive peoples and in folk cultures, myths and legends are a part of the folklore. These stories satisfy some behavioural need and maintain cultural values. Today, such stories are increasingly imposed by a self-conscious leadership which aims at the promulgation of some doctrine or the elevation of some individual. To be sure, leadership in the past has sometimes used myths and legends as an agency of control, but the leadership of the past did not have mass media and sophisticated publicity agencies at its command.

The aristocrats who ruled feudal society by divine appointment (as was then believed) buttressed their own dominion with an elaborate structure of myths concerning the nature of the physical universe. They looked with no tolerance whatsoever upon the early scientific discoveries. Giordano Bruno was burned at the stake, and Galileo was threatened, not because they said true things about the world, but because the saying of these true things was incompatible with the lordship of the aristocracy. Physical science was one of the weapons which the middle class forged against the aristocracy— which had therefore to do all in its power to prevent the weapons from being forged.

The legends of primary groups relate to a relatively narrow range of values, whereas the scope of the subject matter of legends in the great society is much broader. New legends are created in connection with every social movement, and as the attention areas of modern man have widened the number of his legends has increased.

The mythologies of various people contain anthropomorphic devils. Personification of evil pervades folk thinking, and man has persistently imagined epic struggles between good and evil spirits. Vritra, Ahriman, the Ancient Egyptian Seth and the Satan of Christianity are major evil spirits. Throughout the Middle Ages, people attributed obscure diseases, indefinite pains, piercing sensations in

[8] G. Sorel, *Reflections on Violence*, 1906, authorized translation by T. E. Hulme, Peter Smith, New York 1935; V. Pareto, *The Mind and Society* (English trans.) Harcourt Brace & Co. Inc., New York, 1935, vol. I, sections 650 ff.; F. Delaisi, *Political Myths and Economic Realities*, The Viking Press Inc., New York, 1925.

the region of the heart, kidney pains, paralysis, impotence and many other disorders to the devil's invasion of their person. As the conflicts of the religious ideology with rationalism increased, the devil became associated with reason, argument, dissension and questioning. Folk suspicion of learning ascribed a splendid intellectuality to Satan.

A study of mythology indicates that, whereas legends began as a folk product, they were later consciously manipulated by leaders, churchmen, and politicians.

Hero legends usually ascribe certain elements of mystery to the birth of the hero. The male progenitor is often assumed to be someone other and greater than the legal father. So it was with the Lincoln legend. Put about by Lincoln's opponents in the organized whispering campaigns of the 1860 and 1864 elections, it was a natural folk legend, and gained credence from the inclination of Lincoln's admirers to assume a brilliant natural parentage for their hero. In an earlier age such a legend would have persisted. With the better means of communication available in nineteenth-century America the bastardy tale was finally scotched, though not until half a century after Lincoln's death. The human and historic greatness of Abraham Lincoln has been distorted by legends which highlighted those qualities which the common man or the special pleader has found it convenient to emphasize. Yet, with all its vagaries, distortions and emotional elements, the popular legend may be essentially true to the essence of its subject. As time passes, Lincoln gathers more securely the significance of his period about him, and becomes more and more a national mythos. The remarkable thing about the mythos is that, if history and biography are to be trusted, Lincoln was a worthy man to be made into a symbol of justice, mercy, spiritual and intellectual strength, or a symbol of democracy and freedom. The biographers and historians may not be able to make every fact fit into this picture, even though the mass of facts fits naturally, but the mythos is undisturbed because it has seized upon the best of the Lincoln story as poetic truth.

The Coolidge legend, on the other hand, was created very rapidly in the months immediately succeeding his elevation to the presidency. Organized publicity by the Republican National Committee, and the less organized legend-making of the Washington correspondents soon projected the image of a silent, unintellectual, honest, cautious, shrewd, average man. The newspaper-reading public accepted and embellished the legend. It is now agreed that Calvin Coolidge had the "best press" of any American President. Yet here was a man who, a few years earlier, had been considered by many party leaders as too weak and nondescript for the vice-presidential nomination.

(i) Leadership

The roles and functions of the leader, his characteristics and the techniques of leadership vary with the situation. Disparate groups, differing in size, in the nature of their constituents, and in purposes and functions, require different types of leadership. The characteristics of the leader and the leadership process are obviously dissimilar in a board meeting, a theatre fire, a political rally. Moreover, types of leadership and of preferred personalities vary greatly in different cultures and at different periods of culture history.

The sociologist Georg Simmel declared that submission may be exhibited toward a person, a group or an impersonal principle. But, in large groups, submission to personal authority is the kind most frequently and dramatically exhibited. The leader is the most vital authority to the common man. However, in special groups also, thinking and discussion often depend on appeal to personal authority. Dostoevski has his Grand Inquisitor declare that mankind needed "miracle, mystery and authority", stating that "Man is tormented by no greater anxiety than to find someone quickly to whom he can hand over that gift of freedom with which the ill-fated creature is born."[9]

The guide most favoured by mankind has been the medicine man, or priest, reputed to have direct access to divine wisdom; and in his wake came along presently the philosopher who, sinking a shaft into his own mighty mind, and prospecting and introspecting through its darksome galleries, emerged with absolutes essential to the Good Life: Truth, Beauty, Duty, Faith, Loyalty. The philosopher has never seriously challenged his predecessor in popularity, because he

[9] F. M. Dostoevski, *The Brothers Karamazov*, Part II, Book V.

could never tell people in a few plain clear words what to do. Besides, philosophers talked a mysterious jargon and each has contradicted the other. When the old-time priest rumbled into his beard, "Thus saith the Lord: Fetch a goat!" that was something any simpleton could understand. He hurried off to get the goat.

Personal leadership, as distinct from other forms of authority, may be usefully differentiated into *representative* or symbolic, and *dynamic* or creative, leadership.[10] The representative leader serves as a symbol for a group without changing its direction or purposes. Dynamic or creative leadership exists when the personal leader directs or modifies the objectives of the group.

In addition to serving as symbols, modern leaders in large publics are actively engaged in manipulating the symbols which are most effective in influencing opinions.

The most effective leader-symbols are the national, cultural and group heroes. These are personifications of values, causes and critical events. Their names, pictures and statues are a focus of the emotional loyalties of their publics.

The leader symbol of greatest potency is the *charismatic leader*, that is one who is believed to be in some unusually intimate relation with supernatural power, or to have some extraordinary qualities beyond the normally human. Charismatic authority is the leader's authority under conditions where the governed submit because of belief in the extraordinary quality of the leader. Charisma must be potent, active, effective and successful, or it withers rapidly. To fail ruins the charismatic leader, as evidence of departure of power. In any case, modern charismatic leadership would be of short duration in periods of crisis when short-lived mass-emotions are intense.

Among leaders the *agitator* and the *demagogue* tend to adopt the most exaggerated political, economic and social aims. Unlike the true reformer, they do not as a rule attempt to trace social dissatisfaction to a clearly discernible cause, nor always to offer a specific solution. The agitator is not a hero to large publics and does not usually arouse heroic, self-sacrificing emotions, but, characteristically, generates spite, venom and hate between races, classes, parties and nations. To many who feel that in a confusing world they are the

[10] R. Schmidt, "Leadership", Ency. Soc. Sci, 9: 282.

eternal dupes, conspired against by hostile individuals, forces and groups, the agitator offers a simple description of the nature of the menacing plutocrats, the Reds, the racial enemies or foreigners.

The characteristics of successful leaders, and the processes of leadership in influencing opinion differ with the size and type of groups and with other circumstances. There do not appear to be general characteristics of leadership that are everywhere effective in influencing the opinions of followers. Even so and regardless of the situation, large publics cherish the positive statement. Their own requirements may be vague, but the leader of opinion in any large public states a positive programme most of the time, although his programme may be an attack on the existing order. The confident leader with a positive statement is at an advantage, and one that is particularly relevant to success in propaganda. The Fascist leaders purveyed positive programmes in the guise of great spiritual messages. Mussolini uttered grandiose generalities about the rebuilding of the glory that was Rome. This is true not only of Fascist leadership. A depressed and bewildered nation welcomed the positive and confident assertions of Roosevelt. Contemporary insecurities have intensified the quest for leaders with positive programmes.

Although leadership qualities cannot be considered abstractly, but must be related to specific situations, some generalization is permissible. Viscount Bryce said that leaders in democracy must possess initiative, comprehension of the forces that affect the needs of the people, eloquence of voice and writing, self-confidence and the ability to inspire confidence, that they must attract capable lieutenants, and that they must achieve personal publicity.[11] These he considered the minimum general requirements. Political leaders must arouse faith in themselves. In the rapidly changing social order of the world, faith is accorded to the leaders who exhibit speed of decision. Decisiveness, especially in crises, injects something clear-cut into the vagueness and confusion of the situation.

Leaders survive and grow in power who reflect the vague feelings and general aspirations of large groups. Hitler hurled defiance at what many followers considered international persecution. President

[11] J. Bryce, *Modern Democracies*, The Macmillan Company, New York, 1921, Book II, Chapter 76.

Roosevelt retained numerous followers who opposed almost every specific measure his administration had put forward, but who agreed with a general attitude that he seemed to express clearly and with obvious justice. It is in this sense that it has long been declared of leaders in democracy that they are "the common mind to an uncommon degree."

The popular leader must have or build up some elements of personal uniqueness. He must be a colourful figure of distinctive carriage and style. If he does not have these qualities and attains high office, his publicity men ascribe them to him.

A certain reserve and a modicum of mystery and inscrutability are characteristic of popular political leadership.[12] Mystery may be crudely presented, as in Hitler's assurance to mass audiences that he had the plans for the economic regeneration of the German Reich in the drawers of his desk in the Brown House in Munich. The imagination of followers is stimulated.

The leader of large publics must be an organizer and also make astute use of existing organizations. Indeed, Frank Kent insisted that nothing would compensate for the lack of ability to deal with party organization. Leaders of mass movements must competently organize their contacts with lieutenants and must select subordinates who will organize the channels of communication and of administration out to the most distant followers.

(j) Conclusions

Although scholars and researchers have not yet agreed on hard and fast rules governing human behaviour, some deductions are applicable to the formative elements of public opinion. Firstly, public opinion is not formed by a single element. Its components do not function independently of each other, in a manner that would render a selective or arbitrary separation easy. They form a complex unity and interact one with the other. Cultural heritage, for example, affects socialization. Methods and means of socialization at the same time influence this heritage and may even modify it completely. In the

[12] C. H. Cooley, *Human Nature and the Social Order*, Charles Scribner's Sons, New York, 1902. The chapter on leadership is the most brilliant essay in English on leadership and personal ascendancy.

same manner, cultural heritage and socialization leave their mark on the leaders of the future. But when these leaders assume power, they may overturn the dominant cultural and social conventions. Events of particular importance have a role in effective social change, a change which in its turn has its impact on culture and the means and methods of socialization, and so on. What applies to cultural heritage, socialization, leaders and events is equally true of all the other components of public opinion, that is to say personality, customs, attitudes, knowledge, etc. . . . Consequently, it is impossible, from a scientific point of view, to say which of these components plays the most important role, as it is rather difficult to attribute the formation of public opinion to this particular component or that.

Secondly, the importance of the elements composing public opinion is measured by the extent to which they share in defining its four dimensions of attitude, scope, concentration and depth.

Thirdly, public opinion derives its form from the total social framework inside which it acts, and from the social activities taking place within that frame. Hence, the components of the social frame and activities are the elements forming public opinion.

Fourthly, the elements of *static* public opinion are: cultural heritage (values, mores, beliefs, traditions), while the elements of *dynamic* public opinion are contained in the desire for change (aspirations, ambitions, protest, rejection).

Fifthly, when people react to an imposed desire, public opinion, regardless of its elements, may either be inward or overt, but it must be genuine.

5
Formative Elements of Public Opinion: The Media

(a) Basic and ancillary media

Formal media for all types of information, including, of course, public relations and propaganda, are embraced within three concepts: the written word, the spoken word, the visual image. We shall begin by examining each of these in their more conventional manifestations, notably the press, books, broadcasting, the cinema, television. We shall go on to discuss how the three basic concepts of information, expression and exchange are adapted in certain ways, such as tourism, exchanges for cultural and educational purposes, emigration, all of which revolve around the reality of personal contact. We shall consider the contact work of information spokesmen and offices of information, with particular reference to their contribution to good public relations. Finally, we shall consider the relationship of propaganda to the various media, bearing in mind as we do the key role which propaganda plays in the Arab-Israeli confrontation to which our later chapters are devoted.

(b) The written word

The *press* plays a prominent part in the lives of people all over the world, as one of the most important means of communicating facts. At the same time, the press mirrors the lives of the masses. Thus, the press takes from and gives to public opinion. It takes when it voices the wishes, feelings and expectations of the people. It gives when it offers such facts as will help public opinion decide what it wants.

Specialists have agreed that the main functions of the press could be summed up as follows:

Informing public opinion of events which occur both inside and outside the country;

Orienting public opinion by providing explanations and clarifications of the causes and motives of these events, as well as shedding light on the various considerations and influences which control their course;

Cultivating public opinion by opening the public's eyes and minds to modern schools of thought, and especially to developments related to modern theories and ideologies;

Enlightening public opinion, by giving it guidance as to the aspects of events happening both inside and outside the country;

Protecting public opinion by exposing plots and schemes attempting to detract from its freedom and independence and to undermine its rights, especially those planned by the enemies of the public both at home and abroad;

Serving public opinion by guiding it to the best modes of living on all levels;

Representing public opinion by voicing its aspirations, expectations and hopes, thus providing for its participation in government in a desirable manner;

Developing public opinion by raising it from the abyss of division and under-development, thus making it more capable of utilizing the resources of the country and the fruits of the economy;

Evaluating public opinion by measuring and analysing its trends and inclinations, with the object of determining the factors of social change which occur in society and the outcome of this change;

Rationalizing public opinion, by so educating and leading it that it can ultimately judge matters rationally, wisely and with discernment, especially matters relating to the collective role which public opinion should play;

Enhancing public opinion by pointing out its colossal potentialities and tremendous abilities, and by repudiating allegations which may detract from its dignity and status;

Organizing public opinion by establishing concord among the various sectors and groups, in order to enable it to attain such unity as will realize its purpose of collective influence, and the exercise of this influence for the assertion of its demands;

Entertaining public opinion by offering it human interest and light feature material for its recreation and diversion;

Teaching public opinion through light journalistic material to help to raise its cultural level and enlarge its general knowledge, in addition to press campaigns against harmful habits and decadent traditions and superstitions;

Guiding public opinion to the best methods of expressing its will and inclinations on the one hand, and on the other training it on a sound civic basis to make it aware of its duties, to safeguard its social gains and to champion the cause of its country.

From this rehearsal of main functions, it is clear that the press covers most aspects of the life and activities of the community. Many of its functions overlap in whole or in part with those of other media, perhaps most obviously with television, whose immediate impact is in some respects stronger, though its audience is still relatively limited in large parts of the world. Along with radio, the press then is possibly the most important of the information media. Besides, being a reflection of the people's wishes, the press has the power of discussing and questioning information itself. Its strong influence has gained it the appellations "His Majesty the Press" or "The Fourth Estate" from students of public opinion who considered it as complementing the executive, legislature and judiciary. In carrying out its functions it has recourse to news features, news analysis, scientific research, items of recreation and entertainment, official communiques, as well as visual images like photographs, cartoons and advertisements.

Of vital importance to the press is the service of *news agencies*. Drawing on the work of correspondents and reporters in many parts of the world, these provide the press, as well as radio, television and other organs of information, with news, features, official communiques, analyses and photographs related to events at home and abroad. Realizing the significance of their role in influencing public opinion, most countries have established governmental or semi-governmental news agencies, in order to deprive foreign news agencies of the chance to misrepresent facts in ways inimical to the national interest.

From the intellectual viewpoint, *books* are the most effective and lasting media in the field of publications. Compared with newspapers, magazines and pamphlets, they remain much longer in the hands of the reader and demand from him a keener concentration, besides presenting their material more comprehensively, in further depth and usually with greater seriousness. While their audience is relatively very limited, this does not imply a proportionate limitation of their ultimate effect. One has only to recall the profound consequences of books such as Rousseau's *Du Contrat Social*, or Adam Smith's *The Wealth of Nations*, or Karl Marx's *Das Kapital*. The particular section of the public addressed by the book is highly specialized; it is also often potentially powerful. The book's success in convincing this section may then have a lasting and indeed dramatic effect on the realization of the objectives propounded in its pages. Similar considerations hold good for *pamphlets* and for specialized periodicals. A word of warning may be in place. When assessing the properties of other media, we must avoid the conclusion that their more immediate appeal necessarily discourages the use of such publications. A reverse trend is in fact observable in some countries. For example, in the case of television, interest having been stimulated by a well devised programme, the viewer may be encouraged to pursue subjects further through the relevant literature. This happens with both serious subjects and more recreational reading; the successful TV dramatization of works of fiction and plays has on occasion had an immediate impact on public book-buying and book-borrowing habits.

Reference to book-borrowing reminds us that in many countries the establishment of *public libraries*, with reference and lending facilities, the latter often free, has made books accessible to entire populations. Moreover, the *paperback* revolution of the nineteen-thirties onwards has actually brought the purchase of books within the means of large sections of the public.

One very important way that books as information media have directly affected the Arab struggle results from their contribution to the development, both in the Arab World and elsewhere, of a popular *historical awareness* undreamt of a generation or two ago. Until the mid-nineteenth century, even in the relatively developed countries of West and Central Europe, knowledge of history was confined to a minuscule section of the literate classes, themselves a small proportion of the whole. And for that wealthy, often aristocratic, section history tended to mean background information ancillary to the classical studies of Greek and Roman literature and philosophy, which along with mathematics represented the traditional curricula of the older universities. It was only with the awakening of an interest about mediaeval and modern times, largely as a result of nationalism and the Romantic Movement, that the concept of history as a link between the events of former times and those of today began to be accepted, following the work of writers such as Taine and de Tocqueville in France, of Ranke in Germany, of Carlyle, Stubbs and Froude in Britain. Once recognized as a legitimate major university discipline, historical studies permeated the mainstream of primary and secondary education. In time, the spread of literacy, the popularity of historical novels, the greater availability of books and literature of all kinds, reinforced by historical films, radio and television features, ensured that large numbers of people in many countries came to be aware of the principal events and developments which over recent centuries had shaped the societies in which they lived. Although this awareness is still orientated towards their own countries or regions, the revolutionary change in the outlook of mass society towards the past means that there are now far more people in the outside world for whom the Arab struggle possesses some sort of relevance. We shall have more to say about this in our next chapter, as also about the equally important consequences of the existence of a sense of history among the Arabs.

In a review of the media of the written word it would be unfortunate to omit the *poster*. Despite obvious limitations of presentation and of subject matter, well devised posters, especially those incorporating visual image as well as written word, provide an information service not available through other publications. Thus modern publicity pays attention to poster preparation especially in the promotion of tourism and the arts and for other specific commercial purposes.

(c) The spoken word

Broadcasting is of course the most widespread and influential of the audible media, for the following reasons: the long period of time which the public spends listening to the radio, and the resulting effect of constant projection and follow-up; the abundance and variety of information and general interest material which broadcasting offers to the listening public, and the consequent ability to address its various sections and categories; the effectiveness of the techniques which are employed by broadcasting in presenting its information material, and the resulting impact it has upon the public; the facility of its use and the ease of obtaining information through it, and consequently its availability to the masses at any time; its flexibility and mobility, as it is permanently available for the presentation of information; its ability to influence certain mass sectors which the press, books, pamphlets or posters may not have access to, such as the illiterate or those with a marginal interest in current affairs; its ability to act as a substitute for the press, books and pamphlets for those unable or unwilling to make use of them; its ability to exploit sensory, mental and psychological influences in a more extensive and effective manner than the printed word and thus the more easily to produce a direct response; its ability to combine both information and entertainment at the same time, which also means the ability to draw attention.

Modern information understandably gives special attention to broadcasting, which as a last resort can be a substitute for most information media based on the written word. This, perhaps, explains why in many countries broadcasting comes under the supervision of the state or of public bodies. It may also be the reason for the introduction of schools', workers' and farmers' programmes.

As information media, *orations* are to be considered in the form of speeches and lectures. A *speech* or an address is usually aimed at an unspecialized audience which consists of several categories and cross-sections of the public, as for example the address delivered by officials on significant occasions or commemorations, speeches delivered at international gatherings such as the United Nations, and speeches given at mass rallies and organizations. On another level, a speech is also represented by the Friday sermon at mosques, church sermons and similar forms of direct communication with the masses through the spoken word. Although an address normally deals only with one subject, it often presents a significant and serious information service, for it contributes to information, orientation, cultivation, enlightenment, development, guidance and rationalization. In fact, a successful speech is no less effective than other information media on certain occasions. Thus, rulers in some countries make a point of addressing the people on important occasions. And of course major speeches, or at any rate significant portions of them, will be reproduced in the press, along with appropriate comment. A *lecture* differs from a public speech in that it aims in most cases at a specialized audience, and usually deals with specialized subjects. *Seminars* are different from orations in that they are spontaneous talks among several persons. Seminars may deal with several subjects, although a central theme can bind these topics to assume a certain trend of thought or conduct. They include discussion sessions, symposia, conferences and like activities, at which several participants talk to a public which normally has the chance to put questions and discuss the issue on hand. Though directed towards a limited public and usually dealing with narrow topics, seminars extend an information service similar to that presented by other media.

Our review of the media of the spoken word would be incomplete without mention of *recorded material*, gramophone records and tapes, as a means of preserving broadcasts, orations and discussions, as well as being a medium for the presentation of original material such as audio-aids for schools. The facility they provide for recalling past utterances, in an environment possibly more conducive to critical thought and yet in a more vivid way than the reading of a press transcript, invests them with long-term influence. Admittedly, available in many countries to only a small section of the public, recorded material becomes of greater significance as its production and accessibility increase.

(d) The visual image

The importance of the *cinema* derives from several causes: its supreme ability to achieve sensory, mental and psychological effects due to its manipulation of the reaction-producing properties of sound and light; its ability to combine information and entertainment with its consequent capacity for first attracting and then holding attention; its capacity for inducing audiences to identify with what they see on the screen; its use of reality and its potential for exploiting it; its ability to present diverse material and thus to address almost all sections of the public. Although entertainment is the dominant characteristic of the cinema, its information effect is potent, for what it presents, however recreative or amusing, usually involves such information functions as education, enlightenment and guidance. Even the small measure of these available through the cinema is very effective, because it is coupled with sensory, mental, and psychological impacts producing strong responses and reactions. Modern information therefore accords special attention to the cinema, and is constantly adapting it to new uses, such as school, vocational and technical films.

Because of the immediacy of its impact and its capacity for the virtually instantaneous depiction of events, *television*, combining as it does the properties of press, radio and cinema, has the greatest potential of all. Once it has become generally available throughout the world, it will predictably be the principal means for the dissemination of information of all kinds, as it already has become in countries possessing wide TV coverage. The functions of the press listed earlier hold good for television, which indeed draws heavily on the expertise of working journalists and of men and women with journalistic training in the planning and presentation of its programmes.

In historical terms cinema and TV are recent. As a visual information medium, the *theatre* is much older. On occasions it has been very important in educating and influencing the public, especially in ages of mass illiteracy, and indeed until the comparatively late appearance of the popular press; even daily newspapers, which were at the time hardly of a popular nature, only appeared in England, France and the USA in the course of the eighteenth century. Advances in the other media have inevitably overshadowed and in real terms lessened the overall influence of the theatre, which in many ways is now patronized by specialized and often relatively affluent sections of the public.

Nevertheless, its function as an information medium, most noticeably perhaps in the field of propaganda, is by no means negligible, for, like books, it can sometimes influence groups which, while numerically fairly small, themselves possess potential power as moulders of opinion and determinants of action. At its most effective, the theatre, due to an intimacy of atmosphere and to the *rapport* between actors and audience, is capable of an emotive impact as great as that of the modern mass media. For this reason in the past—and still to an extent today—some governments have maintained a close watch on, and at times a strict control of, the theatre. Much the same considerations apply to *processions and displays* of all kinds, including military parades and demonstrations, whose organization and effects contain some of the properties of theatrical representation.

Although we have devoted this section to the visual image, it has to be pointed out that modern media are largely *audio-visual*. The cinema and TV are in some ways just as dependent on the spoken word, on music and on atmosphere-creating background sound, as is the radio, though in the case of the radio the dependence is of course total. Among art forms *music* is particularly important to the information media, on account of its function in attracting attention. Because of its evocative properties, it is highly prized by radio, film and TV producers in the creation of mental images and of frames of mind appropriate to the programmes in question. It can also be subliminally conducive to the hearer's receptivity to propaganda and to publicity, a fact of which full use is made by political campaigners and commercial advertisers respectively.

(e) Personal contact

We have taken the written word, the spoken word and the visual image as basic, for without any of these there can be no circulation of information. It is in this sense only that other media, all of which imply the pre-existence of one or more of the basic ingredients, are *ancillary*, a term that implies no depreciation of their importance. Pre-eminent among the ancillary media is a whole range which may conveniently be grouped under the head of *personal contact*, namely tourism, cultural and educational exchanges, emigration, official visits by important government personalities and others. After reviewing these we shall conclude our study of the ancillary media with the activities of official statements and of information offices.

Any assessment of the potential of relationships is open to varying emphasis depending on an optimistic or pessimistic view of human nature. In adopting a positive attitude to the advantages of personal contacts, we do not ignore the risk of their resulting in attitudes contrary to those intended. Physical meetings between individuals are by no means the inevitable precursors of a parallel meeting of minds. Depending largely on extraneous circumstances, they can lead to misunderstanding, conflict and dislike, as well as to greater insight, co-operation and friendship. However, in the absence of special circumstances, we believe most people to be predisposed towards harmony, and that, in any personal contact of the type about to be considered, it is normally sufficient for one of the parties to possess a genuinely friendly disposition, and for the other to display the normal human response, for the encounter to be of value to both as individuals and to the nations or other social groups which they represent.

Among the media of personal contact, *tourism* has within a generation developed from the privilege of the well-to-do into an industry catering for a mass public. Never before has it been possible for so many people to make direct contact with areas beyond their own locality and even beyond the frontiers of their own country. Enormous opportunities exist here for the removal of misconceptions and prejudices relating to the characteristics of national cultures and attitudes, in other words for the development of true understanding and even personal friendship through the exchange of information. The opportunities become greater still as and when the host country is able to make available facilities for encouraging direct contact with the tourists, as for example social and sporting clubs, lectures, film shows, easily accessible tourist offices at home and abroad.

In parallel with tourism, *cultural and educational exchanges* assume a growing importance. They go deeper than mere tourism, inasmuch as the participants normally possess a positive orientation towards the country to be visited and towards its people, whereas the tourist may simply be motivated by the desire for relaxation or a change of scene. In terms of the dissemination of information about the Arab World, both abroad and within the area itself, we may mention: the propagation of Arab thought by Arab academics who lecture abroad, with its effect on influential sections of foreign public opinion in respect of Arab issues; the influence of those Egyptian teachers who work in Arab and Afro-Asian countries; the excellent information service performed in many countries by Arab cultural centres; the contacts formed both by Arab students complementing their education by studies in foreign universities, and by foreign students attending institutions of higher education in the Arab World. Centres and institutes of Arab culture have achieved much success in Sudan, Syria, Lebanon, Somalia and Spain. Arab information itself can derive large benefits from studied and planned co-operation between information centres on the one hand and institutions of cultural and educational exchange on the other, and it is to be hoped that the countries of the Arab World will collectively apply a unified information policy in order to enable Arab information to play its full role in the present confrontation with Israel.

Also of special interest in terms of that confrontation is the opportunity for developing personal contact through *emigration*. In a sense emigrants are unofficial ambassadors, while, as representatives of the customs, traditions, culture and ideals of their motherland, they provide an information service through their interaction with the peoples of the countries where they settle. In considering the success achieved in this context by many Arabs abroad, we note that Arab doctors occupy prominent positions in American hospitals and universities, that some Arabs have become members of the US Congress, that one emigrant owns and runs an Arabic broadcasting station, that in Boston and Detroit many of the more influential personalities are Arabs.

The key role of personal contact in the information process is acknowledged by government personalities and officials, no less than by businessmen and professionals, in a widening range of activities from the strictly academic to the purely recreational. *Heads of State, ministers and senior officials* of most countries exchange visits with the purpose of establishing direct contact with their opposite numbers. As well as contributing to the exchange of ideas and providing opportunities for the removal of possible misunderstandings, especially where the meetings are not unduly formalized, the visits also disseminate much information, in that for the time being they focus the public attention of the visitor's nation on the host nation and vice versa. Public interest having been aroused in this way, the formal information media of each country proceed to satisfy it by a proliferation of news reports concerning the visit, of interviews, speeches, official communiqués, and of background data, which on occasion ranges over a multiplicity of topics, social, political, economic, cultural and historic. Moreover, a really important visit may become world news and evoke a parallel blossoming of interest in many lands. For example, President Richard Nixon's visit to Peking in February 1972 focused attention on China, thus intensifying a process that had been evident for some time, particularly since the visits to China in April 1971 of the US, British and other table-tennis teams.

Personal contact need not be physical. Exchange visits by leading personalities imply contact not only with their formal hosts, but also with the vast unseen audience of newspaper readers, radio listeners, cinema-goers and television viewers. To a greater or less extent all receive impressions of the character, disposition, ability and other qualities of the personality portrayed. In recognition of this fact, public relations consultants rightly direct their efforts to moulding the *public image* of their employers. This is true as much in the domestic sphere as in the international, in the private sector as in the public. After all, most people have no physical contact with the leaders of nations, district government or large corporations. But at an accelerated rate the modern media enable them to *meet* these leaders in a none the less real sense.

From the strictly physical point of view, contact is normally limited to encounters with the administrative agents of government or of large organizations—so-called *officialdom*—for example traffic police, tax inspectors, postal clerks, the executives of personnel departments in private industry. The orientation of officials of this sort towards the public at large is a prime influence on mass attitudes, according to whether it is friendly and co-operative or overbearing and *officious*. More and more, therefore, large organizations acknowledge the value of personal contact in the encouragement of harmonious public relations, and consequently have recourse to professional guidance in this field.

(f) Spokesmen and offices of information

Frequent as they may be, visits of the type just mentioned cannot supply the need for a constant and instantly available fund of information on the attitudes of governments and other organizations about a host of topics. As we saw in our third chapter, acknowledgement of the need finds expression in the use of public relations experts, whose function becomes increasingly professionalized and who are employed in the public and private sectors alike. The official spokesman of an organization has an assured place in modern society, and the work of professionals such as press officers grows apace. Most governments maintain spokesmen, whose job it is to answer the questions of journalists and others seeking the background of events in the country, to comment on matters with a potential for national or international repercussions in the information media, to announce important official statements dealing with the broad lines of home and foreign policy, to expose malicious or untrue propaganda. As well as a flair for personal contact, the ideal spokesman must possess high credibility. To this end he must be thoroughly informed about the facts of both current affairs and of any other public matter likely to concern the interests of the state. He therefore relies on an efficient news and information apparatus, and upon experts in all the relevant fields. In these circumstances, it is customary to provide spokesmen with the facilities available through information centres at home and abroad, specialists in public opinion analysis, comprehensive archives, a complete library, an efficient translation staff. Reflecting the two-way essence of public opinion, spokesmen need to acquire information through research so that in their turn they may transmit education to others in a form relevant to the needs of the situation and of the governments which employ them.

The scope and complexity of public affairs are nowadays such that no single spokesman or even team of spokesmen can reasonably hope to cover their entire assignment without the backing of staffs and colleagues, highly trained in the arts of information gathering, interpretation and projection. It is in this sense that the work of the information centre has become indispensable. Each centre should include: a press section for the preparation of press bulletins, for contacts with pressmen providing them with information, photographs, films and the like, and for the study and analysis of the foreign press; a publication section to supervise the publication of books and booklets, to cultivate contacts with writers, authors, and researchers, and to provide them with any reference works they may require, to study and analyse cultural activities; a radio, cinema and television section to provide the media as well as private bodies with recordings and films which realize the desired information service, and to keep abreast of radio, cinema and television activity; a library section; a translation section; a studies and research section; and an archives section. From the point of view of the present confrontation, the existence of efficient and properly equipped Arab information centres is vital to the development of a proper understanding of the Arab cause and to the convincing exposure of hostile propaganda, in a word to the maintenance and spread on a world-wide basis of good public relations. In point of fact, the successful and often strenuous efforts exerted by Arab information centres and offices abroad during the periods of tension in the contemporary Arab World may rightly be considered a good start. There is added incentive and motive for the consolidation of these offices and centres in a manner that would enable them to achieve greater success.

(g) Propaganda media

Like his public relations counterpart, the propagandist relates his use of the media to the major components of public opinion discussed in the previous chapter. For example, he will exploit to the full any pre-existing habits and attitudes that may accord with his purpose. Indeed, the content of propaganda in its more corrupt forms turns on the positive consolidation and exacerbation of prejudice against objects, individuals or groups which society habitually viewed with suspicion, fear or even hatred. In his manipulation of these components, the propagandist employs the same media as other professionals in the information field. In general, there do not appear to be any instruments of exclusive relevance to the propagandist. While an exception may appear in the case of rumour, it is doubtful whether, in the context of this book, this is really an exception at all, because rumour is a medium not so much of information as of mis-information.

The antithetical relationship between the two is so obvious, however, as to justify some reference to the potent effects of rumour in connection with a variety of propaganda activity.

Rumour may be spread either intentionally or in the unintentional form of *gossip*. Both sorts are disseminated because they bring some kind of satisfaction to him who passes on the tale and to him who receives it. Gossips may be receiving vicarious sexual satisfaction, they may be expressing their own latent or not-too-latent hostilities, they may be seeking some form of public recognition from the tales they spread. Rumours during wartime more or less spontaneously arise because people are afraid, aggressive or deluded by their own wishes. Most rumours are far from idle; rather they are profoundly purposive, serving important emotional ends. The propaganda use of rumour is especially associated with war. In peace time, the deliberate use of rumour for propaganda purposes is usually called a *whispering campaign*. In the United States, organizations exist whose sole function is the spreading of rumours on behalf of paying customers. These groups are said to have circulated false stories concerning a disease allegedly flourishing among workers in a competitor's factory; to have employed actors to pose in public places as innocent conversationalists praising a certain brand of tyre or raincoat in a loud voice; to have hired women who feigned anger when stores did not sell certain articles; to have helped break strikes by having bogus salesmen express potent criticism of unions to the workers' wives.

Regardless of their origin, rumours undergo rather violent changes as they are passed along. Although these changes seem to follow some vaguely stated psychological principles, there are so many different distortions which can occur that it is rather difficult for the propagandist to predict the precise fate of the tale he wishes to spread. What he can do is to fabricate a statement which has some small basis in fact, and leave the task of spreading it, and adding to it, to the people. In this case, the people will act as propagandists.

Rumours are psychologically effective partially because they float about as concealed rather than as revealed propaganda. The intentional or unintentional objective of the rumour-monger is not appreciated, and hence at least one conflicting response in the victim is eliminated. Much also depends on the prestige of the rumour-monger.

Propaganda machinery, therefore, lends considerable attention to rumours, especially during wartime. During the Second World War, the American government set up special offices called "rumour clinics" to combat demoralizing rumours in the United States. In the words of Allport and Postman, government officials believed that "to smother a rumour with facts is better than to single it out for disproof." When nasty rumours could be anticipated or when they were discovered, an agency like the domestic branch of the Office of War Information stimulated the release of relevant facts without ever mentioning the rumours. In the interests of discounting rumours in general, slogans and posters were devised which warned against rumour-mongering or "careless" and "loose" talk, but not against specific rumours. The privately organized rumour-clinics approached the problem by first collecting the current crop of rumours and then debunking them with facts—when facts were or could be made available. Approximately forty newspapers and magazines in the United States and Canada employed this technique. "Most of the clinics," Allport and Postman report, "invited their readers to become 'rumour-reporters', and interested readers became their principal source of supply." There were no radio clinics, because it was felt that the audience might hear the rumour and not the counteracting facts; and because one experiment demonstrated that listeners could recall the rumours more readily than they could the facts. Rumours are considered as a special application of the notion of binding propaganda to the feelings of the victims. The psychologists Gordon, Allport and Postman, who conducted wide analyses of rumours, state that rumours vary according to two factors: the significance of the material involved in the rumour, and the vagueness of information surrounding the rumour.

As indicated above, propaganda benefits from the *concealment* of its real objectives. The consideration is paramount in respect of false propaganda, which is destroyed by the revelation of its lies and distortions. Even where its doctrines are genuinely regarded as honest and true by the propagandists, they often prefer to present their case under the guise of purely factual information, so as to avoid drawing attention to their full purpose and thus to avoid the risk of stimulating resistance among sections of the public until the proper time for a full declaration of their aims. They therefore seek to employ the arts of selectivity in ways that will be unnoticed, and they are aided in this by the practical impossibility of being other than selective in a situation where the information media must of necessity pick their way among an ever growing body of fact and incident.

The adept propagandist, like the professional public relations man, must adopt an essentially psychological approach. That is to say, he must sense the nuances inherent in all the regular media, must for example foresee the impact of a newspaper headline on the reader who habitually confines his study of the press to a perusal of headlines, and must know the proportionate value of his opinions as against those of readers who normally persevere through the whole of an article. Before launching his campaign the propagandist must also be aware of and be capable of evaluating the nature of the pre-conditioning of various sections of the public on matters relevant to his propaganda. This is really tantamount to re-emphasizing our previous remarks on the need for an in-depth appreciation of the major components of public opinion.

In time of war, the importance of the psychological aspect of public opinion is even greater, as evidenced in the very term *psychological warfare*. The manner in which this may be pursued without recourse to any lie in the literal sense may be illustrated by two cases. The first concerns the great talent manifested by the Nazis in the Second World War in creating noteworthy events conducive to their purposes. According to one journalist, American reporters in Berlin before 7 December 1941 tended unintentionally to spread Nazi propaganda. They cabled to their papers accounts of how the Nazi press was reacting to world events, reactions which may have been intentionally created by Goebbels, because he knew they would be cabled to the world and presented as news, not propaganda. Our second case dates from the period just before the Six-Day War. Early in June 1967, to lend credence to General Dayan's statement that Israel wished for a peaceful solution to her differences with the Arabs, foreign correspondents were taken to see Israeli soldiers happily relaxing on a beach. Two days after seeking to convince the world's press of her peaceful intentions, Israel struck.

PART TWO
The Arab Cause

6

Steps Towards Recognition of the Arab Cause before 1952

(a) Information as the key

To comprehend the part played by information and its media in the affairs of the Arab World over the past quarter of a century, one has to consider it both from the standpoint of the Arab peoples themselves and from that of the outside world.

From the Arab standpoint, how far did Arab governments and peoples come to accept Pan-Arab policies and attitudes in parallel with, or even at times overriding, the interests of individual Arab states? In other words, can one speak in a practical rather than in an ideological sense of the growth of an Arab public opinion and of an Arab identity of purpose? And, if so, what have been their causes, especially in the field of information? The conflict with Israel, and other aspects of the Arab struggle, are not of recent origin. It is therefore necessary to relate present conditions to the events and tendencies of past generations, particularly during the nineteenth century and the earlier years of the twentieth. Current collective Arab opinion is the result of ways of thought and motivations which the elaboration of the information media has spread both wide and deep. It has been perhaps most profoundly affected by the ideals of liberty and nationalism, and also quite significantly by the world-wide phenomenon of growing historical consciousness.

The view which a social group entertains of its own character affects the esteem in which it is held by others. If the peoples of the Arab World think of themselves as Arabs, other nations will be inclined also to think of them as Arabs, and will in consequence develop policies relevant to relations with the Arab World as a whole, as distinct from policies appropriate to relations with individual Arab states. Our examination of the growth of an Arab identity will therefore lead us to a review of the changing attitudes towards the Arab World in other countries, especially in those whose historic associations or current strategic or economic interests have dictated close contact with the area. In speaking of these reciprocal influences, we shall observe that at practically every turn the inter-relationship has depended both qualitatively and quantitatively on the availability and nature of information about the Arab World. It is in this sense that information is described as the *key*, not only to a factual understanding of the elements of the present conflict, but also to an appreciation of the motives of governments and nations whose actions at the time, taken in light of such information—or mis-information—as was available to them, determined the character of today's confrontation.

From these facets of the corporate image of the Arab World, in its own eyes and in the eyes of others, we shall go on to consider the effects of, first, the concept of the state of Israel, and then its emergence as a hard fact. We shall attempt to assess the enormous influence which it has had and continues to exercise on attitudes to the entire Arab World area on the part of both Arabs and others, and in particular we shall refer to the direct consequences of the establishment in 1948 of the state of Israel on the internal affairs of Arab countries over the succeeding four years.

By concluding this chapter at the point of the Egyptian Revolution of 1952, we underline the importance of Egypt's contribution to the character of the Arab struggle. Because of its geographical position at the heart of the Arab World and because of its political history, both in Ottoman times and later in the days of paramount British influence, Egypt developed in ways that have proved significant to the present conflict. Moreover, since 1952 she has possessed and employed the means for further encouraging the Arab nations to an acute appreciation of their mutual interests and common destiny. The present author has been privileged almost continuously since 1952 to participate in the provision of information designed to promote this encouragement, as also to project the Arab case to an outside world all too frequently dependent for its information on the statements of Israeli propagandists or on the incomplete data available from other sources.

(b) Growth of Arab identity

The great nationalist movements of the nineteenth and twentieth centuries drew their inspiration sometimes from the collective memory of the inhabitants of once sovereign states subsequently obliterated by dynastic or other ambition, sometimes from a deep sense of cultural, or racial, or religious identity. Poland is an example of the first motivation, Italy of the second. In the Arab World we find both tendencies.

In terms of the earlier existence of a single sovereign state, or more accurately empire, Arabs can look back to the glories of the caliphates: the Umayyads of Damascus (661–750) and the Abbasids of Baghdad (750–1258), as well as to the overlapping Fatimids of Cairo (909–1171) and Umayyads of Spain (929–1031). But some six centuries went by before the Arabs were exposed to the force of nationalism. Meanwhile they suffered internal dissension, the havoc of successive attacks from the Saljuq Turks in the tenth century, from the Crusaders in the eleventh, from the Mongols of Jenghiz Khan in the thirteenth and from the Tartars of Tamerlane in the early fifteenth, till the remnants of their empire, like the remnants of Byzantium, succumbed in the sixteenth century to the rising Ottoman power. Strictly speaking, the last truly Arab part of the old empire had disappeared much earlier; when the Ottoman Turks entered Cairo they were in effect annexing an Arab area for long ruled by foreigners, the Circassian upper class of the Mameluk empire.

The establishment of Ottoman hegemony did not represent a dramatic change of existing patterns within any recognizably nationalistic concept. Moreover, the period of Ottoman conquering zeal was comparatively short; even though the empire was to expand territorially for some considerable time, almost engulfing Vienna in 1683, its real strength was spent well before the late seventeenth century. With the eighteenth century, and the rise of Russia under Peter the Great and Catherine the Great, the Ottoman Empire was well on the way to becoming "the sick man of Europe". At its greatest extent it spread along the entire North African coastline, the valleys of the Tigris and Euphrates, Asia Minor, the Balkans and Hungary. Given the sheer size and the relatively poor communications available, it was inevitable that the Turkish Sultan in Constantinople should allow much local autonomy, though this was not necessarily exercised by governors and governing classes of the same nationality as the peoples for whom they were responsible. As power at the centre declined, regional governors were tempted to carve out semi-autonomous or even independent states for themselves. In this respect and for some of the same reasons, the Ottoman decline follows a course similar to that of the Moghul Empire in India or the Holy Roman Empire in Central Europe. Just as, long before the demise of the latter in 1806, the Hohenzollerns of Brandenburg had turned Prussia into a major power, though still theoretically subject to the Holy Roman Emperor, so Muhammad Ali of Egypt was for much of the first half of the nineteenth century to eclipse his suzerain at Constantinople. His dynastic successors as khedives (viceroys) of Egypt ruled over a country whose independence was in practice limited not by the Ottoman sultan, to whom until 1919 it theoretically owed allegiance, but rather by the realities of foreign pressure, which in the end came to mean British control.

The power vacuum arising from Ottoman enfeeblement, coupled with the impact of nationalistic and liberal ideas from Europe, coupled in turn with the spread of communications of all sorts, could hardly fail to evoke a response in the Arab lands and to stimulate half-forgotten memories of Umayyad, Abbasid and Fatimid glories. Despite broken political continuity, the peoples of these regions managed to preserve some sense of identity, though admittedly not an exclusively Arab one. Cultural affinities derived from a heritage in large measure Arab or Byzantine, and overwhelmingly Islamic. In consequence the area was potentially receptive to the doctrines of nationalism. Before these were consciously accepted, local unrest assumed the more basic form of exasperated revolt by subject peoples against cruel or unjust government. On occasion such protest might be manipulated by local potentates or by adventurers to further personal ambition. At times public and private interests coalesced. For instance, incipient Arab nationalism would align itself with local dynastic ambition in pursuit of the common aims of both: the removal of outside domination, be it exercised by the titular suzerainty of the Ottoman sultan, or by the more effective economic and administrative dictation of Great Britain or France.

Parallels exist between the state of public opinion in both Arab and Balkan parts of the Ottoman Empire. At much the same period the Pan-Slav movement gathered momentum both within the Ottoman Empire and in the contiguous areas of the Hapsburg Empire of Austria-Hungary, that other sprawling amalgam of nationalities, where in 1848 a Slav congress was held in Prague under the inspiration of the nationalist Frantisek Palacký. Pan-Slavism differs from the Arab cause inasmuch as at its outset it could look to the presence of a major Slav power, Russia, while from quite an early stage there was an independent Serbia. Even so, the similarities between the two movements are instructive. Both aimed at the removal of alien domination, whether German or Turk. Both suffered from the conditions of their respective historic development. Sooner or later both had to recognize and attempt to resolve the contradictions implicit in some of the alliances with dynastic and other interests whose opposition to the foreign ruler stemmed less from an acceptance of cultural, linguistic and religious affinities than from personal or family ambition. Pan-Slavism at the turn of the century suffered from the Karageorgovitch-Obrenovitch feud in Serbia, and later from the Second Balkan War of 1914 when Bulgar fought Serb. When the map of Europe and the Near East came to be redrawn after the First World War, it was the local nationalisms of Serbia and Bulgaria, of Egypt and Iraq and Saudi Arabia which triumphed, rather than the wider concepts of Pan-Slavism or Pan-Arabism. It is hardly surprising, therefore, that the outside world should have continued for so long to think in terms of the existence of Egyptians, Iraqis and Saudis rather than of Arabs as a whole.

Even these limited nationalisms may be seen as a necessary stage towards the realization of a greater Arab identity. We must therefore examine some of the more significant factors at work during the nineteenth century and the first half of the twentieth, insofar as they have a bearing on our study of the information process.

Within the Arab World it was Egypt which experienced the first major contact with the new ideas of nationalism and liberty. It did so from the most potent source of all, France, less than ten years after the collapse of the *ancien régime*, and at the hands of Napoleon Bonaparte, the personification of the militant revolutionary ideal. Not long before, during his first Italian campaign and with his creation of the Cisalpine Republic, he had foreshadowed a future sovereign state of Italy, evoking the national sentiments of a people long fragmented under the rule of local oligarchies, petty dynasties, papal dominion and Hapsburg might. On arriving in Egypt in July 1798, Napoleon found a land which, while legally part of the Ottoman Empire, was for practical purposes governed by the Circassian military aristocracy of the Mameluks, whose rule had survived the Turkish conquest of the sixteenth century. Obvious parallels existed between the position of the Arab majority and that of the other peoples affected by the doctrines spread by the revolutionary armies of France, peoples who, as in Poland and Italy, were subject to rulers who were not only politically unrepresentative but also foreign. Later Napoleon was to pursue his own dynastic interests at the expense of the democratic and nationalistic ideal. But in 1798 his pristine revolutionary fervour was still untarnished, and this, coupled with a declared sympathy with Islam, produced a dramatic effect. Mameluk power was finally shattered following his victory at the Pyramids. The academics who accompanied his expedition prepared the way for the work of Champollion and the discoveries which were to attract continuing attention from archaeologists and historians the world over. With the spread of primary education, these discoveries were to ensure that one aspect of Egyptian history, the Pharaonic age, would in time achieve a place in the school curricula of important countries. To this extent at least, and in her own right rather than as an Ottoman province, Egypt achieved the permanent attention of the outside world, whose curiosity would not always be confined to unravelling the secrets of a distant past. Moreover, contact being a two-way process, Egypt began to seek information about other nations. In terms of the formal media, a start was actually made by Napoleon when he set up a printing press. The flow of information was further encouraged by his penetration the following year into Syria, though militarily the campaign was not a success.

Although Napoleon returned to Paris in 1799 to become initially

First Consul and later Emperor, French influence persisted, providing lines of communication for the ideas that were revolutionizing much of Europe. With the power of the Mameluks broken, with the Turks preoccupied by unrest in Greece and the Balkans and by the threat of an expanding Russia, Egypt was left to her own devices. As a result, the Albanian Muhammad Ali was able to establish himself as virtual ruler. Arriving in Egypt with a Turkish expedition intended to restore Ottoman authority, Muhammad Ali soon became so powerful that in 1807 he was actually recognized by the Turkish government as Pasha of Egypt. From the point of view of Egypt, let alone that of Arab nationalism, his success hardly represented an advance, for it simply meant that effective control passed out of Circassian-Mameluk hands into Albanian-Turkish hands. For years to come the latter were to constitute a major element of the ruling class. But in two ways at least Muhammad Ali's ascendancy was of significance to both Egyptian and Arab nationalists. In the first place, it intensified Egypt's exposure to the novel notions admitted as a result of Napoleon's expedition, because Muhammad Ali encouraged educational contact with France, French officers being invited to undertake army training, while Egyptians were sent to France to study. In the second place, Muhammad Ali, sustained by the superb generalship of his son Ibrahim, laid the foundation of a dynasty which, though not itself Egyptian, came to identify itself with the country over the next century and a half, and was to establish Egypt as a sovereign entity quite separate from the Ottoman Empire, at first de facto and from 1919 de jure as well, albeit after 1882 at the price of British control. For a while it seemed that Muhammad Ali and Ibrahim could expect comparable success in Syria, which they wrested from Turkey in return for services rendered during the Greek war of independence, itself a further ingredient in the gradual conditioning of Egyptian opinion to acceptance of the national ideal. But by the late eighteen-thirties Britain had become seriously concerned over the growth of Russian influence in the Near East, and accordingly wished to maintain the integrity of the Ottoman empire. As a result, and despite strong French support, Muhammad Ali was forced to relinquish Syria in 1840.

Under two of Muhammad Ali's successors, the khedives Said

(1854–1863) and Ismail (1863–1879), foreign and especially French influence grew apace. And with it grew Egypt's capacity for absorbing foreign ideas, ideas to which eventually she was to appeal in her struggle against foreign control. The railway age in Europe had its counterpart in Egypt. An even more spectacular manifestation of the spread of communications came with the digging of the Suez Canal, begun in 1859 by the French engineer Ferdinand de Lesseps and opened ten years later. The Khedive Ismail's enthusiasm for re-modelling the country on European lines stimulated a building boom, especially in Cairo. But, while undoubtedly impressive, it led to bankruptcy and to foreign control. Moreover, the prevailing auto-cracy of the non-Egyptian ruling class conflicted with the climate of the times. By now Egypt was sufficiently familiar with concepts of national self-determination and of liberty to develop her own independence movement. Allied with these influences, the growing sense of history, mentioned in our previous chapter, meant that in due course part of the movement was likely to assume characteristics of Arab as well as of purely Egyptian nationalism. The beginnings of such sentiments are present in the appeal for an intrinsically Islamic approach to reform made by Gamal al-Din al-Afghani and Sheikh Muhammad Abdu, both of Cairo's al-Azhar university. In the case of the former the Pan-Islamic character of the awakening is strongly evident. By the time he left Afghanistan in his early thirties, he had made his mark as a scholar. Both there, and in Constantinople where Gamal al-Din spent the next year or so, an alert and philosophi-cally inclined young man would not have lacked opportunities to sense the growing pressures of industrialized Europe, pressures which were ideological as well as political and military. Arriving in Cairo in 1872, he boldly spoke out at the university against these pressures. In 1878 he joined forces with the young Sheikh Muhammad Abdu to set up the Free National Party, *Al-Hizb al-Watani al-Hurr*. Its threat to entrenched interests was such that they procured the removal of both leaders, Gamal al-Din being sent to India and Abdu a few years later to Syria. By 1883, however, they were together again, this time in Paris. Their choice of the French capital is not surprising in view of what has already been said about the role of France in the context of liberal and nationalist thought. In Paris they published a

newspaper *Al-Urwat al-Wuthqa* (The Indissoluble Bond) which enjoyed much influence over their contemporaries.

Already their teachings had impressed Colonel Ahmed Arabi, who
in 1882 moved for the independence of Egypt, both from the oppression of an alien ruling class and from the intensifying economic interference of the great powers. Arabi's revolt failed, and it provided a
further excuse for direct foreign financial domination. For all that,
it has great significance as the precursor of the later struggle for true
Egyptian independence within an Arab framework, for Arabi won
to his side Arab officers in the army and inspired strong popular
support. A genuinely Egyptian public opinion, with Arab under-
tones, was beginning to be heard in the matters of tax extortion by
the khedives, and of Egypt's standing in the world.

Virtual control of Egypt was established in 1882 under the British
consul-general, an office exercised until 1907 by Lord Cromer and
subsequently by Sir Eldon Gorst and Lord Kitchener. From 1882,
therefore, the objects of nationalist hostility were starkly identifiable.
The new régime undoubtedly sought and achieved financial reform,
yet much of the consequential prosperity benefited only a small
section of the population and helped to make the fortunes of Greeks,
Armenians and other foreigners. Thus the nationalist cause had an
economic motive as well as a directly patriotic one. The interplay of
both sentiments was strong where the social privilege of the country's
economic masters was protected by administrative measures, as in the
case of the *capitulations*, a system exempting foreigners from the juris-
diction of Egyptian civil and criminal courts. Ideas of liberty and of
equality before the law, whose potency derived largely from the
foreign and especially the French contacts of the previous hundred
years, recoiled against the latest examples of foreign influence. They
were to do so with gathering momentum, in step with the elaboration
of the information media and with the receptivity of an increasingly
literate public right up to the revolution of 1952.

Within a few years of Arabi's brave but abortive protest, youthful
and inspiring leadership came from the lawyer-journalist Mustapha
Kamel. Encouraged by the sympathetic attitude of the young khedive
Abbas Hilmi, who succeeded his father Tewfiq in 1892, the nationalist
party was very active in the early years of the new century. The

popularity of its demand for the removal of British rule drew further strength following the draconian punishment—it included some death sentences as well as public floggings—imposed on those incriminated in the killing in 1906 of a British officer at the village of Denshawai; the incident had arisen in confused circumstances involving a quarrel between British soldiers and local civilians. News of the Young Turk revolution of 1908 was another stimulant. However, the outbreak of the First World War temporarily diverted British attention away from internal Egyptian affairs. Already the nationalists had suffered from the death of Kamel in 1908, and from suspicion of their responsibility for the assassination in 1910 of the prime minister, Butros Ghali. It is worth noting that Ghali's unpopularity arose not only from his participation in the judgement following the Denshawai affair but also from his acquiescence in British demands; it was he who concluded the 1899 condominium agreement with Britain over the Sudan, alienating a territory which the nationalists regarded as Egyptian, while not long before his death he yielded to British pressure for the extension for another forty years of the concessions enjoyed by the International Suez Canal Company.

At this point we must consider the parallel appearance of nationalism in other parts of the Arab World. Again in the realm of ideas, the part played by France is difficult to overestimate. French activity from the mid-nineteenth century onwards sometimes reflected expansionist ambition, colonial rivalry with Britain and Germany, and strategic pressure. Nevertheless, while individual French governments and statesmen were far from untainted by chauvinism, the underlying French political ethic, especially after the establishment of the Third Republic in 1871 and even more after the Dreyfus affair of 1896–1906, tended to enshrine the revolutionary ideals of 1789. Even in diluted form, the French message of liberty and nationalism got through to the peoples within areas of predominant French influence. As we have seen, this was true of Egypt, where Mustapha Kamel for example had had a French education. It was true of Syria and Lebanon, where pre-existing French cultural influences were strengthened by the foundation in 1874 of the Catholic Université St Joseph. Eight years earlier in Lebanon a Protestant college was set up by Daniel Bliss, which was later to develop into the American

University of Beirut. Like the American University of Cairo, this was to expose intellectual Arab opinion to a new source of ideas, though, after allowance is made for variations in nuance and emphasis, the ideas themselves carried substantially the same message as that of the French. Syria and Lebanon, though nominally subject to Turkey, enjoyed quasi-independence. Their situation contrasted with that of the Maghreb at the other end of the Ottoman Empire. In Algeria, particularly, French control soon established deep roots, and the same was true of French ideas. The more Algeria came to be regarded as part of metropolitan France, the greater the exposure of her intelligentsia to the activities of French politicians, writers, and journalists of all shades of opinion, including many whose philosophy and opposition to the French establishment held lessons for the beholder, French or Algerian.

Activities such as these made for a cross-fertilization of outlooks. They led to a quickened feeling of identity in much of the Arab World. From outward appearances the renaissance of academic interest in past cultural achievement, whether Islamic or Arabic, was a far cry from a popular nationalism, expressing itself in the idiom of contemporary political agitation, and exploiting the latest information techniques, among them the dramatic impact of popular journalism pioneered at the turn of the century by William Randolph Hearst in the US and by Alfred Harmsworth in Britain. Nor as yet was political agitation carefully organized. Typically it still retained much of the character of angry response to local oppression, whether at the hands of individual rulers, or from the ever more obvious political and economic domination of foreigners. An earlier age would as often as not have borne oppression with resentful acceptance, interspersed with the occasional outburst of uncontrollable rage when conditions became unbearable. That an ever widening circle of opinion now began to regard oppression as not only intolerable but also as unnecessary, and so remediable, was due in large measure to an intelligentsia reared on the ideals of republican France, of the Italian *Risorgimento*, of German nationalism and of Pan-Slavism, an intelligentsia that moreover recognized the opportunities for mass persuasion inherent in rising standards of literacy and in the great improvements taking place in the field of communications. For all their apparent differences, then, the academic and political manifestations of the underlying ferment had by 1914 done much to prepare the way for the later conscious projection of a mass Pan-Arab identity.

This found real, albeit limited, expression in the Arab Revolt of 1916, which focused attention on the nationalistic sentiments of an historically vital part of the Arab World. The revolt's leader, Sheriff Hussein of Mecca, King of the Hejaz, was descended from the Prophet. Arab pride was justifiably aroused by the revolt's important contribution to the destruction of Turkish power in Palestine and Syria, arising from the ability of the relatively small numbers of Hussein's followers to tie down a large part of the Ottoman army. The revolt attracted to its side considerable numbers of Arab soldiers previously conscripted into the Ottoman forces. By helping to remove the Ottoman impediment to ultimate freedom, the revolt enabled the Arab leadership of the future to concentrate on fewer elements, so that gradually after 1918 the struggle centred on the removal of those undue foreign influences which remained. More immediately the success of the revolt gained for the Arabs a voice at the peace conference in Paris in 1919, a conference permeated by the notions of self-determination which in the previous year had been formally enunciated in the Fourteen Points of the American president Woodrow Wilson. These notions were also expressed in a fashion relevant to the Arab World in the Anglo-French promise made in November 1918 of independence to countries hitherto suffering under Ottoman rule. The circumstances of the declaration are themselves an interesting example of the propaganda possibilities of aviation, many copies of the text being dropped from the air in leaflet raids over Palestine. Taken together with the victory of more or less liberal powers over the conservative régimes of Germany, Austria-Hungary and Turkey, the concept of self-determination produced an effect on the minds both of the Arab delegation at Versailles, led by Hussein's son the Emir Faisal, and of populations which the press furnished with at least a rudimentary picture of the proceedings of a momentous international gathering. Optimism generated by the euphoria of the Arab Revolt and the disappearance of Ottoman hegemony was reasonably predictable in the light of certain declarations of intent on the part of leading allied powers. For example, Britain had sought to enlist support for the Arab Revolt by strongly hinting at independence for most countries of Arab Asia; the Declaration of the Seven on 16 June 1918 had promised government based on consent for those parts of the Arab World which were occupied by the Allied forces; in November 1918, as we saw, the British and French had jointly announced their intention of securing the liberty of those peoples who had suffered under the Ottoman yoke.[1]

In the short term, of course, these expectations were not to be realized. Disenchantment was the more bitter because of the betrayal of hopes fervently held and directly encouraged at the height of the first widespread expression of Arab identity in modern times. Understandably the Arabs felt they had been used by the victors of 1918 in pursuit of the latters' national or strategic interests, and that they would continue to be used for these same countries' economic advantage. The British protectorate over Egypt, declared in 1914, remained for some years yet, and, though abolished in 1922, it was replaced by a system which preserved the essentials of British control. The British were firmly entrenched in the Sudan, the French in the Maghreb, and the Italians in Libya. In Palestine, in Iraq, in Syria and Lebanon a system of mandates was set up under League of Nations auspices. Zionist gains at the peace conference, with which we shall deal at more length in the concluding section of this chapter, introduced a more sinister factor.

Nevertheless, things did not revert to what they had been in 1914. Indelible memories had been created in the meantime. On the whole the major powers of the post-1918 era were more sympathetic to change and to the ideal of independence, even though the Arabs lost a strong potential ally after the US Congress had rejected President Wilson's energetic espousal of their cause, and with the subsequent election of Republican administrations in Washington. When due allowance is made for the disenchantment and the feeling of abandonment, and for the resentment over the lack of proper consultation of Arab opinion after Versailles, the settlement of 1919 and of the years immediately following did represent a limited gain. After all, for the

[1] Details of various pledges to the Arabs are given in: Henry Cattan, *Palestine, the Arabs and Israel*, Longman, London 1969, pp. 9–10.

first time for centuries, sovereign Arab states under Arab governments began to emerge. Yemen retained the independence which its Imam Yahya had wrung from the Turks. Before long Ibn Saud was to establish his ascendency over Arabia, where the state of Saudi Arabia emerged in 1932. Elsewhere independence was more restricted. Nonetheless, both Arabs and outsiders could take note of the existence of Arab states, organized on Arab lines under largely Arab governments. This was the case with Iraq, where, after his removal by the French from the throne of Syria, Emir Faisal of the Hejaz was installed as king by the British, whose mandatory responsibility was established at the San Remo conference in 1920. At first fragile, the boundaries of the new Iraqi state were assured by Britain's firm action against Turkey's attempt in 1925–1926 to re-annex the province of Mosul. A further stage was reached in 1930 with the declaration of Iraq's independence, despite the vestigial degree of most-favourednation treatment retained by Britain, and in 1932 Iraq became a member of the League of Nations in her own right. Another British mandate, Transjordan, attained a measure of freedom under another Hashemite ruler, Faisal's brother the Emir Abdullah, as a prelude to its complete independence in 1946. Allowing for the special relationships with France of Morocco and Tunisia, the areas under French rule continued to be closely tied to Paris. While French influence had for long been potent in the Levant, formal political overtones were added after Versailles with the establishment of French mandates in Syria and Lebanon. Algeria remained firmly under French administration. Similar relationships existed between Libya and the Italians, and between Sudan and the British.

Throughout the inter-war years the receptivity of Arab sentiment to notions of independence and of common destiny grew apace. As we saw, the process was already well advanced in certain countries before 1914. Soon, with the intense exposure of ever more literate populations to the effects of the information media, now supplemented by radio, the pressure would become irresistible, the message ever clearer, and the response would be made with unambiguous coherence. Popular interest, roused to a higher pitch of awareness by the Arab Revolt and the First World War, could not fail to detect in the events of the twenties and thirties a relevance to its particular national situation, even to its Arab heritage. These events included: the rebirth of Turkey under Kemal Ataturk; the resistance of Abd el-Krim in Morocco against first Spain then France, culminating in the proclamation in 1922 of the short-lived Rif Republic; the Druze rebellion of 1924–1926 in France's Syrian mandate; the success of Reza Shah in maintaining Iran's integrity.

Just as in pre-war days the Egyptian political scene had provided many of the formative ingredients of opinion throughout the Arab World, so now Egyptian nationalists continued to command an attention that transcended national frontiers. With even nominal Ottoman suzerainty a thing of the past, they could concentrate on a single overriding objective, the removal of British control. In the atmosphere of 1918–1919 with its talk of self-determination, Egyptians reasonably enough anticipated the removal of the British protectorate established in 1914. Their demand for the right to send an Egyptian delegation—a *Wafd*—to the peace conference gave its name to the political party which from then till the revolution of 1952 was to dominate Egyptian political life. It was, however, only after an outbreak of strikes and widespread rioting, affecting not only Cairo but much of Egypt as a whole, had demonstrated the extent of national support for this demand, that Britain's assent was given. The British authorities need not really have worried about possible injury to their position arising out of the statement of the Egyptian case at Versailles, because on their arrival at the conference the delegation found the powers too preoccupied with their own affairs to heed yet another set of grievances from an oppressed people. Indeed the conference went so far as to confirm the British protectorate, which was only to be ended as a result of direct action by the Egyptians themselves. Following an intense campaign under the Wafdist leader Saad Zaghloul, Egypt was declared technically independent under its sultan Fuad, who in 1922 became king. But important privileges were retained by the British in the shape of the much resented capitulations allowing them to by-pass the Egyptian courts. Britain maintained overall responsibility for defence. She soon showed the strength of her residual authority, when in 1925 her high commissioner Lord Lloyd was actually able to prevent Zaghloul becoming prime minister, despite the Wafd's victory at the recent election, and despite the fact that Egypt was now supposed to be a constitutional monarchy. Grievances of this kind aggravated a public opinion less and less willing to accept foreign dictation, overt or concealed, which responded with cynical disbelief to repeated British declarations of an intention to confer complete independence once the tangled question of the Sudan, technically a *condominium* of Britain and Egypt, could be satisfactorily resolved. To resentment expressed in purely political terms was added economic resentment at the way in which the benefits of spreading industrialization were largely monopolized by a small group, strongly non-Arab and non-Egyptian in character and composition, whose ostentatious wealth was a standing scandal to every principle of political and economic nationalism. It was moreover a scandal that was to figure decisively in shaping public opinion permanently, both against the influence of the British and of those foreigners who grew rich under their protection, and against the establishment, including the king and the court, that sustained these conditions, an establishment still presided over by the descendant of the Albanian Muhammad Ali.

Before this régime ended even the Wafd had succumbed to the permeating corruption of wealth within the upper strata of society. The last days of the dynasty were clouded by rumours of the financial malpractices of the wife of the Wafdist leader Mustapha Nahas. The unsavoury circumstances of its demise, however, ought not to blind us to the valuable services performed by the Wafd, especially in its earlier years before Zaghloul's death in 1927, in moulding a harmonious public opinion on behalf of the country's essential interests. Drawing to his side some of the nation's best minds, Zaghloul did not lose sight of the necessity for a direct and continuing appeal to all classes. To these he directed his rare gift of oratory, speaking to the people in terms they could recognize as relevant to their worries and aspirations. With the rise of the Wafd, Egypt possessed a genuinely popular party, capable of speaking for virtually the entire nation. The recognition on the part of the Wafdist leadership of the two-way character of public relations, as both a teaching and a learning process, was shown by their constant travels throughout the length and breadth of the country, a policy that paid off in the party's impressive electoral record. Despite a growing association with the wealthy and the conservative, and despite the appearance in 1937 of the frankly capitalistic Saadist party of Ahmed Maher's, the Wafd had no rivals for mass support until the overwhelming transference of that support to the Free Officers movement.

Until the mid-1930s Britain was the prime target for Wafd agitation. The ambitions of fascist Italy, which now found an outlet in Mussolini's Ethiopian adventure, posed a threat to both parties. This resulted in a period of co-operation between Britain and the Wafd which was to last till the end of the Second World War. It began with the conclusion of the 1936 treaty, which gave Britain the right for twenty years to maintain up to ten thousand troops in the vicinity of the Suez Canal, and which provided for mutual assistance between Egypt and Britain in time of war. Egypt now joined the League of Nations as a sovereign independent state. But from a long-term point of view the basis of the *rapprochement* was fragile. The continuing British military presence, whatever its temporary justification and despite its altered basis of legality, was an affront to national opinion, which recalled the part played by British troops in suppressing the patriotic demonstrations at the time of the campaign for representation at the League of Nations in March 1919, and which believed that Egypt could not be really free until the final departure of the British forces. Nor, from the point of view of the Wafd party, can their new-found co-operation with Britain be seen as an unmixed blessing, particularly after the action in February 1942 of the British ambassador, Sir Miles Lampson, in threatening to bombard the royal palace unless King Farouk abandoned his support for Ali Maher, whom Britain regarded as friendly to Germany, and made Mustapha Nahas prime minister instead. To the man in the street Sir Miles Lampson must have looked like Lord Lloyd all over again. Irrespective of the strategic imperatives dictating British concern at the height of the Second World War, Egyptian opinion was insulted by this blatant intervention. Much of the opprobrium rubbed off on the king, who had no practical alternative but to yield to the British threat. Even the image of Nahas himself was affected, for his accession to power virtually on the instructions of an occupying army flouted the principles of years of Wafdist agitation. It is doubtful whether mass opinion fully understood, or, if it understood, whether it was convinced of Nahas' justification for his alliance with Britain, as a means for securing after the war the final evacuation of the British troops which under the 1936 treaty would otherwise remain till 1956. Despite these blows at the reputation of the Wafd, it retained sufficient public support to be able to win the 1950 election.

For the development of Arab identity as a whole, the period was extremely important. Just as in 1916 Britain encouraged the Arab Revolt, which it viewed as a strategic advantage in its war with the Ottoman Empire, so now the British government went out of its way to enlist Arab support. Collaboration with the Wafd was one example of this new attitude. Another was the new British policy on Palestine. British sympathy for the Zionist cause cooled to the extent that in 1939 Britain decided to stop Jewish immigration into Palestine after the entry of a further 75,000 Jews. A third example was the formation with British encouragement of the Arab League in March 1945 between initially Egypt, Iraq, Lebanon, Saudi Arabia, Syria, Transjordan and Yemen. In fostering the association, Britain was acting not out of respect for Arab consciousness so much as from a wish to end a power vacuum in a strategically important area, and one which was to become vital to Britain, given the economic necessity of safeguarding oil supplies, and given in the following years the intensification of the Cold War. The Arabs, however, saw the matter differently, and soon came to use the League as a means of hastening the achievement of Arab independence and nationhood, and, above all in the years to come, of combating the problems posed by militant Zionism.

From the end of the Second World War the Palestine question came to dominate most Arab issues. Its implications in terms of the mass media and the Arab struggle deserve close attention, and we shall therefore revert to them at the end of this chapter. To the qualified extent that it is possible at all to consider any developments in the area in isolation from the Palestine question, we see that the Arab cause, both on the national plane and on the supra-national, has been largely consolidated. In varying degrees, and due in no small measure to the work of political leaders supplemented by the much greater awareness brought about by closer contact with the mass media, a widespread and patriotic Arab public opinion existed. The defeat of the European despotisms in 1918 had brought much of the area within the control of the more amenable democracies, though Italian rule in Libya was a notable exception, while France and Britain could act in a thoroughly undemocratic fashion when they felt their interests to be at stake. Just as the verdict of 1918 marked some improvement, or the possibility of improvement, so the verdict of 1945 showed that the sort of quasi-colonialism which we have examined above could no longer be sustained, logically, equitably, or economically. Europe's global hegemony had passed to the US and Russia. With its passing Britain and France lost the power base on which in the final analysis they depended for their domination of the Arab World. France's mandate in Syria and Lebanon disappeared in 1945. Over the next dozen years or so she was to lose effective control of the Maghreb, an area to which outside Arab opinion now devoted more attention; for example in 1947 a Maghreb bureau was set up within the Arab League.

In Egypt Britain still placed difficulties in the way of evacuation, postulating the need first to achieve a mutually satisfactory arrangement for Sudan. The Cold War brought a new factor, because, with its crystallization, Britain was the more concerned to maintain her oil supplies and her strategic position in the Middle East. Similar considerations on the part of the United States muted the latter's earlier dislike of colonialism. In the circumstances the most Britain was prepared to offer was withdrawal of her military presence as part of a package deal which would include Egypt's accession to a Middle East Defence Organization, consisting also of the US, France, Turkey and Britain, and which would require the return of the troops if later deemed necessary for strategic purposes. In Egypt's eyes the latter proviso conjured up the prospect of indefinitely extended foreign military interference, and as such it was no better, and potentially worse, than the existing Anglo-British treaty, under which after all the British troops would have to leave in 1956. This prompted the Wafd, which returned to power for the last time in 1950, to abrogate the 1936 treaty. Thus Mustapha Nahas sought to complete the work begun after the First World War by the Wafd's founder Zaghloul.

Ironically, the party, which had done so much to heighten public awareness of the issues affecting their country's basic interests, gained no benefit from this decisive assertion of Egypt's rights. Apart from its reflection of the popular demand for independence, the Wafd was by this time closely identified with the small aristocratic and moneyed class, largely foreign in composition, whose ostentatious wealth and recent suspect financial activities utterly alienated the Egyptian people from the establishment. Specifically we note the unpopularity of an alien monarchy which had yielded to the crudest form of British pressure in the choice of a prime minister in 1942, the contempt for a king who seemed to be concerned only with selfish personal interest at a time of enormous hardship for the Arab peoples in Palestine and elsewhere, the responsibility of the government for Egypt's military inadequacies shown up in the 1948 war with Israel, even revelations about court involvement in the supply of defective munitions. Already antagonized by causes such as these, the Egyptian people, as indeed the entire Arab people, were traumatically moved by the available information, not only about the defeat of the Arab armies in 1948, but also about the oppressive Zionist policies vividly exemplified by the Deir Yassin massacre and by the plight of the Palestinian refugees.

Economically and socially unprogressive, their image sullied through the shabby venality of their associates, the Wafdists were a spent force. The political running lay with groups which, regardless of the disparity of their aims and the wide differences in their methods, were alike in attitudes of commitment to their particular causes. These ranged from outright and strident nationalism, to local variants of international left wing politics, to the Islamic ideals of the Muslim Brotherhood. The support these groups now commanded bore witness to the efficacy of the information media. Far from recapturing the political initiative for the largely discredited Wafd, Mustapha Nahas' abrogation in October 1951 of the treaty with Britain caused an escalation of events which he and his party were powerless to control. A wave of guerrilla activity and sabotage directed against the British forces in the Canal Zone culminated in massive rioting in the capital in January 1952. Abortive government reshuffling and accompanying confusion over the next few months prepared the way for the Free Officers' revolution of July 1952. We shall have more to say about that movement in our next chapter. For the moment suffice it to say that, while correctly reflecting the underlying climate of national opinion, the Free Officers wisely eschewed the excesses of some other nationalist groups, and quietly concentrated on perfecting their organization. In consequence, when the inevitable break with the past took place, it did so with a minimum of disruption and suffering.

By crystallizing the influences to which opinion had for long been subject, the July revolution was decisive for both Egypt and the Arab World. It was no longer possible, either for the Arab nations or for affected countries elsewhere, to harbour illusions as to the existence of Arab identity. It existed as a plain fact for all to see. In Egypt it expressed itself in the overthrow of a dynasty which had given the country a form of unity and some of the qualities of independence since its establishment by Muhammad Ali, but which had never broken free of its essentially foreign character. Elsewhere Arab identity took the form of irresistible pressures for independence in those areas, such as the Maghreb and Aden, which had still to free themselves from foreign domination. In every Arab land it received incalculable impetus from the establishment of the state of Israel. More than anything, this transformed the struggle of individual nations, whose nationalism was essentially in the tradition of the nineteenth-century European movement, into a supra-national cause, informed by deep-rooted and coherent aspirations towards an Arab unity, based on a shared language and culture, on shared memories of a noble past, and to a great extent, on shared allegiance to Islamic ideals.

(c) Changing attitudes towards the Arab World

To see the corporate image of the Arab World in perspective, we have to examine it from the standpoint of the outside world, and more especially of those countries which have had contacts with the area, as well as from the standpoint of the Arabs themselves. From the early nineteenth century both Arabs and others experienced broadly similar determinants of public opinion: the concepts of nationalism, liberty, economic and social equity, self-determination, and the proliferation of the mass media of information. Their respective situations differed in respect of the timing of the response to these stimuli. For the Arabs, there was immediate relevance in viewing these factors in terms of national or supra-national problems, just as elsewhere the same factors were translated into terms of an Irish consciousness, a Slav consciousness, an Italian consciousness and so on. For people not directly concerned with events in the Arab World, no equivalent compulsion existed towards recognizing the inhabitants of that region as possessing common qualities or affinities, or even towards thinking about them at all. A long time lag therefore exists between on the one hand the formulation of internal Arab ideas of identity, and on the other hand that of the external appreciation of the same identity.

To the extent that Arab matters did concern the outside world early in the nineteenth century, and for long afterwards, they fell under the heading of foreign affairs, a field of activity which, even in constitutional states, tended to be left to the governing group, and to be of no interest to the public at large, except when issues arose touching on the national honour and thus capable of evoking outbursts of elementary patriotic emotion. With few exceptions, most notably perhaps France and the young American republic, government was still aristocratic. In consequence, its foreign relations bore the imprint of the ideas of the ruling classes, including very importantly that of their education. In the early nineteenth century and for decades to come this was still typically centred on the classics and often ignored any history later than the fall of the western Roman empire in A.D. 476. We saw in our previous chapter that the rise of an interest in historical studies, as we understand them today, did not begin until well into the nineteenth century, while these studies did not affect the mass of the population until much later. For these reasons, the governments of the leading powers were for the most part ignorant of the existence of an Arab identity in any sense that would be acceptable today. Even when they began to be affected by the new ideas of nationalism and liberty, they had no thought of applying them to the Arabs, or for that matter to most other subject peoples. The great exception was the attitude of the ruling classes to the Greek War of Independence, the activities of Lord Byron and other aristocrats on behalf of the Greeks demonstrating the results of a fusion of a classically orientated education with the ideals of the French Revolution.

Individual fervour for a people seen as the descendants of the Greeks of classical times was one thing, the day to day foreign policy interests of governments was quite another and normally regarded as far more important. It was in pursuit of the latter that most of the great powers were sooner or later to establish contact with the Arabs. At first they tended to do so in the context of their policy towards the Ottoman Empire, which as the nineteenth century progressed was seen increasingly by Britain and Austria as an essential buffer against Russian expansion. To outside observers, the Islamic character of the Ottoman Empire was far more important as a distinguishing charac-teristic than the presence within its frontiers of large numbers of Arabs. Moreover, in the case of two of the great powers, Russia and Austria, there was nothing unusual in the proliferation of nationalities within one empire. Having no intention of allowing the aspirations of their own subject peoples to affect government policy, they could hardly have been expected to regard the Arabs in a different light, or to pay any particular attention to their existence. The situation was rather different in respect of outside attitudes to the Arabs as Muslims. Islam as a distinguishing characteristic was something which the great powers could recognize. As the Hapsburgs extended their influence and their dominion into the Balkans, they came into increasing contact with Muslim peoples, just as they had done in the past when recovering Hungary from the Turks. Russia experienced similar contacts following her expansion into Central Asia, as did Britain in India.

The gradual process of liberalization, and in the West even democratization, of government among the great powers did not necessarily conduce to a more liberal or understanding view of the character and aspirations of subject peoples. Ironically it sometimes encouraged the reverse tendency, for the extension of the franchise obliged governments to take account of the aggressive emotions of a public opinion which inevitably absorbed its information on foreign issues in an over-simplified form. The effects of a rudimentary pri-mary education, and the impact of a press designed to attract the attention of the products of such an education tended to encourage the cruder forms of popular prejudice and to foster attitudes such as the jingoism of late nineteenth-century Britain. The harm of which they were capable is vividly, not to say disturbingly, illustrated by the respon sibility of the popular journalism of William Randolph Hearst in causing the Spanish-American war of 1898.

While in the short term the spread of democratic participation in government may have hampered rather than encouraged international understanding, it did contain some promise of later improvement. Among the public sentiments which governments could no longer ignore was that of religion, whose significance appears the greater when we realize that not infrequently the first formal educational influence on future voters was that of a church school. In time, however limited their subsequent exposure to the information media, children in Britain, the United States, Germany, France and Austria-Hungary could no longer be entirely ignorant of the existence of Palestine, as a result of the rudimentary biblical studies which became more or less universal in those countries. With the introduction of elementary historical studies, children heard about another Arab country, Egypt, even though their knowledge was restricted to pharaonic times and few of them, and possibly few of their teachers, consciously appreciated the Arab character of contemporary Egypt. Of these developments the religious was probably the more significant. It certainly goes far to explain the persistence of the inclination throughout the outside world to equate the Arab World with Islam. On occasion it had a direct effect on the actions or freedom of action of governments. For example, the British statesman Gladstone used the religious sentiments of a large section of the British electorate in his political campaign against the then prime minister Disraeli, following the Ottoman reprisals of 1876 against their rebellious Christian Bulgarian subjects. Despite Britain's continued opposition to any weakening of the Ottoman Empire—a policy which itself enjoyed considerable popular support—Gladstone's anti-Turkish pamphlet *The Bulgarian Horrors and the Question of the East* was an immediate success, and his campaign prevented Britain from siding with Turkey in the subsequent Russo-Turkish war. Similar public reaction was evinced some twenty years later at the time of the Armenian massacres, which outside opinion again saw in religious terms. Significantly, no such spontaneous anger arose following repression carried out against Arabs within the Ottoman Empire. To the semi-educated publics of Europe and North America, the words Ottoman, Muslim and Arab amounted to much the same thing.

Of course this is to generalize. The crudities of opinion formation inherent in rudimentary education and in the over-simplified stimuli, administered by interested political and other groups through the medium of a sensationalist press, were a necessary stage, which even advanced countries had to traverse before they could attain a well informed and circumspect public opinion. In time too some appreciation of the greatness of Islam percolated through to western and central Europe. This is evidenced by the histrionics of the German emperor William II on the occasion of his visit to Tangier in 1905, though these perhaps more properly belong to great-power political interest in the area, the Kaiser's motive being to win over Arab sympathy for his struggle against threatened French control of Morocco. In the more disinterested sense of the growth of curiosity about Arab culture for its own sake, the way was pioneered by France, which as we have already seen did much to stimulate Arab consciousness in these years. In saying this, we do not mean to underestimate the factors of global power politics and of domestic chauvinism as major causes of the French penetration of the Maghreb after 1830. But over and above these material explanations, it is true to say that, of all the great powers, France was the one most involved with the peoples of the regions, as Arabs rather than simply as Muslims. In the case of Algeria, the attitude was assisted by the relatively close proximity to France, which contrasted with the great distance separating Britain from those parts of the Arab World with which she was mainly concerned, Egypt and Sudan. Large numbers of Frenchmen settled in Algeria and large numbers of Algerian Arabs settled in France. Both groups maintained ties with families and friends in the homeland. Catholic churches were built in Algeria and mosques in France. From a comparatively early stage, then, a variety of dialogue emerged between Algerians and Frenchmen, and both sides learnt a great deal about each other, to a large extent sharing the same educational and political system, and often being exposed, as individuals rather than as members of their national groupings, to the same information processes and stimuli. Somewhat similar contacts, though less intimate and not so long-lasting, existed between France and

Tunisia, where France's protectorate dated back to the Bardo treaty of 1881, and between France and Morocco, where such a relationship was established by the Fez treaty of 1912. The development of mass journalism, as later that of radio, found in France an audience predisposed to interest in events in the Arab World. The background to the work of Marshal Hubert Lyautey in Morocco before and after the First World War was, therefore, far better understood in France, and in consequence the interest which it engendered among the French newspaper-reading public was far more intense than similar activities would have been concerning Arab lands dependent on any other one of the great powers. The same is true of the exploits of Abd el-Krim at the time of the Rif Rebellion of 1925, and also, at the other end of the Mediterranean, of the contemporaneous Druze Rebellion in France's Syrian mandate, for, while France's association with the Levant differed greatly from that with the Maghreb, her cultural links with the Levant dated back even further. This is equally true of the reciprocal impact of France and Egypt.

Elsewhere the concept of the Arab World as an entity, distinct from the larger world of Islam, was still far from generally accepted. The first major step in this direction was probably the Arab Revolt of 1916. Its importance in this sense, however, was retrospective, for at the time publics were too engrossed in the crucial issues being decided elsewhere, on the battlefields of the western front, to spare much attention for the exploits of the Emir Feisal and Colonel Lawrence. In the more leisured inter-war years, the events of the Arab Revolt, and perhaps some of its significance, began to be appreciated by an important section of the book-reading public in Britain and America with the appearance of T. E. Lawrence's book *The Seven Pillars of Wisdom*. Although the importance in terms of the Arab World of the career of "Lawrence of Arabia" was appreciated by only a minority of the British public, large numbers of people had heard of him. A working predisposition towards the absorption of later intelligence about the Arab World was at least available. Subsequently of course it was to be vastly expanded by the popularity of the motion picture dealing with the Arab Revolt and the career of Lawrence. But that was in the nineteen-sixties and long after the momentous events of the Second World War and its Middle Eastern aftermath had dispelled much outside ignorance about the Arab World.

The Second World War is important in the context of information, because it brought large numbers of foreign conscript troops into the area. Even in the case of a peacetime army of regular soldiers the potential for public concern increased in step with the media. For example, in the thirties the media relayed to Britain news of unrest in Palestine verging on revolt resulting from Jewish immigration under the British mandate. For many conscript soldiers wartime service in the Arab World amounted to their first contact with any country apart from their own. They were naturally curious, and in correspondence relayed their impressions to families and friends back home. The sheer extent of the conscription process during the Second World War meant that very few people in the homeland were without some sort of contact with a relative, friend or acquaintance serving abroad.

While generally tolerated as inevitable in war, public attitudes to conscription, especially where it involves personal danger and pro-longed foreign service, are very different in peace time. After the Second World War there was strong public pressure for the demo-bilization of the conscript armies. Yet in many countries conscription persisted. This was not too greatly resented in countries like France, where for generations national service of this sort had been accepted as part of a citizen's duty. In Britain it was otherwise, for conscrip-tion had in fact been introduced only a few months before the out-break of war. In consequence, British governments faced mounting public concern at the continued presence of conscripts in the British forces in the Canal Zone and in Palestine, especially when the ever more accessible and sophisticated news media, which now came to include television, left no doubt as to the element of personal risk run by these conscripts, vivid examples being Zionist terrorist attacks on British soldiers in Palestine, and guerilla activities in the Canal Zone after Egypt's denunciation in October 1951 of the 1936 Anglo-Egyptian treaty. Concerned wives and parents were forced by these events to take an interest in what was going on in these Arab lands, and consequently some appreciation of the Arabs as a people or as an issue must have rubbed off. This relatively new personal orientation towards events in the Arab World harmonized with a reaction in post-war Britain against heavy overseas commitments. The decolonization process began with the independence of India and Pakistan in August 1947. While it amounted to a great victory for the nationalist movements of those countries, its timing was significant as a response to feelings of war weariness, allied to a desire to concentrate on the task of reconstruction after the disruption wrought by six years of global conflict. The British people, like peoples elsewhere, were concerned as never before in peace time with events taking place beyond their frontiers. The advances in public education, interacting with the availability of instant news, stimulated widespread study of important national and other movements, including those of the Arab World. As we saw in our previous chapter, facilities for such study were now readily available through public libraries and as a consequence of the paperback revolution.

Nor was the interest confined to the general public. Governments of the great powers had long been concerned with events in the Arab World, even though they might underestimate its distinctly Arab characteristics. Egypt, Sudan and the Maghreb were important elements in the great power rivalries at the turn of the century. It was the settlement of the Anglo-French disputes in those areas which, by ending Britain's so-called "splendid isolation" of the previous two decades, prepared the way for the realignment of the great powers in the years immediately preceding the First World War. In 1916, as we saw, Britain went out of her way to encourage the Arab Revolt, which was strategically valuable to her. In the inter-war years the need to maintain oil supplies added a new Middle Eastern dimension to the traditional motives of the maintenance of the balance of power and of strategic links with India. In the Second World War the key geo-political position of Egypt was of direct concern to both Allied and Axis powers, while in 1945 Britain again made a conscious attempt to enlist Arab support, this time by encouraging the formation of the Arab League. Later the continuing importance of oil and the extension of the Cold War dictated the attempt to set up a Middle East Defence Organization, consisting of both Arabs and non-Arabs, which proved to be an important link in the chain of events culminating in the Egyptian revolution of July 1952.

By 1952, therefore, large numbers of people in the outside world, including governments, had begun to grasp the truth that the Arabs possessed an identity apart from that of their membership of the Islamic world. We must beware of overstating this discovery. A majority of people in Britain, for instance, would have found it impossible to explain precisely how Arabs differed from other Muslims, or to have traced with any semblance of accuracy the boundaries of the Arab World, or to have enunciated a tolerable definition of the Arab cause. The endeavour to fill in these enormous gaps has been a major assignment of the Arab information media over the past twenty years, and is of paramount importance to the Arab cause in general and to success in the conflict with Israel in particular. We shall devote much of the rest of this book to an examination of the ways in which Arab information has worked and continues to work to discharge this grave responsibility. But first we must turn our attention to the particular circumstances of the formation of the State of Israel and its immediate consequences, events which have a direct bearing, not only on the elaboration of an Arab identity, but also on the recognition of its existence by other countries.

(d) Israel emerges

For obvious reasons, the Israelis themselves must feature as one of the subjects in any complete assessment of identity consciousness on the part of or in relation to the participants in the events and conflicts taking place in the Arab World. It has been said many times, and, to avoid misunderstanding, it must be said again, that the words *Jew* and *Israeli* are not synonymous. Large numbers of Jews are neither Zionists nor sympathetic to the State of Israel, either in terms of its conceptual basis or in terms of the policies of its leadership. While not for a moment denying these truths, one has to recognize that the current image of Israelis owes an immeasurable debt to a centuries-old awareness of the Jewish identity on the part both of Jews and of others, and to certain attributed characteristics, whether real or imagined, possessed by the Jewish people as a whole. Resulting from intense persecution at the hands of the Romans, the Jews have for nearly two thousand years been dispersed throughout the

world, so that by the beginning of this century only a very small proportion of them inhabited Palestine. Settling in other lands, they
avoided assimilation with their neighbours, retaining a continuous
sense of their own identity, even though, particularly in more recent
times, this sense of being different, of an essential Jewishness, has not
implied acceptance of the religious tenets of Judaism; there have
been and are Jewish atheists, agnostics, Protestants, Catholics and so
on. As we saw, the public image of any group is conditioned by the
private image it cherishes as to its own qualities. In the case of the
Jews this interplay of opinion has been acute. Whether by holding
themselves apart as a "chosen people", or by merely engaging in
pursuits discouraged by the dominant ethic among other groups, for
example their successful conduct of finance in a mediaeval Chris-
tendom which typically eschewed such activities, the Jews drew
attention to themselves in most of their adopted countries. They did
so in ways likely in the long run to arouse the suspicion and often the
envious hostility of the rest of society. Hence the intermittent perse-
cutions which, given the basic resilience of the Jewish character,
served to guarantee their survival as a group apart. Moreover, the
extent of their dispersal meant that, over an extremely long period,
very few countries escaped contact with the Jews. In consequence the
Jewish issue figures both in the formal history and in the less formal
attitude determinants of many nations. In this respect the development of the appreciation by others of the characteristics of a Jewish
identity contrasts strongly with the dearth of information about the
Arabs. Broadly speaking the Arabs were concentrated in a particular
region, and their outside contacts were for long periods of time with
a more restricted range of individual nations and states. We must
beware of overstating this difference, because the Arabs did establish
wide connections in Africa and Asia. Nevertheless, in centuries when
the main and sometimes the only effective element of public opinion
formation lay in personal contact, the Jews made their presence felt
throughout much of the civilized world, from India to the Americas,
from northern Europe to South Africa. Their large concentrations in
Russia, Germany and the lands of the Austro-Hungarian empire held
ominous implications for the future.

Anti-semitism, in its modern form and in its widely accepted connotation, owes much of its importance to the spread of those nine-teenth-century ideals of nationalism and liberty referred to earlier. The resulting greater public accountability of governments, even autocratic governments, obliged them to defer more to public opinion. Where the latter was ill-informed and largely an amalgam of incoherent folk attitudes and prejudices, the ground was fertile for the flowering of debased forms of populism such as fascism. Recog-nizing the possibilities of such movements for clouding real issues and hence for diverting public attention away from governmental shortcomings, the ruling class or party in several despotic states had no compunction in providing plausible scapegoats for popular dissatis-faction. Being easily identifiable, as a group often wealthy, and always a minority, the Jews fitted the part to perfection. A fair degree of anti-semitism of this type was to be found in the later years of the nine-teenth century in France and Austria-Hungary. But it was in Russia that we see it in its major and potentially most significant form. It is at this point, at a time when the information media were about to attain an abundance and potential hitherto hardly dreamt of, that we pass from a Jewish issue, widespread but scarcely sinister, to the problem of *Zionism*.

Beginning as the individual response of a Russian doctor, Leo Pinsker, to the official harassment of the Jews—there were about five million in Russia—Zionism was taken up by the Hungarian Theodore Herzl and propagated in his pamphlet of 1895 entitled *The Jewish State*. At first it had little appeal among settled and prosperous Jewish communities in the more advanced nations. There indeed a significant proportion were and have remained hostile to the very concept of a separate Israeli state, sometimes seeing it as a potential danger to their own security, on the grounds that the existence of a Jewish state could provide anti-semites with a plausible argument for seeking to expel individual Jewish communities. By contrast, to the harassed Jews of the agitated and insecure Russia of the early twen-tieth century, Zionism made far more sense. By skilful publicity, the concept had by the end of the First World War attracted sufficient attention to become embedded into the atmosphere of national self-determination then prevalent. Already, before the turn of the cen-tury, more than half a million Russian Jews had taken refuge in the

US, where they exerted some effect on public opinion. With this in mind and keen to enlist American support for the Allied cause, Britain, in the *Balfour Declaration* of 1917, appeared to place on record her support for the concept of a Jewish national home in Palestine, though with safeguards for the rights of the Arab inhabitants. By 1919, therefore, the Zionist cause had gained an important amount not only of recognition but also of qualified sympathy from the leading powers of the victorious alliance, France also adopting a comparable policy. Hence the admittance of a Zionist representation to the peace conference, and its far greater success in enlisting support than the Arab delegation achieved.

The immediate outcome of these Zionist exertions was the form of the Palestine mandate conferred upon Great Britain at the 1920 meeting at San Remo of the victorious nations. By requiring the mandatory power to consult a *Jewish Agency* in its administration of Palestine, the arrangement gave the Zionists a privileged position *vis à vis* their Arab neighbours. At first the Zionist gains hardly attracted the sustained or widespread attention of the developing media. The Jewish element in the population of Palestine was under 10 per cent. Jews already settled there before the mandate lived on reasonably good terms with the Arab majority. Immigration was small and in one year, 1927, the number of Jews leaving Palestine actually exceeded the numbers entering the country. This does not mean that the situation was accepted without misgivings by the Arabs, especially by the more farsighted, and there was much underlying disquiet. But, by comparison with later momentous developments, Zionism could hardly be called a big issue in the twenties and early thirties.

A major and as it later proved decisive new element was the coming to power of the Nazis in Germany in 1933. The policy of this party is the supreme example in modern times of the misdirection of popular prejudice as a means of drawing attention away from the inadequacies of the ruling group, the supreme example of populism in its most debased form, involving the abandonment by the government of one half of the two-way function of public relations, which, as we saw in our third chapter, implies a responsibility for guiding no less than for assessing the movements of public opinion. Having secured their power base, the Nazis lost no time in demonstrating their attitude to the national scapegoat. Notable landmarks in the mounting harassment and eventual outright persecution of the large Jewish minority were: the Nuremburg Laws of 1935 against mixed marriages between Jews and other German citizens; the massive destruction of Jewish property on 9 November 1938 known as the *Kristallnacht* from the quantities of window panes shattered in the course of the operation; and the attempted genocide of the entire Jewish race, the so-called *final solution*, from 1942 onwards. These Nazi excesses are important to our study for several reasons. In the first place, they were far more efficient than the anti-semitic activities of earlier times, for the Nazis set about their task with a new systematic ruthlessness, aided by the technical capabilities of a highly developed modern state, including their own brilliant albeit sinister professionalism in the manipulation of the propaganda media. The latter consisted not only of the press, film, and radio activities of Joseph Goebbels, but also of the racialist philosophy of Alfred Rosenberg, and of the popular journalism of Julius Streicher's *Der Sturmer*. Secondly, as the Nazis from 1938 onwards came to control in one way or another most of the European continent, their anti-semitism was no longer restricted to German Jews; the plight of European Jewry, with its contacts all over the world, added a global dimension.

As a direct consequence of the Nazi persecution, then, the Zionist cause and the position of Palestine in particular had by the outbreak of the Second World War achieved an international relevance and urgency totally unforeseen when Britain took up her mandatory responsibilities in 1920. Diplomatically Britain found herself in a dilemma. On the one hand, many British people, and not only British Jews, endorsed the swelling international concern for the persecuted Jews of Germany and Central Europe. And in the case of Britain, as of other countries threatened by Hitler, human response coincided with national self-interest. With gathering momentum from the *Anschluss* with Austria in March 1938, and decisively after the outbreak of war in September 1939, the tendency was for the Jewish cause to be regarded as part of the cause of the free world against the Nazi menace. On the other hand, Britain was in a much better position to calculate the extension of Arab fears in Palestine. Just as in the First World War, so now strategic considerations, including the far greater importance of Middle Eastern oil supplies, dictated the sort of policy calculated to enlist Arab support in the coming struggle or at least to ensure the friendly neutrality of Arab governments. The rise of Jewish immigration into Palestine in the later 1930s, much of it illegal, generated more or less continuous interest on the part of the Palestinian peoples, fearful of eventually becoming a minority in their own country. This unrest, and the appeals of the Mufti of Jerusalem, Haj Amin El Husseini, to other Arab states against the manner in which Britain was exercising the Palestine mandate, forced Britain to act in a way that was to arouse the bitter and on occasion murderous hostility of the Zionists, for in the White Paper of 1939 Britain made a determined effort to allay justifiable Palestinian fears for the future. Palestine was promised independence within ten years as a country in which the Jewish element should not exceed one third of the whole. Meanwhile, in an endeavour to ensure a demographic balance, it was laid down that all Jewish immigration would end within five years, and that with immediate effect it was to be limited to an annual intake of 75,000.

Faced with this plain declaration of British policy, the Zionists, immensely more powerful now that they could plausibly identify with the manifest plight of a vast segment of World Jewry, turned their attention to the US. The large Jewish community in that country had been swelled by the refugees from Russia at the turn of the century and was to be further increased by the influx of victims of Nazi persecution. The Jews in the US constituted an important political lobby, whose votes might be essential at election time. Moreover, in contrast to Britain, the political motivation was not balanced by strategic necessity, for there were massive local supplies of oil ready to hand, and in any case the US did not enter the war till December 1941. After that date the strategic argument no less than the political acted to the Zionists' advantage. Britain, hard-pressed economically after 1945, relied heavily on American good-will and munificence. She was in no position effectively to defend Palestinian interests against diplomatic, human and political pressures, which became overwhelming after the revelation of the full scale and horror of the Nazis' *final solution*. Practically speaking, the

British government found it impossible to implement the terms of the 1939 White Paper. For the Zionists Britain was now the main impediment to the fulfilment of their dreams of a Jewish national home. To dislodge the British, their para-military organizations, notably the Stern Gang (named after the terrorist Abraham Stern, killed in 1942) and Irgun Zvai Leumi, attacked the British police and military in Palestine. A wave of terrorism occurred. The most famous examples were firstly the blowing up on 22 July 1946 by the Irgun Zvai Leumi of the British military headquarters and Palestine government secretariat situated in Jerusalem's King David Hotel, resulting in 91 British and Palestinian deaths, and secondly the hanging in July 1947 of two British soldiers allegedly in execution of a so-called sentence imposed by the Irgun. Zionist terrorism against the British was not confined to Palestine. Already on 6 November 1944 in Cairo two members of the Stern Gang had murdered Lord Moyne, British minister of state in the Middle East, who had attracted Zionist hatred for his suggestion that a future Jewish state might be sited in East Prussia. In 1947 the Zionists added a new horror to their arsenal, the letter bomb; contrary to later popular misconceptions, it was the Zionists who pioneered this barbaric misuse of the postal services. Among their would-be targets were the British prime minister Clement Attlee, the British foreign secretary Ernest Bevin, and the British governor of Cyprus.[2]

Exhausted after six years of war, lacking either the resources or the will any longer to sustain an imperial role in the teeth of prevalent world opinion, Britain handed the whole question of Palestine to the newly-formed United Nations Organization. Following the report of the UN Special Committee on Palestine, which had conducted an investigation *in situ* in the summer, the United Nations General Assembly on 29 November 1947, by a vote made suspect by extraordinary pressures, adopted a resolution for the partition of Palestine into two states, of which the one assigned to the Jews represented slightly over half the total area. On 14 May 1948 the State of Israel was proclaimed and was recognized by both major world powers. The British mandate was formally at an end.

[2] A detailed account of Zionist terrorism at this time and since is available in a booklet *The Terrorists* (Prism Publications, Cairo, 1972).

From the point of view of our present study, the period between the UN resolution and the proclamation of the new State is crucial. In those five and a half months the Zionists were able to use the peculiar situation obtaining in Palestinc to enormous advantage, and in a manner which determined the character of the continuing crisis of the succeeding quarter century. A veritable power vacuum existed, for the UN had failed to lay down clear and effective ways in which the partition was to be achieved, while, understandably in view of the terrorist attacks to which they had been exposed, the British forces concentrated their attention on trying to ensure for themselves as smooth an evacuation as possible. Both Arabs and Jews were left largely to their own devices. But, whereas the latter had over the years built up their own organization, starting with the Jewish Agency and continuing with the para-military bodies directed at the British presence after the 1939 White Paper, the Arabs did not possess any parallel machinery capable of safeguarding their areas from Zionist inroads or even of maintaining basic public amenities. The situation was therefore propitious for the consolidation by the Zionists of their future position, and for the manufacture of a series of alleged facts which they could use in their later propaganda attacks on the Arab case.

In particular the Zionists were concerned by the large Arab population resident in those areas of Palestine assigned to them by the 29 November 1947 UN resolution, for even now the Jews represented only about one-third of the entire population of undivided Palestine. Allied with this problem was the fact that less than 10 per cent of the entire land was actually owned by Jews. It was therefore necessary to find some way of achieving a mass Arab evacuation, as a result of which the Zionist information media might later seek to demonstrate to the outside world that the overwhelming proportion of the land within the frontiers of the future state of Israel was both owned by and occupied by Jews. The Zionists pursued this objective with the same sort of ruthless efficiency as that employed by the Nazis in their persecution of the Jews only a few years earlier. The terror campaign, which included murder and the callous destruction of Arab property, culminated in the calculated massacre of Deir Yassin on 9 April 1948. Modern communications media were em-

ployed to evict whole Arab communities from their homes in important towns simply by ordering them out, a process that continued
after the promulgation of the new state of Israel, while the Zionist
mastery of psychological warfare showed itself in constant and
shameless reminders of the fate of the 250 innocent Arab villagers
murdered by the Stern Gang and the Irgun at Deir Yassin. This then
was the origin of the Arab refugee problem with which the world
has since become painfully familiar, but which it almost totally
ignored at the time. Perhaps a million Arabs lost their homes in this
way. They did so as a direct consequence of ruthless Zionist pressure, and not in obedience to alleged instructions from various Arab
governments, as the Israelis falsely attempted to claim.

Already before the end of 1948 there could be seen the beginnings
of an outside awareness that the solution to the Jewish problem
would be far more difficult than had at first been imagined. In an
endeavour to protect the Palestinians from Zionist oppression, including Jewish occupation of areas not assigned to Israel by the
29 November 1947 resolution, the armies of Egypt, Iraq, Lebanon,
Syria and Transjordan intervened. This provided an early test of the
UN's capability of achieving the objectives for which it had largely
been created, the peaceful settlement of disputes. A truce was
arranged, and a UN mediator, Count Folke Bernadotte, was
appointed to try to ensure that it was kept by both sides. Irrespective
of any pre-existing interest in the Palestine problem, international
attention was focused on what must have seemed the proving
ground of the world body on which so many of the hopes of mankind
rested. The attention became the greater when the world audience
received news of Bernadotte's assassination on 17 September 1948
at the hands of Zionist extremists. Israel had emerged as an object of
world attention, and one which the expanding mass media were
equipped to bring to the notice of a world-wide audience. In the
process there was much over-simplification and blurring of vital
data. This happened sometimes because the media operators considered the undiluted facts to be barely assimilable by an audience
untutored in the essential background; at other times the operators
were themselves partisan and so had an interest in suppressing or
distorting parts of the truth.

At first, as we shall see in the next chapter, the Israelis had much the best of it in the matter of mass opinion formation. Nevertheless, the persistence of the crisis in the Middle East meant that in course of time the world audience would demand more information about the Arab states and peoples, whose attitudes and aspirations were and are essential to any understanding of Israel's international image and of great-power policies towards her and towards the area in general. Nor did the world have long to wait for news of purely Arab developments. The defeat of the Arab armies at the hands of Israel in 1948 had repercussions in several Arab countries. It stimulated dissatisfaction with or at any rate a questioning of the old order, which had apparently done little to prevent the emergence of the threat posed by the birth of the Zionist state. An early reaction to these feelings of disillusionment, betrayal and downright anger was the overthrow of the Syrian government in 1949. A more portentous reaction occurred some three years later with the Egyptian revolution, to which we now direct our attention.

7
Beginnings of an Information Response, 1952–1956

(a) The Egyptian Revolution

We have already drawn attention to the climacteric importance of the Egyptian Free Officers' movement and of their revolution of 23 July 1952 in the context of the Arab peoples' deepening identity perceptions. Both the movement and the revolution articulated public sentiments which were Arab no less than Egyptian. The sentiments were an amalgam of anger at the injustices inherent in the creation of the state of Israel, of pity for the plight of the Palestinians, of frustration resulting from a sense of national and Arab dishonour. The last of these elements was uppermost in the Egypt of 1952.

Egypt had cause enough to feel dishonoured. Memories of the defeat at the hands of Israel four years earlier were still fresh, and were the harder to bear because of a mounting realization of the government's military unpreparedness. The defeat was decisive in alienating the nation from an establishment, largely foreign in composition, which enjoyed enormous material advantages beyond the dreams of practically the entire population. That establishment, moreover, flaunted its social and economic privileges in the most insensitive way, cared little for national pride, and damaged the national image at home and abroad by its gross financial corruption. Egypt inevitably suffered from the universal opprobrium attaching to its enervated ruling class. She still smarted from the presence of the British in the Canal Zone.

These discontents were as often as not expressed partially or even incoherently. It could hardly be otherwise in a country still burdened by a high incidence of illiteracy and of inadequate education, where the principal medium of information was severely handicapped, for up to this time, and indeed up to 1960, the newspapers were for the most part financially dependent on capitalists and feudalists reluctant to allow the publication of anything likely to jeopardize their vested interest in the old order. The Wafd enjoyed much press influence, but, as we have seen, the party was by now integrated with the establishment. Its policies accorded with the popular will only insofar as the Wafdists maintained their demands for British evacuation. And even their continued campaign against the British was not so much a genuine espousal of the national interest, as an attempt to divert public attention away from the self-seeking financial activities of party members.

Given massive dissatisfaction, there was a real danger of an outbreak of blind uncontrollable fury, which indeed might destroy the existing order, though at the price of anarchy. As in the case of Ahmed Arabi's revolt of 1882, this would simply give foreign powers an excuse for further interference. The danger was compounded by the presence of groups which might be tempted to exploit an already inflammatory situation for sectarian ends; the two most important groups of this kind were the Communists and the Muslim Brotherhood.

Fortunately for Egypt, the Free Officers rose to the challenge of the times. They did so by their political shrewdness, their correct timing, their mastery of the techniques of opinion formation. From the outset they realized the need to conceal their identity, both because, as we have seen, propaganda from concealed sources is often the most effective, and because a premature revelation of the personnel of the leadership would have been tantamount to an invitation to the government to kill the movement through close surveillance if not the actual arrest of its organizers. The latter had to balance the demands of secrecy with the need to circulate widely such information as was not readily available through the normal media, particularly information dealing with government shortcomings. It achieved this information role largely through the mimeographed tracts of Khaled Muhieddin and others, which were carefully distributed by trusted members of the movement. Colonel Gamal Abdel Nasser and the leadership managed to preserve their anonymity until the psychological moment. Once their identities were revealed, it was seen that the movement was essentially led by officers who had distinguished themselves in the 1948 war, and who had had no part in the incompetent and corrupt activities of the government of the day. In this way the Free Officers restored to the nation a measure of the self-confidence which it had lost as a result of the defeat four years earlier, and also restored a sense of pride in the national army. The Free Officers recognized too that, whereas a nation may wish to rid itself of the evils of an unpopular establishment, it is seldom prepared for the destruction of every feature of its accustomed way of life. A great part of public opinion is profoundly conservative, and has a deep-rooted craving for the sense of security resulting from the continuity of the new with the old. To be permanently acceptable, the revolution must not therefore entail too drastic a break with the past. Conscious of this, the Free Officers wisely selected as their leader the much respected and personally popular Major General Muhammad Neguib. He was to prove highly successful in investing the revolution with the necessary image of continuity.

As far as timing was concerned, the Free Officers realized that the January 1952 anti-British riots in Cairo had brought matters to a head. Neguib was made president of their association in that same month. If they delayed too long, events might escalate beyond their control, as they had already done in the case of the Wafd, particularly in the confused political situation after the dismissal of Mustapha Nahas. In that case the way would be open to the extremists, notably the Communists on one side and the Muslim Brotherhood on the other. Yet it was important to avoid providing grounds for possible later accusations of having acted precipitately, or out of personal interest. For maximum public support, the Free Officers needed to strike at a moment when the entire nation was actively united in hostility to the establishment. The perfect opportunity came when General Sirry Amer was named as the new Minister of War. The establishment press had not been able to conceal from the people as a whole the fact of General Amer's deep involvement in the scandals which had contributed to his country's defeat in 1948. His appointment to the Ministry of War, of all ministries, could not fail to evoke deep seated memories of the national dishonour, and, in this context, it amounted to an almost calculated insult to the national consensus. By acting as and when they did in July 1952, the Free Officers ensured that they were in step with national opinion. Opposition was in consequence negligible and the revolution virtually bloodless.

The conditions in which it took place meant that the revolution of July 1952 would not later be haunted by the memory of the deaths of victims, memories which in other times and places proved divisive of national interests, as can be seen from the history of France after Louis Napoleon's coup d'état of 1851, or of Russia after the Bolshevik Revolution of 1917. There might be disappointments or differences of opinion on particular aspects of policy, but there were no grounds for a legacy of permanent hatred. Their immediate objective attained, Colonel Nasser and the Free Officers were careful not to antagonize even their enemies more than absolutely necessary. For this reason, the King was allowed to depart in peace, and Ali Maher continued as Prime Minister for several months. Throughout its development, and later after its attainment of power, the Free Officers movement displayed a certain pragmatism, a refusal to adopt hard doctrinaire positions for their own sake. And pre-eminently it was distinguished by its correct order of priorities, in keeping with the fundamental aspirations of the public, and with the over-riding consideration of speaking and acting on behalf of the whole nation. These motivations came out clearly in the following excerpt from a broadcast message to the nation a few months later.[1]

> "We were not a mere individual or a mere army on the night of July 23rd. We were a whole people. Indeed, we were a whole people when we began to purify the land from the traces of the past.
>
> We were a whole people when we smashed the shackles that manacled our hands and fettered our heels—the handcuffs of exploitative domination, the chains of imposed imperialism.
>
> We were a whole people when we granted ourselves the right to determine the way we are to follow in the international field.
>
> We were a whole people when we decided that no obstacle should stand in the way of our strength. We were a whole people when we decided that what was Egypt's should be restored to Egypt."

The reference to Egypt is significant. Later President Nasser was

[1] Cairo Radio Broadcast of 23 February 1953.

to bring Arab opinion to a keener awareness of its identity. But for the present he saw that Egypt could hope to make an effective contribution to the Pan-Arab cause only after it had put its own house in order. In looking first to Egypt's interests, President Nasser was not ignoring wider Arab interests, but was quite simply getting his priorities right.

The first priority was, physically and with a minimum of dislocation and resentment, to remove the hands of the old establishment from the major levers of power. This much was begun in July 1952. It had to be followed by effective consolidation, for the members of the old establishment were still for the most part resident in Egypt, and were still influential and potentially powerful. Common sense dictated that their capacity for disruption be brought within bounds. The same was true for other groups, such as the Muslim Brotherhood and the Communist Party, who, out of ideological commitment, laudable enthusiasm, self-interest, or for whatever other cause, failed to confine their activities within the permitted limits of the national consensus represented by the July revolution. But merely preventive measures were not enough. Something positive had to be done for the economic and social progress of the mass of Egyptians, who had suffered from an outdated feudal system and from heavy taxation and primitive standards while others grew rich at their expense. We have to remember that, despite inadequate educational facilities, the masses were not unaware of the possibility of a better life. The attention paid by the Wafd to the political grass roots over thirty years, now reinforced by the accessibility of radio, meant that the masses were no longer passive or even inarticulate. Finally, and very importantly, Egypt could not ignore the matter of her foreign relations. At the very least, the new government must redeem the nationalist hopes on which its July 1952 success rested. In other words, it must build up the nation's defence capability, and must bring about the rapid and permanent departure of the British military presence from the Canal Zone. The latter task had to be tackled in such a way as to avoid the creation of a power vacuum which could be construed as a standing invitation to foreign interference from a different quarter. Put another way, the government of the Free Officers had an inescapable obligation to assert and to maintain Egypt's sovereignty in the world community.

These were far-reaching aims. Their pursuit would stretch the young government's capabilities. Even so, they were limited aims, and Colonel Nasser, always the realist, was careful not to embark upon grandiose projects that had little or no chance of success at this time. For example, he and his advisers knew that, given the prevailing climate of world opinion and especially of great-power opinion, there was little hope in the mid-1950s of taking on Israel, either single handed or in concert with other Arab countries. Egypt neither wanted nor sought any additional dispute with Israel, and the crisis of 1956 was not of Egypt's choosing.

The new government lost no time in taking practical steps for the material benefit of the mass of the people. The obvious priority of the tasks now undertaken stemmed from the causes of the revolution and harmonized with the evidence adduced by the government's own attention to public relations. The purpose of these tasks was synthesized in the *Six Principles of the Revolution*, namely: to combat imperialism, to abolish feudalism, to put an end to the domination of capital, to build a strong national army, to create conditions of social justice, to establish a sound democratic life. There was nothing in these aims which need offend that widespread popular distrust of over-abrupt or over-rapid change which we have already mentioned. Rather the Six Principles accurately reflected the underlying aspirations of the overwhelming majority. By keeping the principles to the forefront of their planning, and by skilfully demonstrating the correlation of the principles with the demands of public well-being, the administration preserved that essential harmony between government and governed which is the hallmark of true democracy.

In domestic affairs, the major early reform was the agrarian reform of September 1952. It limited the amount of land which any individual could own to the not inconsiderable level of 200 feddans—though this figure was reduced later—and provided for the redistribution of the excess among the fellahin who actually worked the soil. In implementing this measure of reform, the government was careful to abide by accepted usage, and provided for proper compensation of the previous owners. It also made full use of the available media in explaining the details, and in projecting an appreciation of their essential fairness and justice to the nation at large. Still within the first four post-revolutionary years, the government embarked upon the Aswan High Dam project. While the scheme took on diplomatic overtones, to be discussed in our next chapter, it was in essence a vast measure of social and economic improvement.

The matter of the British in the Canal Zone was more difficult. But here Egypt could count on the support of the prevailing international dislike of anything savouring of colonialism, a dislike still shared by opinion in the US, and to an increasing degree evinced by important sections of British opinion, despite the return to power of the Conservatives under Winston Churchill in the election of 1951. Moreover, as we saw in the matter of the last years of the Palestine Mandate, British opinion was disturbed at the risks run by conscript soldiers called upon to serve in unsettled regions at a time when Britain's vital security no longer seemed to be at stake. The much increased British exposure to news reports, now often evocatively portrayed through television, helped to feed an insistent demand for the evacuation of the Canal Zone, and hopefully for the end of conscription altogether. For their part the Egyptian information media, with which the present author was closely associated from that time, made it their business to reinforce these feelings by means of programmes directed through a secret transmitter specifically at the British troops. The message was not one of hatred and threats, but rather took the form of a reasoned appeal to reasonable people, with whom the Egyptians wished to establish normal good relations. By their continued presence in a military form, the British were spoiling the prospect for genuine friendship of the sort that can only develop on the basis of a sovereign equality, and they were doing so in conditions of heat and discomfort which bore heavily on the average conscripted serving man. The Egyptian message is a good example of the use of the media in the interests of better understanding, of information for peace. Within two years of the revolution, Gamal Abdel Nasser and the Free Officers had discharged the task implicitly assigned to them by the verdict of July 1952. The problems of Sudan, whose settlement the British had for long regarded as a pre-condition for evacuation, were amicably solved. An arrangement was concluded with Britain, later formalized in the treaty of October 1954, under which the troops would leave the

Canal Zone by the beginning of 1956. Egypt at last attained her independence in the full meaning of the term, and for the first time in the modern era, for even before the start of British intervention Egypt, as strictly speaking still part of the Ottoman Empire, had not been fully sovereign. But the settlement was not seen by Egypt as a defeat for Britain, whose essential strategic interests and whose obligations to her allies were respected in the proviso that British troops might be allowed to return, if at some future date any member of the Arab League or Turkey were attacked by another country apart from Israel.

Satisfactory as it was in the context of both Britain's and Egypt's true national interests, the conclusion of this arrangement had political repercussions in Cairo. We remarked earlier upon the importance for the new Egyptian government of ensuring that political activity should remain within the bounds implicitly set by the national consensus of July 1952. The first major threat—from the Wafd— was overcome without undue difficulty, thanks largely to the internal divisions among the Wafdists themselves and to the almost universal affection in which General Neguib was held. Indeed, slightly earlier an important break with the past had occurred, when Neguib had replaced the veteran politician Ali Maher as Prime Minister, upon the latter's refusal fully to endorse the new government's land distribution policy. With the political figures of the old establishment now removed from the seats of power, the time had come to formalize the national context of political activity. This was done in January 1953 with the dissolution of the existing political parties and their replacement by the National Liberation Rally, followed in June by the promulgation of a republic with Neguib as its first President. By this time the Communist threat was a spent force; like the Wafd the Communists were the victims of their own internal dissensions, while in any case it is doubtful if they could ever have made much headway in an Islamic country at a time when Communism was still largely regarded as synonymous with irreligion if not with actual atheism.

Far more serious from the point of view of the revolutionary régime was the position of the Muslim Brotherhood, for the latter evoked a sympathetic and genuinely Islamic response, not only in

Egypt, but throughout the Arab World. While in no way questioning the sincerity of many members of the Brotherhood, the government knew only too well that to yield to the organization's ideological demands would be to place at risk that working national consensus without which Egypt could neither establish her revolutionary gains on a sure and permanent footing, nor later hope to play her proper role in nurturing the larger unity, strength and well-being of the Arab World. By their uncompromising and doctrinaire stance on matters requiring diplomatic finesse and political agility, the Muslim Brotherhood threatened the very foundations of Egypt's new-found liberty. That liberty was not yet and could not yet be complete, for in the final analysis the new republic's security depended on the army. Understandable impatience was felt in some quarters at the continued restrictions on normal political life in the fullest sense. The new government hoped in time to restore this greater freedom in a new and purer form, unsullied by the hidden controls exercised by the ruling class of the old establishment. But, in its realistic way, it knew that it must adhere to the self-imposed order of priorities, without which there would be no freedom worth the name for the vast majority of Egypt's population. Thanks to thorough and pains-taking public relations, it understood the needs and wishes of the masses better than did any of the other groups. It simply could not afford to see the erosion of its position by yielding to either the well-meaning though divisive policies of the Muslim Brotherhood, or to the facile arguments of politicians in favour of so-called political democracy. Ironically, in view of his immeasurable contribution to the initial success of the revolution, a major threat came from the person of Neguib himself. An amateur in the art of political judge-ment, he was an easy prey to the blandishments of professional politicians, while his immense and continuing popularity throughout the country meant that, once he had been persuaded to support a cause or a policy inimical to that of the Free Officers, their own tenure of power was likely to be short lived, and with it the fundamental security of the revolution itself. Ultimately these conflicts were brought to a head by a plot against the life of Gamal Abdel Nasser devised by some members of the Muslim Brotherhood, in response to what they deemed the unduly favourable treatment accorded to

Britain in the arrangements governing the evacuation of the Canal Zone. Fortunately the plotters were apprehended and eventually condemned, but not before a connection had been established between Neguib and other members of the Muslim Brotherhood. Sadly, there was no alternative to Neguib's resignation in November 1954.

By the time he assumed the Presidency, therefore, Gamal Abdel Nasser had already earned the permanent gratitude of the mass of the Egyptian people, and had shown beyond a shadow of doubt his supreme gift of recognizing their true interests, and of framing his policy in ways calculated to secure those interests and to harmonize with the essential components of national opinion. He had restored justifiable national pride, he had brought order in place of political confusion, he had with a minimum of dislocation and resentment carried out a monumental agrarian reform, he had obtained international recognition for his country as a truly sovereign entity, he had composed Egypt's differences with Britain in a civilized and reasonable manner. As we shall see in the last part of this chapter, he did not forget the causes of Arab independence and unity, nor the global struggle against imperialism. And, while not for a moment accepting the basis of the Israeli state, he had endeavoured to avoid disputes with that country. Yet, in Zionist eyes the rise of Egypt's stature was not to be countenanced. Over this same period the Zionists lost no opportunity of exploiting their special relationship with the world's information media to undermine the gains of the July revolution, as also the position of the Arab World in general.

(b) Israel's propaganda advantage

In the coming Arab struggle for recognition and justice, the balance of advantage in 1952 appeared overwhelmingly in Israel's favour. It was long to remain so. Progressive Arab governments, such as that which had attained power in Egypt, faced what, on any reasonable calculation, must have seemed a well-nigh impossible task. In its timing, the Zionist achievement of the sovereign state of Israel was impeccable; not only did the Zionists maximize the sympathies of a world opinion still stunned by the revelations of the Nazi horror, but they were able to enlist the resources of the world's richest nation,

America, to reckon on the goodwill of the Soviet Union, to exploit the currently anti-imperialist attitudes of international bodies, and to pose credibly enough as a small inoffensive state whose citizens, having suffered unspeakably, wished no more than to be allowed to rebuild their lives in peaceful harmony with the rest of mankind, a threat to no one.

Specifically, as we saw in our previous chapter, their cause had been whole-heartedly taken up by the US, to which the Zionists turned after Britain in the 1939 White Paper had appeared to opt for the Arab interest in Palestine. Twenty years earlier, though already possessing a sizeable Jewish community with some electoral importance, the US had by no means been committed to Zionism. It is interesting to note that the two-man fact-finding commission which visited Palestine in 1919 on behalf of the victorious powers was made up of two Americans, Henry C. King and Charles R. Crane, and that, in reporting against a Zionist solution to the matter of Palestine's future, they were decidedly influenced by the need to act justly towards the Arab inhabitants. Such circumspection is difficult to imagine on the part of any American in the highly charged emotional climate of the years immediately following the Second World War. In the case of Americans, the universal horror which greeted the mass media's revelations of the Nazi's *final solution* was compounded by a national burden of guilt, because until the outbreak of war official US policy had been to deny entry to the victims of Hitler's persecution. Large numbers of Americans now felt they had a duty to make amends for the wrongs suffered by international and ubiquitous Jewry. They vastly augmented the importance of the Jewish political lobby, and in so doing subjected the administration of President Harry S. Truman to irresistible pressures. Because of the dominant economic and military position occupied by the US in the post-war world, these pressures inevitably bore on the world community and in particular on Britain as the power most intimately concerned with Palestine, with the consequences which we noted in our previous chapter. Moreover, American wishes exerted what is now seen as undue influence on the passage of the UN General Assembly's 29 November 1947 resolution, which effectively laid the basis of the future Israeli state. It would of course be misleading to suggest that the outcome would have been unfavourable to the Zionists except for the wholehearted American support of their cause. Sympathy for the Jewish survivors of Nazi persecution was world-wide. But it may be doubted whether, without US assistance, the solution would have been quite so acceptable to Israel. As it was, the heavily partisan attitude of the Americans, coupled with sheer American power, and with the dramatic impact of the information media of press, radio and cinema in bringing the revelations of the Nuremburg war crimes trials to the attention of a world audience, ensured that American consciences should be salved at the expense of the Arabs. At a climacteric stage, the latter were handicapped by the incompleteness of their own identity perceptions, and still more by the utter inadequacy of the fragmentary awareness of that identity on the part of the world in general. Allowing for the rather greater appreciation possessed by some countries, notably Britain and France, it is fair to say that still the Arabs were a people of whom little was known, by comparison with the enormous fund of information available about the sufferings, aspirations, achievements and interests of ubiquitous Jewry.

From the Arab point of view, it was a pity that specialized knowledge of their case was so largely confined to Britain and France, countries whose importance in the post-war world was eroded by the emergence of the two super-powers, countries moreover which were regarded with suspicion as representing an obsolete colonialism out of tune with contemporary world opinion. On anti-imperialist grounds alone, Britain's misgivings about handing over a large part of Palestine to the Zionists would have been seen as self-interested by both the US and the USSR, who in 1948 found themselves agreed in welcoming Israeli independence.

This combination of pro-Jewish sympathies and of aversion from vestigial colonialism gave Israel a great propaganda advantage. It was to remain resilient for many years to come, even though in time Russia would considerably revise her attitude to the crisis in the Middle East. In the years before the 1956 Suez war, which primarily concern us in this chapter, this combination of attitudes, hugely fostered by the mass media, proved decisive. This is because it served to obscure, almost to render irrelevant, the activities of the

Zionist terrorists, in a way that in other circumstances would be incomprehensible. After all, these were the years when the activities of the Stern Gang and of the Irgun Zvai Leumi were at their nefarious height, activities which, after using the campaign against the British army and police as a sort of testing ground, were conducted with still greater ferocity against the Palestinians, and in a manner clearly reminiscent of the Nazi campaign of terror on which the Zionists based so much of their claim to the sympathy of mankind. Although reports of individual acts of Zionist terrorism were disturbing, they were easily dismissed as the uncontrollable reflexes of a people who had suffered too much. In any case, Zionist control of the media, especially in the US but elsewhere also, was such that relatively few reports of this nature were circulated in a form likely to create international repercussions. Where an inconvenient truth did slip out, it was generally under-played, while most of the world's press was ready to accept at their face value explanations that the terrorists were acting in defiance of official Zionist wishes, or later in defiance of the Israeli government. In this way the Israelis were able to preserve a favourable international image. This was in spite of their official policy of harassing the Palestinians out of their homes, and by that means of creating so called "facts", which at a later date might be employed to nurture such propaganda crudities as the claim to have established a people without a land in a land without a people.

It is very important to remember that Zionist terrorism against the Palestinians was not restricted in its duration to the period immediately preceding Israeli independence. Had it been, then even such actions as the Deir Yassin massacre of 9 April 1948, and as the wholesale expulsions from Tiberias, Haifa and Safad in the weeks before the end of the mandate, might have been seen by some as understandable aberrations on the part of a people desperately concerned lest the prize, hope of which had so long sustained them, should be denied at the last moment. The events of the next eight years, however, showed these activities in an altogether different light, for, regardless of the formal emergence of the Israeli state on 14 May 1948, the terror went on, not as isolated outbreaks attributable to despair, but rather as part of a calculated policy to rid the Zionist nation of as much of the residual Arab population as possible. The expulsions of Palestinians from Lydda and Ramleh took place on 12 July 1948, from Beersheba on 21 October. Further wholesale killings occurred, most notably the massacre at Qibya on 14 October 1953 involving fifty-three deaths at Israeli army hands, and the massacre of fifty-seven people again by regular soldiers at Kafr Kassem on 28 October 1956. These events were in their motivation on all fours with Israel's adamant refusal to allow the return of the refugees on any acceptable terms, despite pressure from the United Nations and even from the Americans.

And still to all intents and purposes Israel's image throughout most of the outside world remained unimpaired. The world community's patience suffered perhaps its greatest strain at the time of the murder of the UN mediator, Count Bernadotte, in Jerusalem on 17 September 1948 by a group of Zionist terrorists. The crime was particularly serious because it outraged an international sentiment of comparable potency to that of sympathy for the Jews, namely the contemporary belief that mankind's chief guarantee of survival in the atomic age lay in the efficacy of the new world organization. Also by this time the UN mediator had begun to insist on respect for the rights of the Palestinian refugees. Even so, pro-Israeli emotions were strong enough to ensure acceptance for official Israeli disclaimers of any part in the murder. The phenomenon of Israel's public relations success is explicable, partly in terms of the Zionist control of much of the international media, partly in terms of the difficulties of maintaining mass interest in any particular issue which possessed neither an immediate relevance to the concerns of individual newspaper-readers and radio-listeners, nor an abnormal capacity for prolonged sensationalism. As far as much of the world was concerned, the Jews had through their sufferings of the Nazi epoch earned themselves a state of their own; that state had been established and seemed to be prospering, despite the apparently selfish complaints of a colonialist power, Britain, and despite the incomprehensible agitation of Arab communities of which the world knew little and for the most part cared less. Other and more pressing issues had to be faced, for example the threats implicit in the Cold War, or the activities of Senator Joseph McCarthy in the US. For the outside world the Palestine issue was closed. Nothing could have suited Israeli propaganda better.

Although powerless to frustrate Zionist ambitions, Britain's attitude is interesting as evidence that international support for Israel was less than complete. In common with most of the members of the alliance against Hitler, Britain harboured genuine sympathy for the victims of Nazi oppression. The ordinary British people were no less appalled than those of other countries by the revelations of atrocities appearing from the 1945 Nuremburg War Crimes trials. They too wished to see the victims compensated and rehabilitated in the best way possible and, in their eyes, these victims included the Jews. But, to the extent that they thought about Palestine at all, their preference for possible solutions was likely to be more selective, if only because it was conditioned by an element of self-interest. Owing to Britain's mandatory commitment, Palestine featured in British domestic news to a greater extent than it did in the internal media of many other countries. British troops continued to serve in Palestine well after the end of the Second World War. These were conscript soldiers, whose families were no longer prepared to contemplate their indefinite absence abroad on a mission with no obvious relevance to Britain's own security, or even to any identifiable major British foreign policy interest. Resentment at the continuation of conscription, on the part of tax payers and of the relatives of serving men alike, became the more acute when spreading Zionist terrorism under-scored the risks to which British conscripts were daily exposed. Large sections of the British public, therefore, had a personal reason for interest in Palestine. In this way, although not itself a direct motive for British public concern, the Arab cause was probably better 'understood, or perhaps less misunderstood, in Britain than elsewhere, and the radio and press coverage of events, at any rate until May 1948, was presented in greater depth and in a more continuous manner than was the case in most other countries. It is probably true to say that, for British public opinion as a whole, Zionist claims never acquired the idealistic overtones with which they became endowed elsewhere, especially in the United States. Indeed, as time went on, the typical British response to references to the future state of Israel was far more likely to be irritation if not

positive anger. This was especially true after the publication on
1 August 1947 of the photograph of two dead British soldiers hanging from a tree in Nathanya after their so-called 'execution' by order
of the Irgun. For the average Britisher, the declaration of Israeli
independence was not seen as the well-deserved reward for a hard
and gallant resistance against colonialism—the reaction of many
British people towards for example Indian independence in August
1947—nor was it seen as atonement for collective international
neglect of the Jews of Nazi Germany. Rather it appeared as the un-
merited success of a gangsterism which demonstrated callous ingratitude for a nation which from 1939 to 1945 had done more than most
in support of the cause of the free world, which was also the Jewish
cause. Deep-rooted resentments had been created, and they were slow
to subside.

In Israel's eyes British attitudes were of little moment. Inter-
nationally Britain seemed to be a declining quantity. As a surviving
imperial or at any rate colonial power, her susceptibilities could presumably be flouted with impunity. The ironical thing is that, in
flouting them and in getting away with it, Israel was also flouting the
feelings and damaging the interests of the Arab nations, which in
the years since 1952 have done so much to support subject nations
against surviving colonialism of the older type, especially as in the
long run Israel was busy laying the basis for a new colonialism that
was to prove much more harmful to Arab interests. Far from causing
the Zionists embarrassment in international circles, the British
response may even have assisted the propaganda campaign in quite
unintentional ways. In an attempt to preserve some sort of order,
Britain, as the mandatory power before 14 May 1948, was obliged to
carry out punitive measures against the grosser forms of Zionist
terror and illegality. By adept use of the information media, the
Israelis succeeded in projecting these perfectly legitimate counter-
measures as a species of oppression, at worst indistinguishable from
that of the Nazis, and so sufficient to obscure the activities of the
Zionist terror gangs. And Israeli propaganda received an unexpected
bonus when in mid-1947 the British authorities refused entry to 4,500
illegal Jewish immigrants, who had arrived by sea on the ship
Exodus; with naïve disregard for the emotional impact of their

decision, the British ordered that these refugees be returned to Europe, where they were eventually lodged in camps situated in— of all places—Germany. Israeli expertise in the manipulation of world opinion made the most of this, and in time the journey of the *Exodus* was to acquire an almost legendary aura, a process much assisted by the subsequent motion picture on the subject. A more immediate and practical advantage was the effect produced by the seemingly callous British response on the minds of the UN Special Committee on Palestine, whose recommendations were to form the basis of the UN General Assembly's resolution of 29 November in favour of partition.

The Israelis probably calculated that even British hostility would not last long. After all, British public opinion would wane rapidly once the military involvement was ended, while any residual dislike would be a declining factor as memories of Stern Gang terrorism became overlaid with more relevant topicalities. We have to remember too that, contemporaneously with the news reports of the dangers facing British conscripts in Palestine, the media provided disturbing information about anti-British unrest in Egypt, equally involving British conscript soldiers, and that, while avoiding the atrocities characteristic of the Zionist campaign, the struggle of Egyptian nationalism was to engage public attention in Britain for longer, and was eventually to become entangled with strategic issues of a global character. Lacking the emotional appeal of the Palestine problem of 1946 to 1948, the latter were nevertheless by the mid-1950s important enough to the average Britisher to feature more insistently in his unexpressed scale of priorities than any lingering dislike of the Israeli state. We have to recall that, even at the height of popular hostility to Israel, there were in Britain significant Zionist groups possessed of disproportionate power in the orientation of the media. Some of these groups were, and have remained, influential within the British Labour Party.

Indeed Israel's traditional ethic of socialism, manifested in both the economic and social spheres—for example in the kibbutz co-operatives—made a good impression on several governments, as also more generally on the international socialist movement. Many leading socialists from Marx onwards were Jews. Ideological

inclination then worked in the Israeli interest. It may even have contributed to Soviet goodwill at the birth of the new state. It was not,
however, allowed to upset good relations with capitalist America, on
which in the final analysis the continued existence and prosperity
of Israel depended, nor to frighten off subventions from Jewish
capitalists. By avoiding the more strident manifestations of socialism,
the Israeli leaders saw to it that, in their use of political ideology, as
in other matters, their nation should have the best of all worlds. They
recognized that independence would be unusually expensive: not
only must they provide for a continuous and massive defence
capability against the justifiable anger of their immediate neighbours,
but they had to give their citizens sufficient material inducement to
endure indefinitely the restrictions of a siege atmosphere. In these
circumstances all contributions were welcome, and none more so
than the enforced reparations from the Germans, which, continuing
till 1965, provided an invaluable steady income.

The "heroic" phase of their struggle accomplished, and the initial
stages of consolidation progressing satisfactorily, the Israeli leaders
could to a large extent count on outside events, expertly projected by
Jewish propaganda, to do their work for them. The major contri-
butory factors were the intensification of the Cold War, the alienation of much of Africa and Asia from the international politics of the
great powers, and the growing weight of anti-colonialist sentiment.
As we saw earlier, increasing concern on the part of Britain for the
maintenance of her strategic position in the Middle East, a motive
going back to Ottoman times, prompted Britain's support for the
formation of the Arab League in 1945. With the evaporation of US-
Soviet war-time cordiality, the lowering of the Iron Curtain in central
Europe, the definition of the terms of the Cold War in the last years
of Stalinism, and the outbreak of the Korean War, the US developed a keen interest in the concept of a strong bloc in the Middle
East. Already, as we saw in our previous chapter, the attempt to
draw Egypt into the Middle East Defence Organization precipitated
a chain of events bringing with it the exacerbation of Anglo-
Egyptian relations and the Revolution of July 1952. In spite of this,
Britain was drawn more and more into the strategic calculations of
the US, particularly after 1952, when under the Eisenhower adminis-

tration American fears of communism and of the USSR reached their height, finding practical expression at home in the witch-hunting activities of Senator Joseph McCarthy, and abroad in the tireless attempts of the Secretary of State, John Foster Dulles, to surround Russia with a ring of interlocking military alliances, which eventually resulted in the simultaneous existence of the NATO, CENTO (or the Baghdad Pact) and SEATO alignments. The attitudes towards Israel of important powers such as Britain and France, which were drawn into the US orbit, inevitably underwent a change. They may still have disliked the new state, but in the politics of polarization there was little room for the niceties of personal preference. The more the Arab nations adopted a neutralist line, the more Britain and France came to accept as inevitable a working accommodation with their principal ally's friend in the Middle East.

Nor were the motives for the rapprochement confined to the geopolitical sphere of the Cold War. Latent imperialist nostalgia on the part of the older powers was stimulated by what looked like a chance of recovering some of their pre-1939 hegemony, this time underpinned by the US. It expressed itself in a reaction to imagined insults at the hands of some of the countries in the Middle Eastern area, for example to the political campaign conducted against the British military in the Canal Zone and, outside the Arab World though still in the Middle East, to Dr Mussadiq's nationalization in 1951 of the British oil interests in Iran. For France the transition from imperialism was more traumatic; hence the inclination to salvage something by means of an alignment with Israel may have been the greater. The beginnings of the Algerian revolt in 1954, the fall of Dien Bien Phu in the same year, and the loss of Indo-China, probably had a greater impact on public opinion in France than did any parallel process of de-colonization on British opinion. When the Suez crisis came in 1956, therefore, emotional reasons existed which inclined important sections of opinion in both countries to look with some favour at the Israeli position; in fact in 1954 France entered into an arrangement for supplying war planes to Israel. So here again Israeli propaganda fell upon receptive ears.

Even with the logic of events flowing so strongly in their favour, the Israelis did not relax their attention, and they neglected no opportunity to elicit a still more favourable world opinion. On the other hand, the US itself was to feel the consequences reserved by the Israelis for those who stepped out of line. In developing her global Cold War strategy, the US was worried by Cairo's neutralist posture after the 1952 revolution. To improve relations, she contemplated making a loan to Egypt. Any resulting rapprochement between Cairo and Washington would naturally have caused alarm in Tel Aviv. To prevent it, the Israelis devised a series of outrages on American premises in Egypt, hoping that these would be attributed to anti-American sentiments on the part of Egyptian nationalists. Fortunately the ruse failed, a couple of Jews being caught red-handed in December 1954 as they were about to deposit their bombs. At their subsequent trial the culprits furnished a full explanation of the purpose behind the outrages, and attributed their planning to Israel's Minister of Defence, Pinhas Lavon. In terms of her international standing, Israel suffered little or no harm from the *Lavon affair*. Most of the world was too preoccupied by its national and regional business, or by speculation as to the effects of the Cold War, to spare much thought for isolated acts with little bearing on what were regarded as the major issues. Thus again Israel escaped the embarrassing consequences of an operation whose planning bore the characteristic features of a willingness to distort the truth and of a propensity to manufacture media-worthy "facts". Once more Israel was free to settle down to deriving the maximum advantage from the tide of events.

It is probably true to say that in the years preceding her emergence and for some time afterwards Israel relied most heavily on Jewish-centred propaganda, that is to say on the dissemination of information calculated to evoke feelings of pity for Jewish sufferings, feelings of goodwill and encouragement towards Jewish resilience, and feelings of admiration towards Jewish achievement. During this period Israeli propaganda largely ignored the Arab issue, and in doing so no doubt hoped the rest of the world would remain in relative ignorance of the Arab cause. In this the Israelis, whether consciously or not, were pursuing the same psychological line as that of the US government's war-time *rumour clinics*, which as we saw in Chapter 5 purposely refrained from referring to the target of their activities. Similarly, the Israeli propagandists may have recognized that excessive references to Arab statements and Arab activities would be counter-productive, because such references were likely to encourage unwanted world attention towards the Arabs. However, the Zionists could not expect to maintain a negative posture towards the Arabs indefinitely. Sooner or later the prevailing goodwill of most of the world community towards Israel would be eroded, either by the passage of time or by a growing realization of the continuing injustices perpetrated by the government of Tel Aviv. Eventually the world powers, which also possessed not inconsiderable information media, would begin to assess the extent of the human suffering inherent in the Palestinian refugee problem. In addition, as the fifties wore on, the reality of the Arabs' awareness of their own supranational identity could no longer be ignored, assisted as it was by the world's needs for Arab oil, and by the strategic interests of the great powers.

In consequence, the Israelis developed a more overtly anti-Arab propaganda, for consumption not only by the outside world but also by the Arab peoples and governments. In its latter aspect it took on the characteristics of psychological warfare. The Israelis made it their business to foster widespread doubt among the Arabs, and particularly within the ranks of the armed forces, as to the latters' capacity for achieving ultimate victory. They endeavoured to sow similar doubts as to the domestic capabilities of individual Arab governments, for example pursuing a sustained campaign against the Egyptian leadership after the revolution of 1952. Equally they aimed to encourage dissension between one Arab state and another, seeking for this purpose to exploit local nationalism, or the social and economic differences between socialist Arab states and those pursuing more traditionalist ways. For consumption in the US and among the countries allied to the US, the Israeli propaganda aimed to humiliate the Arab people before the world at large and to demonstrate Israel's alleged military invincibility. In pursuing the latter train of thought, Israeli public relations men had to be careful not to overplay their hand. To have done so might have given the impression of arrogant militarism, and thus have risked arousing the human reaction of sympathy for the under-dog. Rather the image should be one of a small peace-loving country surrounded by powerful belligerent neighbours, and being reluctantly compelled against her true character to look to her defences. Seen in these terms, Israeli militarism would be accepted as an inescapable necessity and as the self-evident consequence of any government's duty of looking to the security of its citizens. Israel's success in fashioning a formidable fighting machine, and in maintaining it in a state of constant readiness, would then earn encouraging admiration, while retaining world sympathy. It has to be admitted that, at any rate until very recently, Israeli public relations succeeded in perpetuating this favourable image for their country's military policies. It certainly served them well in 1956 and even more in 1967. We must also admit that its credibility was enhanced by statements from some Arab journalists. In their altogether justifiable anger at the misrepresentation perpetuated by the Israeli propaganda, a number of them were less than explicit in describing the targets of their wrath. Thus, to many outsiders it seemed as though the Arabs were threatening, not only the Zionist state, but also the Jews in general. The Israelis exploited for all it was worth this opportunity of equating the Arab media with those of the Nazis.

At every stage then the Israelis were able to keep alive latent world sympathy for the Jews of the ghetto and of the concentration camp. In doing so of course they showed as little sense of discrimination between Jew and Zionist as did the Arab journalists just referred to, and with less cause. Their operation was immeasurably assisted by the presence on the staffs of their information and propaganda services of highly articulate professionals, skilled in the techniques of the mass media, and by the close links of those professionals with their opposite numbers in some important countries, and pre-eminently in the US. To a very great extent Israeli and American practitioners in the arts of opinion formation dealt in the same idiom. American capital investment in Israel gave these links real power, so that it is fair to say that a veritable censorship of views and data unfavourable to Israel existed, and still exists, among US newspaper and book publishers. The predisposition of the media towards Israel could be seen in other countries too; examples have been cited of the dismissal of a leading BBC commentator for showing what was considered undue sympathy for the Arabs, and of a journalist responsible for an article in *The Times* of London exposing close US-Israeli relations. It is estimated that at present nearly one thousand newspapers and periodicals throughout the world act in one way or another as organs for the propagation of the Zionist case, and in this connection we should not overlook the hidden pressures exerted by Zionist money as indispensable advertising revenue.

Ubiquitous, expertly handled, massively financed, the inheritors of world sympathy for persecuted Jewry, and coinciding with the strategic interest of the materially strongest nation on earth, Zionist public relations were far more powerful than outward appearances might suggest. Moreover, their low profile brought further advantages, for, as we have seen, propaganda thrives best where its operations are concealed. It was against this mighty co-ordinated machinery that the Arab cause laboured to secure first recognition, then understanding, and later support. Definite, albeit sometimes halting steps in this direction were taken in the years preceding the Suez crisis of 1956.

(c) The Arab response begins

Gamal Abdel Nasser and his colleagues realized that Egypt was likely to get the worst of any new conflict with Israel until such time as they had met the pressing need for reform at home. In the same way both they and progressive leaders elsewhere knew that the Pan-Arab struggle against Zionism could be brought to a successful conclusion only after essential changes had taken place in the Arab World as a whole. The Six Principles of the Egyptian revolution suggested lines of development and reform appropriate to some other Arab countries, especially to those where conditions were in certain respects comparable with conditions in Egypt prior to July 1952. The Egyptian information media, therefore, had both an opportunity and a duty to inform foreign Arab opinion of the aims and achievements of the government in Cairo.

Of the Six Principles the one which was probably most immediately relevant to the Arab World at this time was the declaration against imperialism in all its forms. In 1952 most of the Arab World was still dominated in one way or another by outside powers, despite two world wars waged in the name of national self-determination and democracy. The whole Maghreb was subject to France to a greater or lesser extent. Sudan and the Aden Protectorate (now South Yemen) were still under the British, who also exerted disproportionate influence in Iraq and Jordan. And, most blatantly of all, the Palestinians suffered the evils of colonialism at the hands of Zionist Israel.

Despite the monumental tasks facing it at home, the Egyptian government lost no time in extending whatever support it could to its fellow Arabs in other lands. The 1954 agreement with Britain concerning the evacuation of the Canal Zone greatly encouraged the cause of Arab freedom. The circumstances in which it occurred were an object lesson of the way the media should respond to and encourage the spirit of the people in favour of liberty and peace, for, as we saw, the message of Egypt to the occupying power carefully avoided personal hostility and held out the hope of future Anglo-Egyptian friendship. The encouragement of cordial international relations is not only desirable in itself, but, from the specific point of view of the Arab cause, it is strategically essential, for a climate of belligerence is all too likely to engender fear and hatred, and hence a refusal to listen to justifiable Arab claims, let alone to entertain them seriously. In saying this, we do not for a moment deny that outright colonialism must be combated with determination and by every justifiable means. Pre-eminent among the latter are the facilities for the mass exchange of opinion and information available through the modern media.

Egypt made an early start in this direction with the establishment of *The Voice of the Arabs* on 4 July 1953. Beginning with a radio transmission of half an hour a day the programmes were increased to fifteen hours in 1962, and at present they continue almost round the clock. Currently among the most efficient radio systems in the world, Egypt's broadcasting capability expanded from a modest 72 kilowatts on medium wave only in 1952 to 560 kilowatts spread over both medium and short wave by 1956. Since then the transmission capacity has multiplied about ten-fold. While essentially directed at the whole of the Arab World, *The Voice of the Arabs* from an early stage devised additional programmes for particular countries or regions; examples of these were the broadcasts to Israel, to the Maghreb, to Sudan and to Iraq. Not only did Egypt provide vital information services to an ever-widening circle, but she also recognized the importance of encouraging other Arab countries to develop their own broadcasting facilities along similar lines. Beginning in 1953, the Egyptian Radio Corporation has provided courses in the necessary techniques, these courses being open to professional broadcasting personnel from the whole Arab World. Later, in July 1957, an Institute for Radio Training was inaugurated, and later still similar courses were introduced for television. Egypt has also seconded technicians and engineers to Kuwait, Libya, Saudi Arabia and Yemen, and she afforded technical assistance to Syria in setting up TV stations and studios.

A good deal of this was quite far ahead in 1952. In the first four years after the revolution, *The Voice of the Arabs* directed much attention to the cause of freedom in the Maghreb. For Morocco it encouraged the cause of the Sultan Muhammad V, exiled by the French in February 1953. For Tunisia there was support for Habib Bourguiba and for his Neo Destour party. By the time they attained their full sovereignty in March 1956, both Morocco and Tunisia had received important help and encouragement from *The Voice of the Arabs*. But it was in connection with the French position in Algeria that Paris came chiefly to resent the success of Egypt's radio campaign on behalf of the nationalist cause. The Algerian revolt against French colonialism broke out on 31 October 1954. Its subsequent direction was heavily influenced by leaders resident in Cairo. Spokesmen for the cause of Algerian independence were allowed to use the facilities of *The Voice of the Arabs*. The present author can speak from personal experience of the important effect which these broadcasts and similar assistance had on the calculations of the French government at that time. In 1955 he was sent secretly to Paris for conversations with the French minister, Christian Pineau, who had threatened to provide the Israelis with Mirage military aircraft in retaliation for Egyptian help to the Algerians. During the course of their meeting the present author, acknowledging his personal responsibility for *The Voice of the Arabs,* left Pineau in no doubt that the

French threat to assist Israel could have no effect on Egyptian support for legitimate Algerian demands.

An uncompromising stand on the issues of national integrity and on anti-colonialist solidarity did not preclude friendly relations with the great powers. Egypt's policy as expressed in her press and radio had no place for rabid xenophobia either in the mid-fifties or since. Her clear stand was well illustrated by the sensible and cordial relationship with Britain at the time of the negotiations over the evacuation of the Canal Zone. Egypt also desired similar dealings with France, a country with which her recent history had been closely connected. For the time being friendship was impossible, but, as we shall see, changing French attitudes to the Arab World over recent years have happily brought about an enormous improvement in Franco-Egyptian and Franco-Arab relations. Most difficult of all have been relations with the US. This is not surprising in the light of the massive American support for Zionism, without which the state of Israel would arguably never have come into existence and would almost certainly not have been allowed to expand to the extent that it has done over the past twenty-five years. Yet, even in the matter of relations with the US, the Egyptian government and people and the media through which their views were coherently expressed evinced a similar sense of balance between the calls of anti-colonialism and those of good international understanding. Fair progress had been made by 1954, and signs existed that American toleration of extreme Zionism was approaching its limits, when, as we have seen, Israel deliberately made it her business to disrupt the incipient US-Egyptian rapprochement by means of the Lavon affair.

As the fifties wore on the terms of the Arab response to the major world issues took on a more definite and a more global character. To the desire for good international relations, and to hostility against colonialism, whether in its Zionist guise or in any other, there was gradually added Arab appreciation of common interests with the peoples of what has come to be called the *Third World*. It was not enough to assert Arab independence of the great powers. The rapid polarization of much of world opinion into support of the two superpowers implied a real danger that the Arab World would be drawn into one or other of the Cold War camps. Indeed this happened to

Iraq when, under the leadership of Nuri es-Said, she adhered to the Baghdad pact in February 1955, and, as we saw, Egypt herself had been in danger of absorption into the arrangements for a Middle East Defence Organization before the Revolution. The issues of the Cold War were largely irrelevant to the Arab World. In espousing them, Arab countries risked at worst destruction in an atomic holocaust and at the very least damage to their material progress and to the cause of Arab unity. It was also likely that the attention already won for Arab and anti-colonialist causes, as a result of strenuous efforts by the Arab media, would be dissipated, world concern becoming monopolized by Cold War issues. The Arab cause was not the only one in danger from these developments. Countries that had recently won their independence, such as India and Indonesia, and countries that were still struggling to be free, possessed a common interest, which could best be expressed in a concerted policy of friendly neutralism towards both sides in the Cold War.

The case of Yugoslavia suggested a third option. As early as 1948 Marshal Tito had asserted that country's right to control its own destiny. In the years that followed, Yugoslav independence triumphed in the face of massive Soviet propaganda. It is true that Yugoslavia was materially helped by the countries in the opposing Cold War camp, but Tito was adamant that thanks for aid and friendship in no way implied his country's involvement in their *Weltpolitik*. The West's clear acceptance of this view was not lost on interested onlookers among the uncommitted. Tito had defied the Cold War syndrome, and had got away with it. There seemed no reason why others could not emulate his success. By 1955 the lesson was highly topical for the Arab World. Despite the death of Stalin two years earlier, Cold War alignments were still hardening, and in some respects continued to do so well into the 1960s; after all, the U2 incident occurred in May 1960, the Berlin Wall was built in August 1961, and the Cuban Missile Crisis came as late as October 1962. Moreover, the US drive to encircle the Soviets with a ring of interlocking regional groups—such as that of the Baghdad Pact—was at its height. From motives of self-preservation, as well as out of anti-colonialist and ideological considerations, there was much to be said for the neutralist line advocated by the Indian Prime Minister,

Jawaharlal Nehru. Gamal Abdel Nasser was impressed by the arguments of India's Ambassador to Cairo in 1953–54, K. M. Pannikkar. The following year President Nasser attended the April 1955 conference of African and Asian countries held at Bandung in Indonesia, along with representatives of eight other Arab countries: Iraq, Jordan, Lebanon, Libya, Saudi Arabia, Sudan, Syria and Yemen.

In retrospect the importance of Bandung far exceeds that of the purposes for which it was called—discussion of economic and other matters of common interest and the fostering of increased understanding and co-operation. In retrospect too the unmistakable overtones, sensed as the conference proceeded and heard even more insistently in the following years, obscured for a considerable time a number of quite serious anomalies. The so-called *spirit of Bandung* influenced attitudes and courses of action felt to be appropriate to those countries of Africa and Asia, including the Arab World, for which the rivalries of the Cold War were an irrelevant distraction, and whose common need for economic improvement postulated a common international attitude of neutralism. In point of fact, Bandung was never quite as logically idealistic as this would seem to suggest. Even at the time, the considerable variations in the outlooks of the participating states is evident from the fact that Iraq, Pakistan and Turkey possessed strategic links with the West, while the later stages of the proceedings were largely dominated by Chou En-lai of the Peoples' Republic of China, whose government can hardly be regarded at that stage as uncommitted in terms of the Cold War. Yugoslavia, arguably the most effective neutralist of all, was not even represented. Moreover, below the surface potentially divisive tensions already existed of the type which were later to lead to two wars between India and Pakistan, and to the prolonged Indonesian confrontation with Malaysia. For all that, the gathering struck a responsive chord among the peoples of many of the nations represented. Straddling both continents, the Arab World found itself at the forefront of ideas of an Afro-Asian identity of interest, pre-eminently in the context of the anti-colonialist struggle, ideas which were especially evocative of popular sentiment over the next ten years. Having only recently attained her own independence, Egypt was solicitous of the interests of those African countries to the south of her which had yet to win theirs. President Nasser and the Egyptian people did all they could to foster the cause of African freedom, which was ably championed by the Egyptian information media. The growing Arab espousal of neutralism found a sympathetic echo among many of the twenty-nine countries which had sent representatives to Bandung. Thus in a sense there arose a co-operative interplay between the Arab media and those of the other Bandung countries, which in the years that followed were to work to their mutual advantage, to evoke a sympathetic response among hundreds of millions of people in an enormous and contiguous area, and to present an outward image of considerable solidarity. Consequently, the antagonists of the Cold War were now confronted with a third force, whose existence they might resent but which they could no longer ignore. The spirit of Bandung properly takes its place as a formative element in the Arab response to the Zionist-influenced propaganda of much of the outside world.

Before concluding our remarks on this early phase of that response and of the response to other contemporary information demands, we ought not to ignore the developing confidence and expertise shown by the Arabs in handling the media. This new professionalism is exemplified in the training facilities made available by Egypt. It is also revealed in the greater understanding of the principles and practice of mass persuasion. For example, as we have seen, the Egyptian government was careful not to offend the innately conservative feelings present among most people, especially where matters of property and ownership are involved. It proceeded cautiously, a step at a time, by the so-called *graduation method*. Thus, in enforcing the agrarian reform, it fixed the maximum landholding at 200 feddans, only later reducing it to 100 feddans, and later still to 50 feddans. Closely related to this was the use of the *one target method* based on its appreciation of the truth that propaganda achieves its maximum impact where it deals with one major issue at a time, and so avoids confusing public attention and dissipating the national sense of purpose. Consequently, in the foreign policy of this period the Egyptian information media advocated the re-instatement of King Muhammad V to the throne of Morocco. Once that had been achieved, these media went on to deal with the problem of the British occupation of the Canal. When that in turn had been settled, France's position in Algeria came under fire. Arab expertise in the ways of information and propaganda was to be much extended by the dire necessities of the Suez crisis, and in our next chapter we shall have more to say about the particular methods adopted. Nevertheless, it is worth recalling that the achievements of 1956 and of the period that followed were soundly based on the experience gained over the four preceding years.

8
The Lessons of Suez, 1956–1967

(a) Ingredients of the Suez crisis

The implications of the Suez crisis were not at first fully apparent outside the small circle of the countries immediately concerned, and even there they were not always perfectly understood. At the time attention was distracted by unrest in Central Europe culminating in the Hungarian rising. There the link with the Cold War was direct; it took little to stimulate recent memories of the Central European origins of the confrontation, to whose continuance the Iron Curtain stood as a brutal reminder. Budapest inevitably loomed large in the global diplomacy of the US government, which for this, among other reasons, was anxious to contain the possible ramifications of Suez. As we have already remarked, the US was by the mid-fifties seeking to limit the more obvious expressions of Zionist belligerency, and to do so in the interest of better relations with Egypt, whose attitude was important to US endeavours to secure the Middle East against undue Soviet influence. American public opinion was now permeated with a deep distrust of Russia. As a determinant of popular attitudes, fear of communism was at this time more potent than sympathy for international Jewry. US patience with Israel was wearing thin. It was also clear that excessive American support for Zionism was likely to damage the international image of the US, because Israel's repeated infringements of the temporary frontiers established by the 1949 armistice had earned her a succession of Security Council censures. Sensing this coolness on the part of her protector, Israel endeavoured to disrupt US-Egyptian relations through the Lavon affair. She also cast around for alternative allies, and found them in Britain and France. Her success was to give the

Suez crisis its peculiar character of a conflict cutting across Cold War alignments; the US, far from lending wholehearted support to her Western European allies, sought to restrain them, and in a sense frustrated their objectives by reaching a tacit understanding over their heads with her major Cold War opponent.

To understand Israel's diplomatic success in relations with Britain and France, we must consider the effect of information about affairs in the Middle East upon public opinion in those countries. In Britain particularly, opinion towards Israel, where it existed at all, was mainly unfavourable. To the extent that the new state meant anything to the average Britisher, it conjured up recollections of the ferocity of the Stern Gang and the Irgun. He remembered undeserved attacks against conscript soldiers, who were merely doing their duty in a situation not of their making, and receiving much abuse and little thanks at the time from the world community, including the US. The experience appeared to be characteristic of a world-wide denigration of Britain. We must remember that in 1956 the entire adult British population and a fair proportion of her adolescents had been brought up, in terms both of home influences and of formal education, to regard their country as an imperial power and as one of the world's great powers; as recently as the years immediately after the Second World War it was customary for the media to talk about the "Big Three" of the US, the USSR and Britain, a grouping which somehow was regarded as more important than the "Big Five" which included China and France. There is inevitably a long time lag between, on the one hand, the waning of the substance of world power and, on the other hand, the appreciation of the changed circumstances by the public at large, however well informed it may be. There is an even greater time lag between such appreciation and the full acceptance of the new conditions of international power relationships. In the mid-fifties Britain was barely at the beginning of this two-stage process. The transition was in one sense the slower for being made against the background of the country's achievements in the Second World War. British opinion still looked back with pride to the events of 1940, widely regarded as her "finest hour", and to her subsequent exertions against the threat of global Nazi domination. Britain had spent her strength in the cause of others, no less than on her own behalf. Now that, partly as a result of her efforts, the danger was past, it seemed to the British that smaller powers, no less than the super-powers, evinced little sense of gratitude, but rather sought individual advantage from the country's post-war exhaustion and financial difficulties. In this light, Zionist hostility was seen simply as a grosser form of what was after all a widespread phenomenon of hardly veiled hostility. And it has to be remembered that many people were prepared to make allowances for the Israelis as representative of the sufferings of war-time Jewry, in ways in which they were not prepared to condone, for example, the more justifiable campaign against continued British presence in the Canal Zone.

Zionist influence on much of the world media of information, including much of the British media, greatly assisted the process and largely dictated the form in which British disenchantment expressed itself at the time of Suez. By 1956 it seems fair to say that Israel's image in Britain was no better and no worse than that of other states that had profited at Britain's expense. From what he read in his newspaper or heard over the radio, it seemed to the British citizen as though his country now had little to fear from Israel, whereas other nations of Asia and Africa presented a continuing threat to the future of what was left of the old imperial status. India had fallen away in 1947, and her prime minister now seemed bent on encouraging independence movements elsewhere. The Canal Zone was to be finally evacuated, and in 1955 came news of the creation of an anti-colonialist front in far away Bandung. In 1951 Winston Churchill returned to power at the head of a Conservative administration. Despite his defeat at the elections six years earlier, he still enjoyed enormous prestige as the nation's saviour of 1940. In his years of opposition since 1945 he had left no doubt as to his dislike of the decolonization process, arguing strenuously against the granting of Indian independence. Now that he was back in power, many Britishers felt that the time had come to call a halt to the decline which their upbringing had led them to regard as inseparable from the loss of empire.

To the extent that leadership both personified and shaped an important body of British opinion at this time, the views of the prime minister merit attention. On Churchill's retirement on 6 April 1955, the Conservative administration remained in power under Anthony Eden. Both leaders shared similar opinions and approaches to many international problems. Over the previous twenty years such a close understanding had developed between them that it was natural for the public to expect Eden to continue Churchill's policy. At a formative stage of his ministerial career, Eden in 1938 had resigned the foreign secretaryship in protest against the Chamberlain government's proposed formal recognition of Mussolini's Ethiopian conquest. From then until the beginning of the Second World War he had worked with Churchill and a small group of politicians outside the main stream of party politics, who foresaw the danger of appeasing the fascist dictators. Eden's actions at the time were those of a man of principle and prescience, who gallantly put his career at risk rather than participate in lulling the public into a false sense of international security. Unfortunately, from such irreproachable origins, Eden's attitude to foreign affairs tended to harden permanently into a refusal to consider the merits of any case which he regarded as a threat to Britain's position. Both during and after the Second World War, Eden was much concerned with the maintenance of Britain's standing in the Middle East, encouraging the formation of the Arab League in March 1945. With the onset of the Cold War, the area seemed to Eden to take on an even greater importance; hence the efforts of the government of which he was a member to draw various Middle Eastern states into a defensive alliance against Russia, culminating in the Baghdad Pact of February 1955. Against this background, the Egyptian Revolution appeared as a threat to British interests, especially after the decision to evacuate the Canal Zone, and after the adoption of an unequivocally neutralist line by the Egyptian president. It may also be that Eden, who had begun his career as an active participant in the proceedings of the Europe-dominated League of Nations, subconsciously reacted against the changed conditions of world power after 1945. Psychological factors of this sort may have been at the root of Eden's failure to allow for President Nasser's misgivings over the threat to Arab unity posed by the Baghdad Pact. It is true that for the first few months of his premiership Eden did seek cordial relations with Egypt. But in the longer run he was not prepared to let them interfere with the consolidation of the defensive bloc against Russia. Thus in December a military mission under General Templer visited Jordan with the aim of securing her adherence to the Baghdad Pact. As it turned out the attempt proved abortive, thanks largely to the ensuing demonstrations which left little doubt as to the Jordanian people's hostility to the pact. But the incident further strained already delicate Anglo-Egyptian relations. In some British circles the failure of the Templer mission was seen as the work of the Egyptian leadership. For Eden the decisive event took place on 1 March 1956, when King Hussein dismissed the commander of the Jordanian army, the British General Glubb. Coming so soon after the set-back over the Baghdad Pact, the removal of Sir John Glubb was incorrectly interpreted by Eden as corroboration of Cairo's implacable hostility. Painfully impaired by illness, Eden's judgement succumbed to personal feelings of animosity towards the Egyptian leadership. He came to regard President Nasser as a would-be Hitler, whose downfall would justify almost any damage to Anglo-Egyptian relations.

Eden's subsequent response to the pressures of the developing Suez crisis was informed by an overriding feeling that it would be wrong to give way to President Nasser, just as it had been wrong to appease the fascist dictators in 1938 and 1939. In the earlier case Eden and Churchill had been isolated voices unheeded by the bulk of public opinion. Subsequent events had proved them right. Consequently, it is not surprising that a large part of the British people now came out in strong support of the Eden line towards Egypt and her leader. This was the emotional response of a people smarting from what they regarded as a series of calculated insults to their position as the citizens of a world power, a people still far from accepting Britain's reduced circumstances in global affairs, a people guided by an over-simplified historical view involving spurious parallels between contemporary events and those of eighteen years before. In this case the greater access to world news was the reverse of helpful, for much of the information now influencing British opinion was filtered by pro-Zionist media. Had the British people possessed the full facts, they would hardly have made the mistake of equating the justifiable and essentially peaceable aspirations of the new Egyptian leadership with the inordinate greed of the Nazis.

One must be careful not to overstate the role of Eden's own views and the effect of their interplay with latent feelings of nostalgia for a declining imperial position. These elements were undoubtedly important and at times vociferous factors in the British response to the events of 1956. But the situation was complex, and other factors combined to shape the totality of British opinion. For our purposes two of these are crucial. In the first place, there was by now quite a considerable body of opinion which regarded colonialism and imperialism as obsolescent and which welcomed their decline. The protagonists of this view saw the Second World War as more than a struggle for Britain's survival against Nazi ambition. In a wider sense they rejoiced in the military verdict of 1945 as a victory for freedom and democracy, and hence as a defeat for the impediments in the way of justifiable nationalist fulfilment, as in the case of Egypt, India and Indonesia. Admittedly in terms of Suez the normal concomitant to such views of left-wing politics was a complication; as already remarked, the British Labour Party has, with some notable exceptions, tended to sympathize with Israel, while in 1956 France was led by the socialist Guy Mollet. Even so, the presence of strong anti-colonialist lobbies in both countries did modify the totality of public opinion. The other important factor, which in the long run militated against Eden's policy, was more widespread, although not always so coherently expressed. Most British people had an abiding horror of war after their experiences between 1939 and 1945. While many were glad enough for the moment to endorse a tough line towards President Nasser, they would recoil from it as soon as it seriously threatened to escalate towards protracted hostilities. This was true not only of the mass of the public, but also of at least a part of the British government and of most of the opposition, even though in the initial phases of the crisis the opposition leader, Hugh Gaitskell, may have harboured pro-Israeli sympathies.

We have had to deal at some length with the constituents of British opinion, partly because they were complex, partly because they held lessons for the future, suggesting bounds beyond which Zionist propaganda was likely to become ineffective, and ipso facto revealing areas in which Arab counter-propaganda might reasonably hope to make headway. At this point, we must consider why Israel succeeded in enlisting French support. In a way the explanation is more direct than in the case of Britain. Some of the constituents of public opinion are relevant to both countries. As former world powers both found themselves in reduced circumstances, and the consequences were neither adequately comprehended nor readily accepted by most of the people, whose upbringing and educational conditioning had been broadly similar. Despite the irritations and the bewilderment to which we have just referred, British self-confidence still possessed substantial resources, not least the esteem in which her people still were held for their dogged resistance to the Nazis. Her response to what she regarded as carping criticism from the anti-colonialist and other world pressure groups was one of irritability rather than outright anger. The case of France was painfully different. True, the leadership factor did not count for as much in the formulation of French opinion as it did in the case of British opinion, for probably no member of the French government of the day possessed the national or international stature of Anthony Eden. On the other hand French self-esteem stood in far greater need of rehabilitation. The defeat of her armed forces in 1940 and the subsequent German occupation were enormous blows at France's world prestige, which the courageous exploits of her resistance fighters and of the Free French partly redeemed but could not entirely repair. By the mid-1950s popular views of France's imperial role went through a further state of shock owing to the loss of Indo-China and the news of the outbreak of the Algerian revolt a few months later in October 1954. The impact of the Algerian troubles on French opinion was wide and deep, striking at the roots of popular attitudes, which saw Algeria as to all intents and purposes an extension of the homeland. The French tradition of compulsory military service and other factors had built up over generations the closest links with North Africa. French opinion thus prided itself on its intimate understanding of and special relationship with the Arab World. Unlike Britain there was in France no recent involvement with Palestine and Israel, and hence no emotional impediment in the way of a favourable reply to Israel's offer to purchase French military aircraft. Indeed the French government and public opinion saw the arrangement as a direct and effective response to Cairo's encouragement of the Algerians, a fact which came out clearly in the present author's secret talks with Christian Pineau, referred to earlier.[1]

Israel then succeeded in enlisting the favourable opinions of the British and the French governments, and of important sections of both publics, to the extent that in October 1956 she was able to conclude a secret treaty with these two countries covering the planned tripartite intervention against Egypt. She did so against the background of the growing impatience of the US on which in the last resort her very existence depended. And she did so without abandoning any of her other aggressive policies either towards the Arab states or towards the Palestinian refugees. Some idea of the extent of her ambitious intransigence may be gained from the statement by David Ben Gurion at the Beer Sheba meeting of the Mapai party in 1952, to the effect that he would form a new cabinet only on condition that the country seized every opportunity for southerly expansion. Israel maintained her steady refusal to allow the return of the million or so displaced Palestinians on anything but the most unacceptable terms.

Driven to desperation by conditions in the refugee camps, by the wholesale Israeli confiscation of their lands and even of their personal effects, by Israel's many infringements of the temporary borders set up under the 1949 armistice, it was inevitable that the refugees should strike back. The immediate effect was further Zionist oppression and even Zionist terror, as in the case of the Qibya massacre of October 1953, the Israeli actions at Gaza in February 1955 and again in April 1956, and the Kafr Kassem massacre of October 1956. As far as possible Zionist links with the world media managed to play down press and radio reports of these activities. Where an inconvenient truth seemed likely to attract unwanted attention, the Israeli line was that the action was in the nature of retaliation for border infringements by the Palestinians, including the latter's commando units of *fedayeen*. The Security Council knew better than to accept these protestations at face value, realizing as it did that the aggressor Israel had no case in natural law or international practice for so called punitive or retaliatory action against the attempts of the legitimate owners to recover, or merely as in many cases to revisit, their rightful property.[2]

[1] See p. 167 above.
[2] For an authoritative discussion of this aspect of the conflict and an account of

The succession of Security Council condemnations of such Israeli actions had little effect, failing to attract much attention among the British and French publics, and certainly not interrupting the rapprochement between the governments of London, Paris, and Tel Aviv. Admittedly Britain made a token move towards the recognition of Arab rights, when Eden proposed slight border amendments which hopefully might lead to peace between the Arabs and Israel, but this came to nothing, Ben Gurion in his reply on 10 April 1955 going so far as to say that the UN resolutions on Palestine were dead and buried, and that any contraction of Israel's border was impossible except in conditions involving the annihilation of the Jewish people through war. The statement is a fair measure of Zionist arrogance, especially when we remember that Israel herself had come into existence under the auspices of that same world body which her leader now dismissed with contempt. In retrospect it seems almost incredible that Britain and France should have shown so little concern over the behaviour of their ally, because on balance these two basically liberal states possessed a better understanding of and a deeper relationship with the Arabs than did any of the other major powers. The explanation seems to lie in special circumstances affecting British and French policy at this time, notably the deep misgivings in respect of their future international roles, and their alarm at the Cold War dangers regarded as inseparable from Egypt's policy of neutralism after the Bandung meeting.

It is fair to say that at that period, when the fear of the USSR tended to dominate their diplomacy, the West failed to understand the nature of neutralism. They might however have been expected to realize that neutralism did not imply any carelessness on the part of non-aligned countries for their own security. Indeed in this very connection the pressures on Egypt were becoming irresistible. As we saw, the massive tasks facing her government after July 1952 were such that Egypt sought no new complications in her relations with Israel. At the same time she could not remain supine while fellow Arabs suffered privation and anguish in the Gaza strip and in camps elsewhere. Quite apart from normal human pity, Egypt could not

the sequestration of Palestinian property by Israel, the reader's attention is directed to *Henry Cattan*: *Palestine, the Arabs and Israel* (Longman, London 1969) pp. 61–88.

tolerate Israeli infringements of her territory. Ben Gurion's military operations in Gaza in 1955 brought matters to a head. When he went so far as to congratulate his soldiers for killing forty Egyptians on the border, Egypt understood that she must look to her defences in the face of Israeli expansionism towards Sinai. Through *The Voice of the Arabs*, Egypt broadcast warnings of the danger of a revival of foreign domination, this time at the hands of Israel in collusion with Britain and France. For her own security Egypt looked for sources of arms supply. She still hoped that Great Britain might not yet be irretrievably committed to Israel, and also hoped that recent US coolness towards Israel might predispose the Americans towards the Egyptian request. However, this was not to be. Turned down by London and Washington, Egypt looked to Prague and accepted a Czech offer of arms.

From this point the crisis developed rapidly. Looking at events in stark Cold War terms, the US saw no alternative to reverting to the former friendship with Israel, while still doing what she could to escape the colonialist stigma attaching to the tripartite Anglo-French-Israeli operation. For this reason the US, along with Britain, withdrew an earlier offer of finance for the construction of the Aswan High Dam. Egypt replied on 26 July by nationalizing the Suez canal. At the same time she made it clear that she would respect accepted international practice by paying compensation to the concessionaires, the largely French-controlled Suez Canal Company, and President Nasser also made good his undertaking to keep the canal open to international shipping. The great powers had no real grounds for complaint, while, in terms of Egypt's own development, the nationalization was necessary to provide funds for the construction of the High Dam. Therefore no reasonable case existed for outside intervention on the plea of keeping the canal operational. The only country whose interests were badly affected by the new state of affairs was Israel, which suffered from the *fedayeen* raids in the Gaza area and from Egypt's blockade of the Straits of Tiran, burdens for which she had only herself to blame, for they were the consequences of her own infringements of Egyptian territory. At this point it has to be admitted that Britain was seriously inclining to the American view that the crisis could and should be settled peacefully. But she was overborne by her French and Israeli allies, while the British people, informed inadequately or with biased news, were allowed to draw the wrong conclusions from the events of July to October 1956. On 26 October the Israelis launched their attack and by 5 November, when Anglo-French operations began with a series of parachute drops on Egypt, Israel had attained most of her immediate objectives. At this point the super-powers took a hand, the USSR with a warning of intervention unless the tripartite aggression stopped, and the US with irresistible pressure on her allies, which in the case of Britain was reinforced by a threatened monetary crisis. Within a few hours the British and French withdrew, and on 15 November UN forces took up their peacekeeping assignment in the Canal Zone.

The threatened international confrontation had been averted. But the UN presence, however long drawn out, could be no more than a temporary expedient. Quite apart from the forcible dispossession of the Arab inhabitants of those parts of Palestine assigned to her by the UN resolution of 29 November 1947, Israel held on to the extensive territories which she had illegally annexed in 1948 and 1949. Her leaders still harboured the imperialist dream, defined by Theodor Herzl in 1904 and later by Rabbi Fischmann in 1947, of a "Greater Israel", stretching from the Nile to the Euphrates, and incorporating the whole of Palestine, Lebanon, Jordan and Syria, as well as large parts of Egypt, Saudi Arabia and Iraq. For the Arab World the threat was in no way diminished. The Israeli government's utter rejection of international opinion on this point was demonstrated within hours of the arrival of UN units in the Canal Zone, for in a statement made on 16 November 1956 to *The Jewish Observer* magazine, Ben Gurion reiterated his view that the armistice agreement with Egypt was dead and buried, and would never see life again.

From this brief account of the events of the latter half of 1956, and from our rather closer examination of the ingredients of the crisis, we believe it is clear that Suez need not have happened, if public opinion in Britain and France had been more truthfully and more fully informed. In a sense those two countries acted out of character in November 1956. Their relationship with the Arab World suffered an unnecessary deterioration in consequence of a failure of communications, and it is only in the last few years that the relationships have happily been mended.

Before passing on to a discussion of Egypt's response to the information demands of Suez, we must not omit a further information burden which the Arab peoples had to bear during this period. It took the form of hostile propaganda disseminated in Arabic from Cyprus by the Near East Broadcasting Station, which, though officially owned by a private organization, was in reality run by the British intelligence service. As we shall see presently, the positive counter-propaganda undertaken by *The Voice of the Arabs* succeeded in neutralizing this attempt to mislead and to undermine Arab opinion, and by the beginning of 1956 the Cyprus broadcasts had been rendered ineffective.

(b) Egyptian counter-propaganda during the Suez crisis

Although the course of the Suez crisis could hardly have been foreseen, growing Israeli provocation in the months preceding it left little room for doubt that events were rapidly proceeding along a collision course. Without abandoning their established objectives, of providing an honest information service at home and of supporting the struggle against colonialism abroad, those responsible for the Egyptian media found themselves obliged to devote more attention than before to combating Israeli propaganda. And, as we have just seen, decisive action was needed to protect the Arab image against the attacks of secret radio stations, notably the one operating from Cyprus. The Egyptian response to that particular nuisance was both realistic and effective. On the one hand, it avoided the excesses of the Nazis, who in similar circumstances had treated the listening to clandestine radio stations as a criminal act. On the other hand, while making it clear that active co-operation with those broadcasts was nothing short of treason, the Egyptian government wisely left the door open for the rehabilitation of announcers and others who genuinely regretted their unpatriotic acts. In this way it reaped a propaganda advantage, and also availed itself of technical skills when a number of the former employees of the clandestine stations thought better of their activities and joined Cairo Radio.

From an early stage in the crisis, both the Egyptian people and the world at large had to be given the main facts of the nationalization of the canal on 26 July 1956. In taking the people into its confidence, the

government adopted the correct approach to public relations. It knew
that in the coming struggle with Israel Egypt would have to draw on
every available source of national determination, a quality which
operates fully only where the entire people is convinced of the justice
of the national cause. Once John Foster Dulles, the US Secretary of
State, had refused the loan for the High Dam, President Nasser and
his ministers made it their business to see that the case for the canal's
nationalization was presented in a form that could be readily understood by the entire population of Egypt, as well as by as much of the
outside world as was disposed to listen. Thus in a Cairo Radio broadcast of 27 July 1956 we find the following cogent restatement of
Egypt's position on the issue:

> "The Suez Canal was built by Egyptian hands in 1869 and cost
> Egypt eight million pounds in cash—a huge sum at the time—and
> one hundred and twenty-five thousand conscripted labourers, thou-
> sands of whom paid their lives in digging it, working under the most
> inhuman conditions.
>
> "For nearly a century, the former Suez Canal Company, with its
> headquarters in Paris, established itself as a state within a state. It
> played an effective role in Egyptian policies and became powerful
> enough to topple a cabinet and raise another.
>
> "The canal dues, amounting to a hundred million dollars a year,
> used to pour into foreign establishments owned by international
> adventurers such as De Lesseps. Only a small proportion went to
> the Egyptian treasury.
>
> "The canal dues, after the nationalization of the company, will
> be spent on big national projects meant for the welfare of the Egyp-
> tian people, who are the legitimate owners of the international water-
> way. The most vital of all these projects is the High Dam at Aswan,
> which now—after the nationalization of the company—will be built
> by Egyptian money and by Egyptian hands."

The message thus clearly relayed was that, like any other national
asset, the Suez Canal Company could properly be taken over by the
state, provided that due compensation were given to the shareholders
in keeping with accepted international practice, and provided that the
shareholders had the right to bring genuine grievances to the attention of the International Court of Justice. Both safeguards were

scrupulously honoured. Furthermore the internal and external media were employed to demonstrate that the canal remained operational, and that in consequence no disruption of world commerce was threatened.

In one short book it is not possible to describe in detail all the activities of the Egyptian information services at the time of Suez. We must therefore confine ourselves to a few examples, which are either important in themselves or else serve to illustrate typical approaches adopted at the time.

In this context, Egypt's handling of the French prime minister Guy Mollet is significant. Despite the widespread pro-Israeli feelings existing in France over this period, French opinion was far from solid in support of the tripartite intervention; even some members of Mollet's own socialist party opposed him on this count. He therefore sought positive parliamentary backing for his policy. To this end, he told the National Assembly that French troops had advanced from Port Said to Ismailia, where they had hoisted the French flag on the premises of the Suez Canal Company. France, he declared, could take pride in her armed forces which had rescued the company and had presented Egypt with a *fait accompli*. Given the aggressive and demoralized climate of opinion prevalent in France so soon after the outbreak of the Algerian rising, this was just the news which many deputies wanted to hear. Mollet's declaration evoked warm applause, even from his political opponents. Yet, while the presentation of this piece of information secured his immediate objective, it soon rebounded against Mollet and his policy. This is because it was not only untrue but was quickly shown to be untrue while the circumstances of the announcement were still fresh in everyone's minds. The truth was that the French troops had not yet marched into the city of Ismailia. For his part, Mollet thought that Egypt, besieged by air and sea, could not possibly know what was going on in the French National Assembly. But the text of his speech was wired by the international news agencies to Cairo, where it was received only five minutes after it had been delivered in Paris. In Egypt, the Information Administration retaliated instantly. Its chosen theme aimed to bring about a reaction inside the French parliament capable of exposing the lies of Guy Mollet.

A group of foreign correspondents, including British and French newsmen, was at that time confined to the Semiramis Hotel in Cairo, as a measure of protection against possible reprisals by the people at a moment when Egypt was being strafed by British and French aircraft. At the same time the Information Administration saw to it that these correspondents were well-treated and constantly supplied with news reports. Indeed, good relations were maintained with the newsmen over this period. After receiving the text of Mollet's speech, the Information Administration arranged for the foreign correspondents to be taken by road to Ismailia, whence they were able to wire their cables. One of these, sent by Monsieur Dardaud, the director of the Agence France Press, contained the blunt message:

> "Guy Mollet is a liar . . . a liar . . . a liar. I have entered Ismailia with more than a hundred British, French and American journalists besides other journalists of different nationalities. We were faced by Guy Mollet's lies to the French people and to the world. I found the Egyptian flag hoisted over the building of the International Suez Canal Company."

Hundreds of cables were despatched from Ismailia within ninety minutes of Mollet's speech. They reached the National Assembly as the deputies were still congratulating Guy Mollet on his policy, on his attitude of decision and on his success in taking over the Suez Canal. But no sooner had the deputies read Monsieur Dardeau's cable than their cheers gave way to a spontaneous outburst of anger. The National Assembly building echoed to the refrain of the cable's opening words, "Guy Mollet is a liar . . . a liar . . . a liar." Even the members of Mollet's own party joined in. Having demonstrably lost the confidence of parliament and people, Mollet had no alternative to resignation. The Egyptian Information Administration had gained a notable success in the propaganda war, and had done so quite simply by prompt and professional use of the media at their disposal, in conditions guaranteed to secure the maximum attention and impact for their clear statement of the true facts.

Successful counter-propaganda results from the mistakes of opponents no less than from the workings of a clear-cut plan. In saying this, we do not for a moment denigrate the role of the counter-propagandist. A vital function of his job is to maintain a continuous

watch on the activities of the other side, to diagnose errors or potential errors, and, creatively, to fashion possible instant responses
capable of exploiting the advantages of such errors in terms of opinion
at home, of opinion in the enemy country, and of opinion among
third parties. The Guy Mollet episode just described is a perfect
example of the effective use made of an opponent's mistake by the
Egyptian Information Administration. Had its members been less
observant and less well briefed, they might have missed this outstanding opportunity of maximizing the effects of a blatant falsehood
on the part of the highest French circles. Had they been less well prepared, they might have acted too late and so have dissipated much of
the impact on French and on other outside opinion. Moreover, to the
extent that the Egyptian response favoured the cause of truth, it made
its contribution towards the consolidation of world opinion against
the tripartite aggression, and so in a real sense amounted to information for justice and peace.

Sometimes the aggressors damaged their own cause in an even
more direct way, requiring a minimal response from Egypt. The case
of the leaflets which the British, French and Israelis circulated among
the Egyptian population furnishes an example of a propaganda drive
based on false illusions, and countered by the level-headedness of its
target. These leaflets concentrated on the themes that the tripartite
aggressors had not come as invaders, and that they did not bear any
grudge against the Egyptian people, but rather sought to free them
from an allegedly tyrannical leadership. The intended effect was,
however, lost, for they were circulated in Port Said where a large
part of the most densely populated areas had just been destroyed. The
conditions of death and ruin prevailing in the city refuted the message
of the leaflets far more eloquently than any formal argument could
have done. In human terms, it is impossible for people who have just
lost their families and their homes to distinguish, on the one hand,
between the hostility, actual and visible, of the mechanical agents of
their distress—the bombs and war planes—and, on the other hand,
the declared good intentions of the governments responsible for the
destruction. This clumsy propaganda was directly counter-productive,
its overt hypocrisy serving to strengthen the determination of the
Egyptians in opposition to the invaders and in support of their true

leaders. The naïvety of the aggressors in believing that the leaflets could possibly have aroused any other reaction showed the extent of the false illusions which their governments still harboured as to the character of the Egypt of 1956. They seemed to think that Egypt was unchanged since the days when the British High Commissioners had acted as virtually uncrowned monarchs. Sir Winston Churchill appears still to have considered that it only needed a single British destroyer to appear in Alexandria for the rulers of Egypt to accede to all the British demands; such advice from such a source would certainly have carried weight with Anthony Eden in the mood of the period. The British statesmen seem to have ignored the dramatic change which had come about in Egypt after the Revolution of July 1952.

The tripartite aggressors' image also suffered from the acts of violence perpetrated by the British and French troops in Port Said. Such acts were reported and broadcast to the world, and not merely by the Egyptian media but also by British newsmen who were in the area and who witnessed events with their own eyes. The tripartite operations thus served to alienate world opinion still further, as well as reinforcing the resolve of the Egyptian people.

The latter was a crucial consideration of the leadership and of those responsible for the national media, who needed to retain the confidence of the entire population, even more than they needed to win that of the other Arab countries and of the world in general. When the British and French actually landed in Port Said, the announcement of such an event would have frustrated the Egyptian and Arab cause if it had been reported first by the international media rather than by Cairo Radio. In the event the Egyptian Information Administration in Cairo received a long distance telephone call from one of its employees in Port Said on the only line still operating between the two cities. The report read as follows:

"This morning, many British and French aircraft circled over Port Said and Al-Gamil airport, in particular, for a long while. Our air defence troops were in action. But in the afternoon, the British and French dropped some dummies by parachutes on Al-Gamil airport.

"The Information Administration vans, equipped with microphones, immediately patrolled the streets of the city and exhorted the people to make for the airport in trucks to prevent the enemy from landing.

"Many trucks loaded with armed youth made for the airport to the accompaniment of national songs and military tunes. The airport was besieged and the young men took their positions in ditches surrounding the airport. When the first batch of enemy parachutists landed, they were all wiped out by the Egyptian youth.The enemy continued to shell the area surrounding the airport so as to besiege it and prevent any reinforcements from reaching the airport.

"Meanwhile, the enemy parachutists continued to land. Some of them have already landed, while the landing operation is not yet over."

This report was received at 1415 hours. The Egyptian people and the world clearly had to be told about the landing, for otherwise confidence in the country's information media would be irretrievably lost. The problem then was essentially one of timing and presentation. Within a quarter of an hour the Information Administration's response was ready, and the following bulletin went out over Cairo Radio.

"Enemy aircraft circled over the city of Port Said this morning and our air defence troops downed a number of them.

"The enemy aircraft tried to circle over Al-Gamil airport in an attempt to drop parachutists. But appeals were made to the Egyptian armed youth to make for the airport immediately to the accompaniment of national songs and military tunes which were beamed from vans patrolling the streets of the city. Many trucks loaded with young men made for the airport, and formed a defensive barricade.

"When the enemy tried to drop parachutists, a batch of them was wiped out. The engagement is still going on, and the enemy is still trying with large bodies of troops to set up an air bridge-head at Al-Gamil airport. The armed Egyptian people are putting up a valiant resistance."

This announcement conveyed the truth. But the fact that it mentioned the wiping out of the first batch of parachutists, the massing of civilians to resist the enemy, and their success in besieging the airport, inflamed the feelings of the whole people, who thronged the streets and public squares shouting "Allah Akbar . . . Allah Akbar" (God is Great). Moreover, by mentioning the attempts at a landing by large bodies of enemy troops, the announcement served to prepare the public for the subsequent news of the occupation of Al-Gamil airport, and thus to lessen the shock and the danger to national morale.

We must now consider more closely the aims, the principles of presentation, and the methods of those responsible for information, including counter-propaganda, at this critical juncture. Most importantly and urgently the Egyptian Information Administration had a duty to maintain national morale against the military and propaganda onslaught of the enemy. Confidence had to be heightened and the will to overcome the threat to the nation's integrity and independence had to be consolidated in face of odds that at times must have seemed overwhelming. While these considerations were paramount, it was hardly less important to project the correct image beyond the area of immediate hostilities, and so to enlist the sympathy and hopefully the active support of as much of the outside world as possible. These tasks demanded scrupulous adherence to the truth on the part of the Information Administration, both on moral grounds and also to maximize the favourable results of the Egyptian message. The object of world attention, Egypt knew that any lies or attempts to mislead would soon be exposed by the foreign newsmen working at the scene of the fighting, and would be as rapidly denounced by the information media of the other side. Any tampering with the truth would therefore prove directly harmful to those sentiments of internal confidence and resolution and of external understanding and sympathy which it was the task of the Information Administration to nurture and develop. Put another way, it would quickly defeat the aims of good public relations at both the domestic and the international levels.

There is of course far more to the role of a national information service than mere factual reporting. Public opinion has to be encouraged to adopt one option rather than another, and it expects to be offered guidance and comment by its press and radio. These are proper functions of the national media, always provided that, while exercising them, the controllers of the media bear in mind the intrinsic characteristic of good public relations as a two-way operation. They must know what the people are thinking and must be aware of areas in which public opinion is confused. There must be an educative process in the fullest and best sense of the term. Thus, while before, during and after Suez, books were published in Egypt projecting a definite outlook based on the Six Principles of the Revolution, the information media did not attempt to impose a view before subjecting it to open discussion by the intelligentsia in the press and on the radio.

Public opinion also had to be protected from the propaganda activities of the enemy and from the more subtle dangers arising from partisan information disseminated by those nations or groups in the outside world which were sympathetic to Zionism, not to speak of the inadvertent inaccuracies of foreign writers and newspaper columnists who were simply ignorant of the full facts. The Egyptian information media were very active in their exposition of the directly hostile propaganda. For example, on one occasion a Lebanese newspaper, subsidized by Britain, France and Israel, described the nationalization of the canal as an act of suicide. The Egyptian media reacted by exposing the newspaper's highly questionable motives; the response was so effective in terms of Arab public opinion that large demonstrations took place in the streets of Beirut against the newspaper in question.

Among the most serious sources of anti-Egyptian propaganda were the nine clandestine radio stations broadcasting over this period. We have already seen that the one operating in Cyprus for the British Intelligence Service had been rendered ineffective. But others continued, some of them employing Egyptians who had fled abroad after the Revolution of July 1952. One of these, Abdul-Fath, the former proprietor of the Wafdist newspaper *Al-Misri*, was hired by France to run a clandestine broadcasting station called *The Voice of Egypt*, which disseminated lies and allegations designed to undermine the revolutionary régime. A similar station was called *The Voice of Truth*. Such broadcasts aimed to confuse Egyptian public opinion. But, by refuting the lies perpetrated by these means, the Egyptian information media succeeded in destroying their credibility in the eyes of opinion at home and throughout the Arab World. The process was assisted by the widespread realization that the clandestine broadcasts were financed by the imperialist countries, and thus likely to be unreliable, and by the fact that the Egyptians who co-operated in the running of the stations had left Egypt some years before and consequently betrayed their dearth of up-to-date knowledge of conditions in their motherland. This ignorance, coupled with the lack of experience of the personnel of the clandestine stations in the field of mass communication, may well explain the unimaginative nature of their anti-Egyptian onslaught. They tended to hammer away at the themes of the canal's nationalization and of the shortcomings of the Egyptian government, and quite overlooked the latter's public relations achievement which ensured that the great mass of the people were solidly committed to the men who had abolished the corrupt monarchy, had pioneered a popular and extensive agrarian reform, and had secured the departure of the British military presence. Against such a background, the clandestine exhortations to turn against the new leaders appeared in their true colours as merely another variant of the colonialist's "divide and rule" philosophy; the Arabs recalled the oppression and lack of development for which colonialism had been responsible in the past, and had no intention of allowing a renascent colonialism to jeopardize their new-found Arab unity and their hopes for the future. The hostile propagandists therefore betrayed their inexperience and lack of professionalism by overlooking a cardinal precept for successful opinion formation, namely the need to ensure that both methods and content accord with the dominant feelings of the propaganda target. Their attempts to present their message in allegedly uncontroversial terms were pathetic in a situation in which their case was so demonstrably controversial and recognized for what it was by the bulk of Arab opinion. As in the case of the leaflets circulated in Port Said, this clandestine propaganda presented the Egyptian information authorities with much material for counter-propaganda.

In a more positive sense these same authorities showed their professional understanding by the use of information methods such as the graduation and the one-target methods already described. From July 1952 they strove to explain the Six Principles of the Revolution, and to inculcate an effective appreciation of their relevance to the welfare of the people as a whole, exposing the self-interested attacks of foreign propagandists and of those Egyptian feudalists who had exploited the people for so long. During the few years immediately preceding Suez, therefore, the people's conviction of the real advantages brought by the new régime was strengthened and promoted. When the nationalization of the Suez canal was declared on 26 July 1956 the public acclaim and enthusiasm were unprecedented, and, as we saw, the government made it their business to ensure that the people were given the true legal facts. Public support for the régime was at its peak and public opinion was therefore already prepared for the challenges ahead.

This is strikingly borne out by the popularity of the national songs, inspired by the critical events of the time and a direct expression of the people's determination to defend their rights. More than anything else it was the philosophy of new Zionism, now allied to old-style colonialism, which threatened these rights. The Egyptian information media, for the benefit of opinion at home and abroad, rightly sought to reveal the threat in its true light. They brought out a series of books, written in straightforward, non-technical language, explaining the essential characteristics of Zionism, and also employed press and radio to the same end, disseminating throughout the Arab World facts about Zionism that had hitherto been largely ignored. In presenting these facts in terms that could be readily comprehended by a mass audience, whether at home or abroad, the Egyptian information media understood the need for simplicity; official statements, commentaries, and more specialized articles and programmes all strove for clarity and conciseness. Nor was it enough for the message to be clearly understood. It had to be constantly brought before the attention of Egypt and the world. Otherwise the essential facts could all too quickly be forgotten or smothered by the opposing propaganda.

The information authorities therefore recognized the importance of continuity and of repetition. The latter principle requires adept implementation; inexpertly employed it may merely bore the audience and lead to an undervaluing of the message. The authorities accordingly made it their business to ensure that, while few major themes were utilized, they should be presented from as many different angles as possible. Moreover, in the wider context of the Arab World, the presentation was modified to appeal to the peoples of different countries; a theme presented by Cairo Radio would for example be presented by newspapers in Damascus and Lebanon in a somewhat different manner, one calculated to appeal to the peoples of Syria and Lebanon respectively. Despite local variations of this sort, the basic message remained the same and the basic truth was unimpaired. Commentaries broadcast over Cairo Radio were quoted by other Arab broadcasting stations on the same day. Conversely, a daily review of the Arab press was made by Cairo Radio. The latter also became adept in the exploitation of a principle used by the enemy propaganda, that of shifting attention away from unpalatable themes. For example, the landing of British and French troops in Port Said was accompanied by a hostile campaign against Egypt in some of the international press and broadcasting media. Instead of retaliating directly, the Egyptian information machinery recalled the strong resistance put up in Port Said and the atrocities perpetrated in that city as a flagrant encroachment of basic human rights. In adopting this line there was no question of concealment. Rather the Egyptian authorities were providing domestic and world opinion with the means of obtaining the full truth of the situation, in a way that would have been impossible if attention had been monopolized by the enemy media which presented only a part of the total picture.

We therefore see that the Egyptian Information Administration recognized and constantly strove to implement certain key principles of presentation: the overriding principle of instilling an absolute conviction of the rightness of the Egyptian and Arab cause into the entire home population and into as many of the peoples of the outside world as possible; the principle of expounding the enemy's ideology; the principle of simplicity as evidenced in the official publications and broadcasts dealing with particular aspects of the crisis; the principles of continuity and of judicious repetition of the major themes; the principle of shifting attention where the enemy propaganda threatened to distort the facts through over-concentration on selected details.

From this review of the principles of presentation, we must go on to the actual machinery and practices employed. The Egyptian authorities appreciated the key factor of timing in the pursuit of information objectives, and recognized that the information machinery must be fully equipped and capable of performing its duty at any moment. Every piece of information must therefore be sifted, classified and stored so as to be instantly retrievable when needed. The selection of information personnel is of course crucial, for the time factor leaves little room for the process of trial and error. Should mistakes occur, the individual concerned usually has to be replaced without delay. During the Suez war a member of the information staff happened to tamper with a statement put out by one of the mobile vans after the shelling of the radio transmission plant at Abu-Zaabal, near Cairo. This individual had to be replaced immediately, not so much as a punishment, but as an essential safeguard of information activity at a moment when decisions had to be made with the utmost speed.

As well as a complete system of information gathering, sifting and retrieval, and as an entirely reliable staff, the information machine calls for the fullest range of equipment and the capability of employing these media to maximum advantage. The latter requirement again involves the factor of timing. For instance, when the Information Administration requested the printing of a considerable number of copies of the film *Aggression on Port Said*, the operation, which would normally have taken at least a month, was done in a single day. Thanks to the co-operation and the dedication of the technicians concerned, this opportunity for a major and immediate impact on world opinion was not lost.

The Egyptian information machinery used all the media—the written word, the spoken word, the visible image—available to it at the time. During the Suez crisis the Egyptian newspapers rose to the challenge most impressively, displaying a spirit that was at one and the same time both patriotic and responsible. With regard for the truth, they saw to it that facts were not concealed, but equally that the truth should be presented in a way calculated to maintain national confidence and to avoid panic or defeatism. Thus, when the Egyptian troops withdrew from Sinai, the facts were reported without delay, but the newspapers drew a comparison between the operations and the British evacuation of Dunkirk in the Second World War. Where blunders occurred, as they sometimes will in crisis conditions, the newsmen made a point of avoiding undue fuss. Where the newsmen came across data which added nothing to the overall truth but which could be useful to the enemy, they applied a degree of self-censorship in harmony with the national interest, which obviated the necessity for any strict official censorship.

Indeed the authorities did all they could to provide newsmen with the facilities they wanted, including reports and photographs; access was even granted to Port Said, Ismailia and Suez during the hostilities and constant telephone contact was maintained with these cities. It did not occur to the responsible authorities that the publication of photographs showing the tremendous destruction in Port Said would impair morale; rather they believed that, possessed of the facts, the entire people would be the more capable of rising to the greatest challenges. Government co-operation with the press was not confined to Egyptian newsmen. Facilities were extended to Arab and foreign correspondents, a policy which paid off handsomely at the time of the Guy Mollet affair referred to earlier. Some of the foreign newsmen had of course already been influenced by enemy propaganda, but no steps were taken against them, except in the very few cases where they abused their privileged position. The principal concern was to convince all newsmen that the Egyptian cause was to defend the national territory against invasion. A great success was achieved when, following a UN Security Council resolution providing for the withdrawal of the occupying troops, the foreign newsmen asked to be allowed to visit Port Said under the UN flag, the UN emergency forces having already set up their headquarters in the village of Bellah, near Port Said. The UN office in Cairo agreed to the request and permits were issued for the correspondents, including British and French newsmen. They reached Ismailia by car prior to their approach to Port Said. But, to their surprise, the enemy military command in Port Said refused to allow them into the city. They therefore decided to issue a protest, and this historic message was reported that same evening by the international news agencies. In this way much of the international press came to accept the justice of the Egyptian cause and contributed to its defence. This was a notable achievement particularly when we recall the massive influence, direct or indirect, which Zionism exerted over the news media and over the written and spoken word generally in so many countries. The Egyptian information authorities went even further in the rivalry of persuasion, for they published magazines in various languages, including English, French, German and

Spanish, carrying photographs of the enemy's activities inside Port Said, and they published pamphlets in various languages containing historical documents about the Suez canal and proving Egypt's legal right to ownership of the waterway. They made the most of the foreign reaction to all this information activity; for example the protest demonstrations staged in London against the tripartite aggression featured prominently in both the Egyptian and the Arab press, and similar attention was given to the action of Syrian workers in blowing up the oil pipelines.

Other forms of the written word effectively employed included the circulation of leaflets in factories and schools, and the various simply written books on the major facets of the situation already mentioned. Many of these books were sold out as soon as they reached the bookshops and news stands, and had to be reprinted several times. Some of them even aroused international interest. As enemy propaganda used the same medium, the books published in Egypt had to refute the lies and allegations in the enemy books, and had to do so quickly. Timing was again vital. The promptness of the response can be seen from the fact that when Israel published a book entitled *A Hundred Hours to Suez*, hardly a week passed before the publication of the Egyptian riposte *A Hundred Hours in Sinai*.

A more light-hearted though very effective use of the written word exploited the strong sense of humour possessed by most Egyptians. Enemy propaganda attempted to turn this national trait to advantage by publishing a *Book of Jokes* in 1956; they repeated the attempt in 1972 with a further collection of jokes. To endow these publications with apparent authenticity, they came out under the name of a non-existent publishing house called *Free Egypt*. The origins of the jokes included could be traced back to those launched by the Allies against Hitler and Mussolini during the Second World War, names of the Egyptian leaders merely being substituted for those of the German and Italian ones, and the contents being adapted to suit Egyptian circumstances and contemporary events. But the Israeli approach was psychologically wrong, and the Egyptian people not only saw through this crude exercise, but also derived much light relief from it, for the Egyptian broadcasting services and particularly *The Voice of the Arabs* in 1956 launched a counter-campaign revealing the sources of these jokes and their underlying aggressive motive. The enemy aim was defeated. The jokes, now turned against Eden, Mollet, Ben Gurion and other political enemies, circulated among the Arab people because they wanted a good laugh.

This reference to the use of humour reminds us that the most effective information and counter-propaganda operations often use a multiplicity of media. The joke book was an example of the use of the written word, but its propaganda potential was further exploited by the media of the spoken word, especially radio. Broadcasting in fact was crucial to the information authorities at this time, providing a means of instant retaliation to the enemy's propaganda. To widen its effectiveness, the government installed loud-speakers in public places. When enemy bombing temporarily silenced the transmission station at Abu-Zaabal, near Cairo, mobile broadcasting units were organized. These so-called *information caravans* transmitted news bulletins, comment and music throughout Cairo, in other cities, even in the villages. So successful were they that the capture of one of them by the occupying forces in Port Said was regarded as quite an important prize of war. The broadcasting authorities became adept in matching the mood and even the language of their programmes to their intended audiences. Thus, simple, almost colloquial Arabic was beamed to Egypt, whereas broadcasts over *The Voice of the Arabs* were made in classical Arabic which appeals to all Arab countries. In addition more than thirty languages were used in the overseas broadcasts.

Any review of the use of the media of the spoken word, or perhaps more comprehensively the use of audible media, would be incomplete without reference to the role of music. We have already mentioned this in connection with resistance to the enemy parachute descent on Al-Gamil airport. In 1956 lyricists, composers and professional singers responded to the call, and a spate of songs emerged glorifying the struggle against the aggressor. The government did not ignore the possibilities of music as a stimulus to national cohesion. The popular songs of 1956 spread throughout the Arab World and some were later adopted as national anthems by a number of Arab countries. Put to music, the slogan *We'll fight* took on an added dimension and, as a national song, it was soon echoing beyond the frontiers of Egypt. Allied to the strong religious sentiments of the people, the impact of such songs became even more potent, and it is probably no coincidence that the most popular and effective song during the hostilities was one entitled *Allah Akbar* (God is Great).

Even in translation, something of the atmosphere can be savoured from the refrain of one of the popular songs of the period:

> "This land is mine, my own.
> Here my father sacrificed all.
> And to us my father said:
> Tear the invader into shreds."

The lyrics of another song ran:

> "God's might is above the plots of the aggressor.
> God is the support of the oppressed.
> By faith and my arm I will redeem
> My country, with Right's light shining in my hand.
> Say with me, say with me, God is above the aggressor.
> Oh world, look and hear.
> There came the aggressor's army to slay me.
> By my Right and my arm I will destroy him.
> And, if I should perish, so perish him with me.
> Say with me, say with me, God is above the aggressor."

In terms of visual media full use was made of posters and signs such as that of the powerful arm and fist symbolizing strength in the face of aggression. A special use of photography was the despatch to heads of state, UN delegations, leading world personalities and the international press and television organizations, of albums containing photographs of the destruction of churches and mosques and of war casualties. These undoubtedly heightened awareness of the nature of the tripartite aggression among the most influential sections of the global community. It is said that when President Nehru of India saw one of these albums he was unable to hold back his tears. Predictably the cinema played a major role. The film entitled *Aggression on Port Said*, to which we have already referred, achieved international repute. Quite apart from its technical merits, which were considerable, it really amounted to an historical document, giving the lie direct to Sir Anthony Eden's statement to the House of Commons that there had been no casualties among the occupying troops and that no damage had been done to the city of Port Said. The present author vividly recalls the conditions in which the film was made while fighting was still in progress and houses, churches and mosques were being set ablaze by the naval shelling of the city.

In their professional use of the machinery of information the Egyptian authorities did not forget those other media which, as we explained in our fifth chapter, are ancillary only in the sense that they must of necessity apply one or more of the basic media of the written word, the spoken word and the visual image. In that chapter we noted the importance of the medium of *personal contact*. One of the forms this assumed in 1956 was the activity of personnel from the various information offices in the governorates in communicating by word of mouth news which, for one reason or another, the official information authorities considered unsuitable for dissemination by more formal means. This network of verbal communications was often used to minimize the repercussions of bad news; nothing was concealed but the presentation was made in a way calculated to limit the demoralization factor, and so to ensure that as far as possible the public might relate the setback to the overall context of the struggle and not inflate it into a cataclysmic disaster out of proportion to its real importance. Preachers in mosques and priests in churches provided another form of personal contact when they reminded their congregations, Muslim and Christian alike, that the battle in which Egypt was involved was a battle of all citizens, irrespective of creed, for the sake of one nation.

Other ancillary media described in our fifth chapter were rumour and psychological warfare. The latter had been a continuous feature of Zionist propaganda for years. During the Suez crisis, as before it, the Egyptian Information Administration responded in the most effective way of all by developing among the people an irresistible conviction of the justice of their cause as the basis of national confidence in ultimate victory. Rumour of course is a deadly weapon in the armoury of psychological warfare. Recognizing the need for prompt and efficient counter-measures, the Egyptian authorities set up an office equipped with teleprinters for the specific purpose of refuting rumour. The telephone number of this office was widely circulated. A responsible official was permanently in charge of the office, where a record was kept of all rumours and allegations disseminated by the enemy. On one occasion a rumour spread throughout the country that the commander of the Egyptian Air Force had been killed, but the authorities were able to refute it very promptly by broadcasting a radio interview with the commander on the same day, while the text of the interview and a photograph of the commander were carried by all newspapers on the following day. By adopting such efficient scientific methods, it was possible to nip in the bud some very dangerous and demoralizing rumours. What remained were so trivial as to be of the nature of mere gossip rather than real rumours.

Our review of Egyptian counter-propaganda in 1956 has drawn attention to notable successes, such as the use of Guy Mollet's National Assembly statement, and the protest of the foreign press correspondents against the refusal of the tripartite aggressors to admit them into the city of Port Said after the Suez problem had been handed over to the UN. It has also brought out the expertise of the Egyptian information authorities in turning to good account the mistakes of their opponents. But more than anything the Egyptian achievement, *vis à vis* domestic and foreign opinion, lies in their adherence to sound aims: the maintenance of national morale, respect for truth and accuracy, care for Egypt's image at home and abroad, the provision of adequate defences against hostile propaganda. Between the Revolution and the Suez crisis the Egyptian Information Administration had grown experienced in the ways of opinion formation and of good public relations. They had accepted major principles of presentation: the needs to carry conviction, to expound the enemy ideology, to strive for clarity and simplicity, to maintain continuity, to keep the major themes alive by constant repetition while avoiding boredom, to shift attention where enemy propaganda threatened certain events and subjects with over-exposure. They had shown skill in the application of these principles, setting up an efficient method of information gathering, sifting and retrieval, ensuring its running by an expert and dedicated staff, utilizing to the full the capabilities of the major media of the written word, the spoken word and the visible image, as well as those of the ancillary media such as personal contact and the specialized medium of psychological warfare. The achievement was the more impressive for being attained without recourse to falsehood or to gratuitous abuse.

On the latter point the record of Egypt's opponents left much to be desired. Quite apart from the constant and predictable abuse from Israel, Egypt had to suffer defamation from the British press, London newspapers such as the *Daily Express* and the *Daily Mail* resorting to headlines like "Nasser pinches the Canal", or referring to the Egyptian president as "The Small Dictator", or describing the Suez war as "a new Munich". The Egyptian information media retaliated by analysing such expressions without specifically mentioning them. They stressed Egypt's right to nationalize the Canal. They argued that it was Eden and Mollet who had acted dictatorially by conspiring with Ben Gurion behind the backs of their cabinet colleagues. In doing so they were never abusive. Whereas Eden referred to Nasser as "the small dictator", the Egyptian information media always gave these leaders their proper names and titles. The present author recalls that in the year after Suez he was taking part in a TV interview in London at which the British commentator referred to President Nasser as "the Egyptian dictator". He at once retorted "Please note that when I refer to your head of state, I say Her Majesty the Queen; Nasser's title is President Nasser." The commentator at once apologized before all the viewers of this live interview.

Strident abuse and defamation are often symptoms of lack of conviction and of insecurity. Egypt had no need to resort to them. Thanks to good public relations and to the honest expert management of the information services, the Egyptians felt secure in their just cause, confident of their leadership, sure of their ultimate victory. There might be temporary reverses with unpalatable consequences, but the people met these with level-headed resolution. Thus, when the British and French landed in Port Said, their temporary success was turned into a victory for the Egyptians, following that city's gallant resistance. Again, after the Egyptian withdrawal from Sinai, threatened demoralization was averted by the Information Administration's explanation of the strategic necessity for the withdrawal, and by its revelation of the considerable losses inflicted on the enemy, including the shooting down of a number of Mirage aircraft. Examples such as these illustrate the real measure of Egypt's counter-propaganda success in 1956. National morale had been signally pre-served and brought to a heightened pitch of confidence. And exter-nally large inroads had been made in the Zionist domination of much of the world media.

(c) The lessons applied

Thanks to UN pressures and the exertions of the UN Secretary-General, Dag Hammarskjold, Israel was prevailed upon to evacuate the Sinai peninsula in February 1957. The Arab World could now revert to the arts of peace. For Egypt this meant resuming the work of national reconstruction on the basis of the Six Principles of the Revolution so cruelly interrupted by the tripartite attack. Bitter as it was, the Suez experience was turned to good account by President Nasser and his government. Not only had they demonstrated their country's determination to preserve its hard won sovereignty, but, by asserting Egypt's integrity in unmistakable terms, they had earned for her a new respect among the nations, and had raised the morale of her people to new heights of confidence. The conditions were right for renewed co-operative efforts for internal reconstruction, and for the pursuit of an external policy calculated to further aims clearly enunciated before Suez: Arab unity, victory in the anti-colonialist struggle, friendly neutralism towards both sides in the Cold War in keeping with the spirit of Bandung. Both at home and abroad Egypt would need every available facility of the information media. Her ability to make use of these had been much improved by the experi-ence gained in the Suez war. The next eight years were to show that the lessons had been well learnt. Before discussing their imaginative application to the major policy aims adumbrated above, however, we must say something of the expanding capability of the principal media.

Before July 1952 the establishment politicians exerted enormous influence on the press, which in consequence reflected the interests of feudalism and big business. This unhealthy circumscription of press freedom by the Wafd and others was partly removed with the dissolution of the existing political parties in January 1953, though a measure of capitalist control remained until the reorganization of the press by Law No. 156 in 1960. Under this law the ownership of the leading newspapers was transferred to the people. This measure of nationalization did not imply any rigid control of the newspapers. Freedom of the press was respected, and was at last a practical reality, being no longer frustrated by the hidden manipulation of wealthy groups.

To be fully effective, however, press freedom needs a large well-educated readership. The capability of this information medium relates closely with the education system. To outward appearances Egypt's pre-revolutionary education system was not ungenerous. Compulsory education for all children between the ages of six and twelve was introduced in 1933 and in 1944 education at the primary stage became free. But the advantages of these enactments were often illusory. Right up to 1952 the number of school places fell a good deal short of the total population of compulsory school age. Recognizing the high priority of education, the new government undertook a vast school building programme. Thus within ten years of the Revolution the school population had gone up from under two million to some three and a half million. And the improvement was not confined to the primary level. Great strides were made in the provision of secondary and advanced education, especially in the fields of science and technology. Between the budgetary years 1951–2 and 1964–5 expenditure on education rose from L.E. 40·2 million to 96·5 million.

While the connection between literacy and press effectiveness is obvious, there is also a correlation between the value of other media and the existence of good educational facilities. More education, therefore, enabled the people to benefit from the greater opportunities for the circulation of information and ideas created by the expansion of Egypt's broadcasting service, referred to in our previous chapter. Moreover, in 1961 Egyptian television became operational in the Delta, later spreading throughout the major population centres. These improvements in the media of press and broadcasting meant that ever larger numbers of people could have direct knowledge of the government's activities and of its continuous efforts to improve the conditions of the overwhelming proportion of the population. For its part the government possessed increasingly effective means for explaining its policy to the nation and so for cultivating good public relations.

Public understanding was vital at this time of reconstruction and progress. A serious failure of communications could all too easily have obstructed the régime's urgent reform programme, and have presented selfish minorities with opportunities for creating public alarm or confusion through deliberate misrepresentation. It was not enough for the government to act in the public interest, it must also be seen to be doing so through the fullest programme of information and education. In this way the government showed its confidence in the good sense and loyalty of the people. On their side the mass of the population wholeheartedly reciprocated the sentiment. Just as in the dark days of Suez, so now in the process of rebuilding the nation, true partnership existed between rulers and ruled.

Its practical benefits were nowhere more welcome than in the various measures of nationalization introduced over this period. As we have already observed, strong conservatism and fear of change are universal popular traits. Time and again they have frustrated the reforming zeal of progressive governments, particularly where the latter have allowed their convictions and enthusiasms to obscure the practical need to maintain the understanding and support of their peoples. Autocratic government is not necessarily reactionary. It can be enlightened and genuinely concerned with the public welfare. Where it often fails is precisely in the field of public relations. It becomes remote and so suspect. Recognizing the need for constant and meaningful communications, the Egyptian leaders avoided this mistake, and they took infinite pains to make sure that the great majority of Egyptians comprehended the purpose and the implications of the nationalization policy.

This attitude was brought out in a 1962 Cairo Radio broadcast dealing with the socialist laws of July 1961. Placing them in context as an extension of earlier legislation, it acknowledged that the revolutionary change could not have proceeded so smoothly without "the deep faith and consciousness of the people". Thanks to their determination, ability and sincerity, the delicate transitional phase to socialism was achieved without loss of productivity, and industry was saved from attempted sabotage by reactionary elements.

Another Cairo Radio broadcast of the same year explicitly referred to the deep-seated human suspicion of any philosophy or activity which appears to threaten individual property. Observable in most social groupings, this fear is often acute in communities that are predominantly agricultural, as was the case with Egypt at that time. One of the hardest tasks which democratic socialism has had to face is to persuade the masses that there is an effective distinction between the wealth of the community on the one hand and the private property of its citizens on the other, that the community through its proper representatives has a right to use the former for the well-being of the entire nation, whereas it interferes with the latter at its peril. The government's task of education and conviction is the more difficult because the private owners of the essentially national resources normally have both the motives and the means to blur the dividing line between the two species of property. The danger is acute in societies where the mass of the people is only partially educated, and hence vulnerable to well-presented though specious arguments designed to spread confusion and alarm concerning the possible results of the government's socializing activities. To combat feelings of this kind and to prevent their exploitation by vested capitalistic interests, Cairo Radio broadcast the following message in 1962:

"The people's control over all the tools of production does not necessitate the nationalization of all means of production, neither does it mean the abolition of private ownership or any infringement of the legitimate right of inheritance following therefrom. It is of prime importance that our outlook towards nationalization be freed from the stigmas that private interests have tried to attach to it.

"Nationalization is but the transfer of one of the means of production from the sphere of private ownership to that of public ownership. This is not a blow to individual initiative, as alleged by the enemies of socialism, but rather a guarantee to and an expansion of the range of general interest in cases urged by the socialist change effected for the benefit of the people.

"Nationalization does not lead to a decrease in production."

The message went to the heart of the matter. The average listener with the normal human misgivings about any threat to property was relieved that his fears were known to the government, gratified that they had been taken into account, reassured that his essential interests would not be harmed and that the administration was acting, not in pursuance of academic theories unrelated to practical reality, but rather in the interests of the whole nation of which he was an essential part. He was proud of this feeling of belonging to a body which, while more powerful than himself, so clearly demonstrated its awareness of his own fears and interests, and at the same time invited his participation in the realization of its noble objectives. Further reassurance came from the reflection that, in the struggle between the rich and influential and the interests of ordinary people, the government was firmly on the side of the latter and had the measure of stock capitalistic arguments against socialism, such as that of the implied threat to productivity. And in any case the message made it clear that the 1961 nationalization laws were not socialism for its own theoretical sake, but were essentially pragmatic measures, which, by allowing a mixed economy, would leave plenty of scope for individual initiative and justifiable varieties of private enterprise. The entire message is a telling example of the government's professionalism in public relations, of its use of the media for internal peace and harmony, and of an impressive expertise acquired in the testing years immediately after the Revolution and during the months of the Suez crisis. The message's credibility benefited also from the nature of the nationalization. The measures of 1961 were directed largely against the economically over-mighty, such as the Bank Misr conglomerate. On the other hand, as Anthony Nutting has pointed out in his biography of President Nasser, much of the building trade, a very large employer of labour, was left alone, while agriculture remained overwhelmingly in private hands.[3] The respect accorded to agricultural property was especially important, for, as a result of the agrarian reform, many people of modest means now owned land. Any tampering with these widespread vested interests would have risked antagonizing the peasants and smallholders, as a group normally among the most conservative economic elements of any country.

Cairo Radio assiduously strove to maintain a sense of partner-

[3] Anthony Nutting: *Nasser*, Constable, London 1972, p. 299.

ship involving all citizens as valuable contributors in an exciting task of national renaissance. As part of its communications function, it supplied the sort of statistical information which the people could readily assimilate, and which had an obvious bearing on their individual circumstances as the inhabitants of a still predominantly agricultural country, which looked to a well conducted industry to improve the quality of life of all its citizens, urban and rural alike. In this context data simply presented in a Cairo Radio broadcast covering the 1964–65 budget have a bearing on our present study of opinion formation, as well as illustrating the impressive material progress achieved by President Nasser and his administration. The broadcast quantified both the vast improvement since 1952 in government finance for agriculture, and the rise in land ownership resulting from the break up of excessively large private estates. It detailed the investment on the High Dam and allied projects, justifying it in terms of the anticipated accession of national wealth. Matters of day-to-day concern to ordinary citizens were not overlooked, for "expenditures on housing and utilities increased from L.E. 5·9 million in 1952 to L.E. 96·3 in the 1964–65 budget." And, significantly in terms of our present subject, the broadcast supplied the information that "The number of radio transmission hours increased from 15 hours in 1952 to 121 hours, while the number of TV transmission hours increased from 10 hours in 1961 to 22 hours."

At home the period was one of real achievement undertaken as a genuine partnership with the people, in the service of which the government employed the media fully, honestly and expertly. This was both information for harmony and information for progress. In the foreign policy of these years we find the same professionalism in the use of the media in the interests of Arab unity and of freedom from the remaining colonialist shackles, as also to counter the incessant propaganda of Israel and her sympathizers. All these aims implied the necessity for a ceaseless vigil against imperialism in its various guises. A Cairo Radio broadcast described the danger in the following clear terms:

> "What is then the aim of imperialism? This aim is to destroy Arab nationalism, have it broken into little bits, thus allowing for other nationalisms to grow between the broken bits. This aim, however,

is not new. It dates back to the Crusades in the tenth and eleventh centuries, when war was waged against this part of the world under the pretext of religion, while the real objective was the destruction of Arab nationalism and the establishment of an imperialistic rule in the area."

The reference to the belligerent and destructive attributes of imperialism is important as showing that Egyptian and Arab hostility was defensive rather than aggressive. The aim was not to encourage disputes between the nations, but rather to illustrate the dangers to lasting peace unless imperialism and colonialism were checked and ultimately abandoned by the powers.

In terms of the Arab cause *The Voice of the Arabs* therefore continued to campaign for the independence of Algeria and against the continued British presence in Aden. It also came out strongly against the concealed foreign intervention threatened by the strategic policies of the great powers, in particular by the Baghdad Pact and by the *Eisenhower Doctrine*; the latter, recognizing the decline of British military power in the area, set out to substitute a US presence as a bulwark against Russia. These were Cold War considerations with which Egypt and other Arab countries had no wish to become embroiled, particularly after the emergence of a Third World attitude in the period following the Bandung conference. For this reason, Cairo Radio conducted a campaign against the pro-US stand of the government of Iraq under Nuri es-Said. The latter was overthrown in the Iraqi revolution of July 1958. Fearing that the Russians would use the resulting confusion as an excuse to draw Iraq and other Asian Arab states into their orbit, the Americans intervened in Lebanon, and Cairo Radio turned its attention to this latest infringement of the integrity of an Arab sovereign state. The threat from the USSR may well have been real, but Egypt realized that ultimately the only guarantee of true security lay in greater Arab self-help and unity, along the lines of the Syrian response. Fearing excessive Russian pressure, the Syrian leaders had already approached Egypt with the suggestion of a political union, and in February 1958 the United Arab Republic was established. In the event this expression of a common Arab purpose proved premature. It certainly suited neither the US nor the USSR, which both attacked it. Possibly due to the hostility of the great powers, but also as a result of special conditions applying in Syria, the union, which in the meantime had come to include Yemen, was dissolved in 1962. While disappointed, Egypt did not for a moment question the inalienable right of the Syrians to bring the relationship to a close.

Of all the manifestations of the Arab struggle for independence during these years the Algerian rising claimed perhaps the most attention from the media. Throughout the seven and a half years of the war—from its outbreak in October 1954 to the settlement concluded at Evian in March 1962—*The Voice of the Arabs* maintained steady support for the Algerians, while, as we have seen, Egypt was not deflected from their cause by the threats of Christian Pineau to supply military aircraft to Israel. Welcome expressions of solidarity came from Arab and other Third World sources; for example in August 1959 the Monrovia Conference of independent African countries, which included delegates from Libya, Morocco, Tunisia and the UAR, urged its members to give material assistance to the provisional Algerian government and urged France to stop the fighting. The fact that the war went on so long underlines its importance for international perceptions of the character of the Arab World. World attention was further stimulated by the involvement of a leading power, France, and after 1958 by the involvement of a world personality, General Charles de Gaulle. Hitherto some countries had more or less taken at face value the official French policy of regarding Algeria as an exclusively French issue and as hardly part of the Arab World at all. By 1962 the world had learnt to view the Algerians as a distinct people, who now took their rightful place as an independent nation within the regional grouping of the Arab World. Cairo Radio and the Egyptian government have an honourable place in this opinion development. The importance of the Algerian war in the affairs of the Arab World and in international affairs generally is even greater than these consequences suggest. For it had enormous effects on France's internal politics and on her subsequent attitude towards the Arab World.

In the period just before Suez and during the crisis itself, France acted out of character in her hostility towards the Arabs. This was to a great extent due to the decline of French influence following the

Second World War, and to the rude awakening to the revised facts of international relations brought about by the loss of Indo-China, and, in the same year, by the outbreak of the Algerian troubles. In course of time the French education system would presumably have given future generations of Frenchmen a different set of preconceptions about their country's rightful place in the world. But conditioning of this sort is almost invariably slow, sometimes delayed by atavistic tendencies, and usually effective only after a considerable time lag. Fortunately, it was now possible to accelerate the process. By the early sixties, after all, most adult Frenchmen recollected twenty years of dramatic change in great-power relationships. Beginning with the occupation of their country by the Germans in 1940, they had witnessed events which disproved any delusions as to the immutability of the circumstances applicable to their country or to any other nation. To a degree, therefore, a growing number of them were prepared for change in international as in social or political matters, though this does not necessarily mean that they welcomed change. The recognition in logical terms by many Frenchmen of the cold fact of diminished status did not prevent some of these same Frenchmen from acting out of emotional nostalgia of the sort that seemed to be infectious at the time of Suez. It did on the other hand create a predisposition to profit by the Suez experience, and to yield to its proof of the futility of gunboat diplomacy as an instrument of national policy. The predisposition was encouraged by massive exposure to the international news media, which now included television. French traditions of dissent from the establishment and the revolutionary tradition of freedom put large numbers of Frenchmen in possession of the essential facts of the Suez episode, including the fact of Guy Mollet's parliamentary discomfiture. Through the international media they heard accusations of mass murder and of other atrocities perpetrated by their own parachute regiments—*les paras*—by the police, and by the private *Organisation Armée Secrète* (OAS) dedicated to the destruction of the Algerian freedom fighters. As the struggle went on the French public could not delude themselves about the widespread use of torture.

In many ways the development of French opinion proceeded along lines similar to those of British opinion over the Suez period, though in the French case both stimuli and manifestations tended to be more extreme. In France, as in Britain, there were the problems of re-adjustment to the new conditions of international hegemony. Initially the majority of Frenchmen, like their British counterparts, were not at all averse from measures calculated to restore the status and respect which they regarded as their due in international affairs. But in both countries there was always a large and articulate group which dis-agreed with this view, while public opinion as a whole was not pre-pared to support an adventurous foreign policy regardless of its cost. In Britain a reaction to the Suez intervention set in once it became widely recognized that the price of perseverance was likely to include a threat to international peace and growing economic difficulties, of which petrol rationing was merely an early symptom. In France the reaction took longer to reveal itself, partly because the nation's world standing had suffered more grievously from the Second World War, partly because of the fresh blow to national pride from the loss of Indo-China, and very importantly because of the uniquely close rela-tionship of the French people with Algeria. The fall of the Fourth Republic and the return of General de Gaulle to power in May 1958 reflected the continuing determination of France to assert its posi-tion, eighteen months after the lesson of Suez.

Up to that point the French response to Algeria had shown the dominance of upbringing and education, of traditional habits and attitudes, as formative elements of public opinion. From May 1958 a new and countervailing element came into play—leadership—and this was increasingly reinforced by the effects of the media during the concluding years of the Algerian struggle. De Gaulle's patriotism and sense of national destiny were unimpeachable. Had he so chosen, he could probably have prolonged the Algerian war for several more years. Fortunately for most of the parties concerned, and for the cause of peace in general, he rose to the occasion as he had done in 1940, when France's vital interests were at stake. Acknowledging the justice of the Algerian cause, and recognizing the advantages to his own country of good relations with Algeria and with the Arab World as a whole, he lent his enormous authority to the tasks of ending the war and of allowing the Algerian people to determine their own destiny. After a visit to Algeria the previous month, de Gaulle took the French people into his confidence in his broadcast of 16 September 1959, when he explained the need for a settlement and for realism.

"We must settle it. We will not do so by tossing at each other sterile and over-simplified slogans coined by those who are blind to everything save their conflicting passions, interests or daydreams. We will achieve it as a great nation should do, choosing the only path worthy of being followed—I mean the free choice which the Algerians themselves will make for their future."

Such was de Gaulle's reputation that in time he succeeded in carrying the main body of public opinion with him. But the popular feelings that had brought him to power as the intended defender of French Algeria were still strong, not to say aggressive. It therefore needed two and a half more years of fighting before France agreed at the Evian negotiations of 1962 to bring the war to a close. In the end the French government was fighting as much against the extreme colonialist sentiments and activities of a still important section of opinion as against the FLN (National Liberation Front) and other Algerian nationalists. It had to suppress the rising of the Algerian settlers in January 1960 and the attempted military coup d'état of Generals Challe, Jouhaud, Salan and Zeller in April 1961, events whose coverage by the media incidentally stimulated further outside interest in and ultimately appreciation of the Arab cause.

By then, however, the reactionaries were clearly in a minority. Not only were the French people unwilling to go on defraying the costs of the war in face of financial strain and world criticism, but they had been unsettled by the message of the foreign media, including those of the Arab countries. The evidence of atrocities was too insistent to be ignored. Both the war in Indo-China and now the troubles in Algeria brought home to Frenchmen that torture and murder were not the exclusive prerogative of certain other nations. French soldiers and police, and French private citizens, were incontrovertibly guilty of crimes that stood comparison with the Nazi horrors revealed at Nuremburg in 1945. Nor did French opinion have to rely on the revelations of Arab and other foreign media. Even before the return of de Gaulle, the rumours of the use of torture were so widespread that in May 1957 a commission in defence of individual rights and liberties had been appointed to investigate complaints, and its report, published on 14 December 1957 in *Le Monde*, confirmed the public's suspicions of the use of torture and of brutality towards prisoners. Corroborating evidence was provided by the publication on 9 April 1959 in the Catholic weekly *Témoignage Chrétien* of the views of thirty-five Catholic priests serving with the French forces in Algeria. Moreover the revelations often centred on individual tragedies. There was the arrest by the *paras* on 11 June 1957 of the Algiers University lecturer Maurice Audin, who was later strangled by his captors. There was the case of the Algerian trade unionist Aissat Idir who, even after his acquittal by a military court, was kept in internment until his death on 26 July 1959, the result it was alleged of burns received when his bedclothes accidentally caught fire! From the point of view of its effects upon public opinion, perhaps the most important of these human stories was that of the journalist Henri Alleg. Arrested the day after Audin, Alleg was subsequently subjected to torture by electric shock and by having water forced into his nose and mouth. Despite security precautions, he was able to get word of this treatment to the world outside his detention camp, and subsequently his book *La Question* made a big contribution to the revulsion felt in France and elsewhere against the individuals and authorities responsible for brutality of this sort.

The solidarity of much of French opinion in favour of peace was demonstrated on 1 February 1960, when, as a riposte against the abortive rising of certain non-Arab sections of the population, the three main French trade unions—Communist, Socialist and Catholic—in concert with the teachers' and students' unions effected a one-hour general strike. For large sections of the population the government, though proceeding in the right direction, was dragging its feet. Many Frenchmen now began to question the traditional military service. If their national obligation implied support for a reactionary military clique and for the virtually treasonable aims of colonialists in Algiers, then was it not their patriotic duty to refuse to participate in the repression? The attitude was coherently expressed in the *Manifesto of the 121*. Framed in July 1960, this document was endorsed by many well-known people commanding widespread respect or popularity. The signatories included the actresses Danielle Delorme and Simone Signoret, and the writers Simone de Beauvoir, Jean-Paul Sartre and Françoise Sagan, as well as politicians and intellectuals. After castigating the use of torture and the army's obstruction of the government's aim of peace in Algeria, the manifesto went on:

"We declare and consider justified the refusal to take up arms against the Algerian people. We respect and consider justified the conduct of Frenchmen who deem it their duty to help and protect Algerians oppressed in the name of the French people. The Algerian people's cause, contributing in decisive fashion to the ruin of the colonial system, is the cause of all free men."

Although left wing views were prominently represented among the manifesto's signatories, the declaration could not be dismissed as the expression of a mere sectional interest. Profound disquiet at the moral and patriotic justifications for continued support of the military operations in Algeria transcended political boundaries and social attitudes. For example on 17 October 1960 the French cardinals and archbishops, scarcely a revolutionary body, issued a statement to the effect that serving soldiers had a moral obligation to refuse orders to take part in torture. The following month similar sentiments were expressed by the French Protestants, who also pressed for the recognition of conscientious objection to military service. The cumulative effect of all these elements—respect for de Gaulle, resentment at the cost of a seemingly endless conflict, revulsion at the atrocities, disgust for the narrow selfishness of the colonists and of their reactionary allies in the army—was felt in April 1961. It was essentially ordinary French opinion which frustrated the attempted coup d'état of that month. The national service men who made up the bulk of the armed forces simply refused to implement the illegal schemes of Generals Challe, Jouhaud, Salan and Zeller. Like Britain after Suez, France had come to terms with international reality. The role of the media was decisive in effecting the transformation.

The part of the Arab media in inducing a keener appreciation of reality in the public opinion of former imperial powers was not confined to the Arab struggle for independence. Colonialism wherever it existed was both an affront to human dignity and a potential threat to international harmony.

The dedicated work of *The Voice of the Arabs* and of other media in providing information about the evils of colonialism was accordingly a real contribution to peace. The same media were used to encourage the struggle of African leaders, such as Sekou Toure in Guinea, who went so far as to observe that in Cairo Radio Egypt possessed a weapon to liberate Africa. Thus the media played their part in bringing about a climate of opinion which contributed to the wholesale decolonialization policy adopted by Great Britain and France; beginning with the independence of Ghana in 1957 the process was virtually complete ten years later. Other colonialist régimes continued of course, notably those of the Portuguese, Rhodesians and South Africans. Outside Africa colonialism took the less direct forms of US intervention in Viet Nam or of the US economic domination of much of Latin America. Through unflinching declarations of solidarity with the peoples of these regions, the Arab media showed where their sympathies lay, as well as continuing to exercise their educative role in the provision of information conducive to good international relations and ultimately to peace.

The veiled colonialism implicit in the attitudes and policy of the Israelis remained as intractable as ever. Israeli aggression continued in a succession of border incidents against Egypt, Jordan and Syria. Israeli terrorism was by no means confined to operations against the Arabs; in 1962 and 1963, for example, there was a wave of bomb attacks, including letter bombs, on German scientists both in Egypt and in Germany itself. Although Israel had in the end yielded to US pressure against the tripartite aggression of 1956, Washington's attitude at that time resulted from global policy considerations rather than from any lack of sympathy for the Zionist state. In the field of information and propaganda Israel still benefited from clandestine US broadcasts. For instance in 1958 the American CIA (Central Intelligence Agency) financed a clandestine broadcasting station under the pretext that Radio Cairo should not be permitted to transmit freely without receiving any rebuttal.

Hostile undercover attacks of this type were a constant feature of the period. A series of stations was established in the Middle East to undermine the influence of Radio Cairo. In some cases they employed anti-revolutionary elements who had fled from Egypt. President Nasser pointed to the seriousness of these attacks when, during an interview on 6 April 1958 with Frank Kearns, a representative of the US Columbia Broadcasting Corporation, he said:

> "There are nine hostile clandestine stations along with a number of open broadcasts all working against the Arabs and us. Foremost among these is the Baghdad Pact organization whose sole objective is to attack us. In fact, they oppose the Arabs' aspirations and the lawful rights to which they are entitled in having a national policy emanating from their own desires. You forgot the campaigns directed against us, but you remember our self-defence against them. These clandestine stations have instigated my murder."

Israeli deceit made the most of this propensity of much of the world to censure Arab reaction while ignoring the provocation that had caused it. A supreme example of this deceit took place in October 1956 when Ben Gurion expressed the wish to discuss peace with President Nasser, only to embark on the tripartite aggression within a matter of hours. In the following year a member of the Israeli delegation to an international parliamentary conference in London sought to use the publicity attendant on the gathering to convince public opinion of Israel's attachment to peace. The present author went to that conference as a member of the Egyptian delegation, and he recalls pointing out to the other delegates that his normal inclination on hearing such public sentiments from the Israelis was to ask his secretary to book him on the next plane to Cairo, for Israeli protestations of peace were wont to presage sudden attack. If the Israelis had really wanted peace then or since, simple and effective methods existed for indicating their good faith, and there was no need for the limelight inseparable from international gatherings. The fact is that talk of peace was just another weapon in Israel's propaganda armoury, and from Israel's points of view the more publicity it commanded the better. It has to be admitted that until recent years deceit of this type was usually successful.

In course of time the world would come to realize something of the extent to which it had been misled by Zionist propaganda. For the moment and for some years to come the Arab response was bound to take on many of the attributes of a holding operation. For the most part, all *The Voice of the Arabs* and the other Arab media could do was to cling steadfastly to a message which they knew to be right, in the belief that eventually others would also come to acknowledge its truth. Hence their support for oppressed peoples, Arab and non-Arab, and their adherence to the Bandung spirit of friendly neutrality. This determination to escape domination by either of the Cold War groups is shown, not only by Egypt's protests at the activities of the Baghdad Pact and at the implementation of the Eisenhower Doctrine in Lebanon in 1958, but also by her attitude to the USSR and communism. For example, when in 1959 the Russian leader Nikita Kruschev attacked President Nasser for his union with Syria, Cairo Radio responded to Kruschev's speech within half an hour. As to communism, we have already observed that its irreligious implications were at odds with the ideology of the overwhelming proportion of the Arab World, and that the Egyptian Communist Party failed to attract popular support after the July Revolution. Indeed its disloyalty to the national cause was such that the government had no alternative to imprisoning its leaders. Egypt thus maintained a strict neutrality between the opposing world ideologies, no less than between the Cold War military blocs.

By the mid-sixties events were beginning to vindicate this neutralist stand, which only a few years before the US administration had regarded as little short of positive hostility. With the conclusion of the nuclear test ban treaty in October 1963, with the widening gulf between the USSR and China, with the fall of Kruschev and the emergence of steadier Russian leadership in October 1964, the way was prepared for a more permanent international détente than the illusory thaw following the death of Stalin in 1953. China's defection from Russia's side increased the number of options available to the non-aligned. Neutralism had become respectable in the eyes of the great powers. With this change went a greater readiness to listen to the views of nations and groups that had preserved their independence of the Cold War. New opportunities opened up for the Egyptian and Arab information media. Unhappily their capacity for constructive exploitation was delayed by the events of 1967, to which we must now turn our attention.

9
The Six-Day War and After, 1967–1973

(a) Grievous setbacks

In their quest for unity and justice the Arabs have never been able to count on uninterrupted progress. The mid-1960s certainly justified hopes of greater understanding of the Arab cause, but we must not overstate the pace of this development. International relations might be relaxed by comparison with the intransigencies of the previous decade, but the Cold War was not over yet. And in parallel with the détente, the Arab World had to face new problems or the accentuation of old ones, which by 1967 had made the area more rather than less vulnerable to Israeli propaganda.

For one thing the struggle against colonialism was no longer the binding force that it had been among the nations of the Third World in the years immediately after the Bandung conference. By the mid-1960s most of Africa and Asia were independent. Their common purpose attained, it was understandable that the newly sovereign states should develop in different ways, and that on occasion policies should conflict. In the Indo-Pakistan sub-continent discord arose over the manner of independence in August 1947; although the fighting about the ownership of Kashmir was contained, relationships deteriorated to the point of the clashes in the Rann of Kutch in April 1965, and, far more seriously, the war of September of the same year. Further east, American involvement in Viet Nam began immediately after the French withdrawal in 1964, while from January 1963 to August 1966 the confrontation between Indonesia and Malaysia threatened to turn into full-scale hostilities. In Africa many of the independent states acceded to one or other of the rival groupings: that of Brazzaville formed in October 1960 and restructured as the Monrovia group in August 1961, and that of Casablanca formed in January 1961. Faced with the hostility of Israel and handicapped by vested interests and imperfect understanding among the leading powers, the Arab World could afford internal divisions even less than its neighbours to the east and south. On the whole a fair measure of unity remained, though concentration against the common danger inevitably suffered from the differing methods favoured by individual Arab states and from the Yemen dispute which, beginning in September 1962, was settled only in May 1970.

The range of problems facing Arab governments grew in quantity and complexity. It was becoming more difficult to preserve a friendly neutrality towards all. Egypt saw no alternative to heavy reliance on the USSR for completing the Aswan High Dam project, the basis of so many of her hopes of future prosperity. Nor had the West broken completely free from earlier colonialist leanings. Admittedly France had bowed to the inevitable in Algeria, but for a while in the sixties Britain seemed intent on putting the clock back. She retained a presence in the Gulf and showed little inclination to give up Aden, her major remaining foothold in the Arab World. Britain's apparent deafness to the public relations demands of a delicate situation, and British failure to curb the racist activities of Ian Smith's régime in Rhodesia led to the rupture of diplomatic links between Cairo and London in December 1965. The British deal with Saudi Arabia for an air defence system appeared to substantiate a widespread suspicion that, in her determination to recover some Middle Eastern hegemony, Britain would not hesitate to sow dissension between one Arab state and another. The same year also saw the development of closer links between Bonn and Tel Aviv, and the consequent severance of diplomatic relations between Western Germany and Egypt. With Zionist influence on the US media in no way diminished, the credibility of Israeli propaganda in Western circles was as great as ever. In any future outbreak of hostilities between Israel and her Arab neighbours, the West would regard the onus of proof as resting with the Arabs. This was of course an incomparable advantage for Israel. She exploited it for all it was worth during the 1967 June war.

A further difficulty for the Arabs lay in the changed circumstances of the Palestine question. The change was one of degree, because essentially the problem had been defined by the events of 1947 and 1948. For much of the fifties, however, Palestinian interests tended to be overshadowed by other pressing issues, notably the struggle against French and British colonialism. The Palestinians therefore could not expect the undivided attention of the Arab governments and peoples. From 1956 onwards the demands of the Palestinians became more insistent. By the mid-sixties a high proportion of the refugees had reached adulthood, knowing no life other than that of the refugee camp, with all its privations and frustrations. To the extent that they knew about the outside world, they were conscious of a rising affluence created by peace and economic growth and contrasting with the sad conditions which were their lot. They had no personal knowledge of the climate of world opinion in which the Israeli state had been created—universal revulsion against Nazi anti-semitism and against the horrors of war. For many of them war may have seemed preferable to the continuation of a peace which merely served to entrench the interests of the dispossessors.

As the children of the refugee camps attained or approached manhood, a new Palestinian generation arose with none of the memories of more or less normal and sometimes cordial relationships between Arab and Jew, which had existed under the Ottoman Empire and even in the days of Britain's mandate. Generally speaking the older Palestinian generation did not hate the Jews, and even after 1948 many of them could still draw a distinction between the Jews on the one hand and the Zionists on the other. Their sons and grandsons had neither the inclination nor, to be fair, the means for achieving such a nice discrimination. The seeds of unmitigated hatred had been sown by the Stern Gang and the Irgun, they had been nurtured by the Zionist propaganda of the fifties, and they were now about to come to a full and terrible fruition. Individual Arab governments did not forget the plight of the refugees. For example, hard pressed as he was by Egypt's own economic necessities, President Nasser contributed generously to the development of public amenities in the refugee camps in the Gaza area. But in the long term, however well meant these efforts and however great the sacrifices they entailed among the donor states, assistance of this sort could be no more than a temporary palliative. With the anti-colonialist struggle all but won and the demands of the Palestinians too insistent to be denied, it was as inevitable as it was just that the Arab governments should co-ordinate their efforts in search of an acceptable long-term solution to the problems of Palestine.

Decisive steps in this direction were taken during and imme-diately after the summit meeting of Arab states held in Cairo in January 1964. Two prerequisites of effective action were recognized. In the first place there had to be a co-ordinated military capability equipped to counter future Israeli aggression. A start was made by the appointment of a unified Arab command structure headed by the Egyptian Field Marshal Abdel Hakim Amer. Secondly, the Palestin-ians needed an organization which could speak officially on their behalf. Such an organization should as far as possible enjoy the inter-national standing and attributes of a government, and be capable of representing Palestine at Pan-Arab gatherings. It was reasoning along these lines which led to the formation in May 1964 of the Palestine Liberation Organization (PLO) under the chairmanship of the lawyer Ahmed Shukhairy.

Understandable and even essential, these responses to Palestinian need may have determined the form and timing of the crisis of June 1967. The Israelis were alerted about the new co-ordination among their opponents while it was yet in embryo. They therefore had the chance to choose their ground and largely to determine the timing of the coming conflict. Viewed from Tel Aviv, Arab unity had to be broken before the financial contributions promised by the partici-pants at the Cairo summit had created a strong Pan-Arab defence force. Also the Israelis recognized the wisdom of ensuring that the next round of hostilities should take place at a time when their own stock in the West was high and that of the Arabs low. It was not that the Israelis sought active Western participation in hostilities along the lines of the 1956 tripartite intervention, but that they wished to ensure the West's co-operative non-participation.

They had used the years since Suez to add to their military pre-paredness, to the point where they were confident of being able to overcome any individual Arab country or combination of countries, at least for the foreseeable future. What they could not afford to risk was a situation such as that of November 1956, when American pressure deprived them of the chance of inflicting a crushing defeat on their Arab opponents. Next time they were resolved that the issue should be settled before either their Western friends or the Soviet bloc could interfere to reverse or neutralize the military verdict. In other words, just as in their expropriation of the Palestinians before Israeli independence in 1948, the Zionists made it their business to create the sort of facts which were unlikely to be overturned by any subsequent international conference. And pre-eminent among their targets for annihilation was the army of Egypt, whose leader they regarded as primarily responsible for the new determination evident among the Arabs. But here they struck a difficulty, for the Egyptian frontier was in effect protected by a UN force watchful of encroachments by either side. So long as the UNEF remained, any Israeli operation against President Nasser would be branded as aggression by the world body. Although Israel had time and again contemptuously brushed aside Security Council resolutions, she knew that even her friends could not countenance the opprobrium attaching to an outright attack on Egypt involving a clash with the UNEF. The problem for the Israelis then was so to manipulate the crisis as to allow their forces to move against Egypt without infringing the rights of the UNEF, and at the same time to bring matters to a head before the Arab armies had benefited from their new command structure, and from the more sophisticated weaponry and organization which the subventions agreed at the Cairo summit would bring within their reach, and before there was any chance of a change in the pro-Israeli climate of Western opinion.

Although Israel's main target was Egypt, she aimed to involve as many of the Arab states as possible in the coming conflict. Her initial moves were largely concentrated against Syria. She realized that, while both Syria and Egypt were determined in their support of the Palestinians, the character of their individual responses differed. Having dealt at close quarters with the Israeli armed forces in 1956, President Nasser was understandably cautious. He appreciated only too well that the Arab military build-up would need years before it achieved parity with Israel. In the meantime he had no wish to jeopardize the achievements of the 1952 Revolution or to weaken solid Arab gains through a premature trial of strength. He therefore strove to delay the conflict for precisely the same reasons as the Israelis wanted to precipitate it. The Syrians, on the other hand, suffered mounting provocation from Tel Aviv, which calculatedly over-reacted to Palestinian guerilla activities on the Syrian frontier. Especially cynical was Israel's exploitation of the situation in the Lake Huleh demilitarized zone, where she built up a system of fortifications and blocked all Syria's endeavours to submit the issue for UN consideration.

In September 1966, as a reprisal for alleged Syrian attacks in the demilitarized zone, the Israelis mounted a heavy onslaught on Syrian positions. The calculation paid off. In the name of Arab unity President Nasser could not leave the Syrians to face such gratuitous hostility alone. On 4 November he concluded a defensive agreement with Syria. Far from deterring Israel, the agreement was precisely in line with her plans, for now any war with Syria must involve Egypt. To widen its eventual scope still further, Israel moved against Jordan, on 13 November destroying the village of Es Samu. Over the next few months Israel made full use of physical violence as part of her unrelenting psychological warfare in an attempt to sow confusion, fear and division among the Arab nations and peoples. Concurrently with this, she worked hard on her chosen image of a small peace-loving state struggling for survival in face of the implacable hostility of a group of countries that all but encircled her. Thanks to her control of much of the Western media and to persisting frigidity between the Western alliance and leading Arab states, the plan worked. Israel enjoyed a free hand during the vital six days of the June war.

The main events may now be outlined. To persuade President Nasser and other Arab leaders of the imminence of a full scale attack, the Israelis launched a violent air strike on Syria in May 1967. So convincing was it that even the Russians believed Israel to be on the point of invading Syria and warned President Nasser to this effect. In that event he would have to go to the aid of the Syrians under the terms of the undertaking of 4 November. The presence of the UNEF on his border posed a problem. On 18 May, therefore, he requested a partial withdrawal of that force. The UN Secretary General U Thant refused to admit a partial withdrawal and insisted that the UNEF should either remain in its existing position or withdraw completely. President Nasser had no real alternative to accepting the latter option. Moreover, once his troops were in Sinai he was subjected to understandable and irresistible pressure from the other Arab states to impose a blockade on the Straits of Tiran in the Gulf of Aqaba. This would prevent the Israelis and their suppliers from using the port of Eilat, and so hopefully exert effective pressure on the Israelis to desist from their attacks on Syria and Jordan. Further practical expressions of mounting Arab unity were King Hussein's visit to Cairo, and the accession of both Jordan and Iraq to the existing defence arrangements between Egypt and Syria.

Israel's final preparations were now complete, and following the government changes of 31 May the hawks were in the ascendant in Tel Aviv with General Moshe Dayan as minister of war. Not only was Israel ready, but she could afford to wait no longer, for the Arabs had been careful to avoid any aggressive reactions after the closure of the Straits of Tiran, while the Egyptian vice-president Zacharia Mohieddin was about to leave for Washington in an attempt to defuse the situation; had the mission taken place it is arguable that Israel would have been denied the freedom of action she needed. On 5 June therefore she attacked. By 9 June, when the Security Council imposed a cease-fire, Israel had overrun Gaza, Sinai and the West Bank of the Jordan, and had virtually destroyed the airpower of Egypt, Iraq, Jordan and Syria. The manner of her success against the air forces of these countries highlights the contrast between Israel's calculated aggression and the essentially peaceful attitudes of her opponents, for a very high proportion of the Arab planes were in fact destroyed on the ground. Moreover, even after the official cease-fire, Israel prolonged the war for two days, only calling a halt to her expansion after she had secured Syria's Golan Heights.

Israel's achievement would have been impossible without the professional excellence of her military machine and the unceasing efforts of her leaders over the years in equipping and perfecting it. But this is only a partial explanation of her success. Military preparedness alone would not have brought her the spectacular gains in territory of June 1967, which depended on her consummate skill in the manipulation of the media, including an outstanding ability to profit from the mistakes of her opponents. As we saw, she exploited the coolness in the relations between a number of Arab countries and the West, and she struck before the projected Mohieddin mission had had a chance of dispelling some of the misunderstandings damaging US-Egyptian relations. The prevailing coolness admitted a predisposition in the West to believe the Israeli version of events, and either to ignore or to discount Arab disclaimers.

Thus, for example, President Nasser's request for a partial withdrawal of the UNEF was seen in the West as a form of aggression, whereas the fact of the matter was that the UN troops were stationed on Egyptian territory and could legally remain there only with the assent of the Egyptian government. The contrary and untrue impression, widespread in the West and fostered by Israel, that Egypt had somehow broken international law was on all fours with the misrepresentation of the facts of the nationalization of the Suez canal in 1956. Again, Israeli propaganda succeeded in obscuring the truth of the Huleh demilitarized zone. It had played up the declaration of a blockade of Eilat and played down the restraint of the Egyptians in implementing the blockade. Through vicious psychological warfare in the months before the June war, the Israelis deliberately aimed to provoke Arab governments, newsmen and individuals into unthinking anger of the sort which would express itself in declarations of hostility. These could then be quoted as evidence of the sinister and unrepentant anti-Jewish sentiments prevailing throughout the Arab World. Once again Tel Aviv could count on memories of Nazi anti-semitism to do the rest, aided of course by Israeli deceit.

We have already seen how the present author had drawn attention to the latter feature of Zionist policy at the time of the 1957 London meeting of international parliamentarians. Just as in October 1956 Ben Gurion had assured the world that he wished for nothing better than the chance of talking peace with President Nasser, so on becoming War Minister on 1 June 1967 Moshe Dayan declared that Israel was looking for a peaceful solution. To lend credence to this statement, the Israelis drew attention to the relaxed atmosphere of their army when on 3 June a number of foreign correspondents were presented with the spectacle of groups of soldiers enjoying themselves by the seaside. Two days later Dayan launched his *blitzkreig*. For the benefit of foreign, especially Western, opinion, he sought to justify the declaration of war with the explanation that over the radar he had seen the Arab planes setting out to attack Israel. This was a palpable impossibility for, as we have remarked, most of the Arab air power was destroyed on the ground. By apparently substantiating Israel's pose as the injured party, the deceit none the less achieved its purpose in preventing outside intervention during the critical first few days of the June war.

Against this cynical use of lies and deception, allied to Israel's unparalled competence in the use of the media, the Arabs could hardly hope to secure a sympathetic hearing in the West. Moreover they suffered from a decline in their own response to the psychological warfare. It is perfectly true that the Arabs had learnt valuable lessons in the sphere of information at the time of the Suez crisis, that they had attained new heights in the consolidation of morale, and that they had used the knowledge gained to good purpose in the fight against colonialism, as also in the task of internal reconstruction. But these preoccupations had to a degree distracted attention away from Israeli propaganda. For example, after about 1962 Cairo Radio had been largely concerned with the projection of Egypt's five year plan for economic development and prosperity. There were perfectly sound reasons for this diversion of attention. The tasks facing the Arabs at home were so great and pressing that it would have been impossible to have maintained the information machinery on the war footing of 1956. To have attempted to do so might in a sense have helped Israel, inasmuch as it would have risked delaying the economic progress of countries like Egypt. Even so, the fact remains that when the June 1967 crisis broke it found the Arab media unprepared.

All too often irresponsible bombast did duty for carefully calculated information responses to Israeli provocation. For example, immediately before the Six-Day War Egypt claimed to be the most powerful country in the Middle East. A few extremists even went so far as to state that Israel would be thrown into the sea and Jewish women and children deported to Europe. When compared with Moshe Dayan's peaceful pretensions, statements such as these did irreparable harm to the Arab cause, appearing as they did to vindicate Zionist accusations of implacable Arab hatred.

At the same time the Egyptian authorities seemed to have lost their touch in the matter of censorship. During 1956 they had used it sparingly, and, except where secrecy was vital, had tended to welcome the fullest exposure of facts and events, as evidenced by the facilities generously made available to foreign newsmen, even those from France and Britain. In 1967 on the other hand journalists were subjected to petty restrictions. Yet at the same time information likely to benefit the enemy was allowed to leak out. Egypt therefore suffered the unpopularity inseparable from the restriction of news, while losing some of the advantages of censorship in terms of her own security. For example, the French newspaper *France Soir* headlined the allegation that Egypt had launched the June war. This was not due to any dishonesty on the part of the newspaper, but was rather the result of the denial of essential facts to the Western press. We must remember too that communications between Egypt and the outside world were disrupted throughout the six days of hostilities, and that consequently only those reports which were released by Israeli sources were readily available. On the other hand, insufficient attention to vital security interests played straight into Israeli hands. This was in fact acknowledged by Moshe Dayan, who observed:

> "We have benefited from the material which was published by the press of the enemy. Thanks to such material, we set the timing of our attack on Egyptian airports at 9 a.m."

The explanation of this remarkable admission lies in the fact that some articles appearing in Egyptian newspapers and magazines before the June war had indicated that all the senior and junior officers of the Egyptian air force usually took breakfast together at the same time each morning.

While Israel was able to piece together a valuable picture of Egypt's military capacity, the Arabs were all too often in the dark about their opponent. For this reason, and because the Arabs lacked a co-ordinated system of information, it is not surprising that Israeli propaganda met with few serious challenges. Unlike that of the Arabs, Israel's information machinery was both consistent and responsive to diplomatic and military demands. The contrast between the two systems makes it easier to understand why much of the outside world accepted the manifestations of a blatant and calculated expansionism. It goes far to explaining how British public opinion could harbour feelings of friendly neutrality for a government which had just admitted to its ranks the erstwhile leader of the Stern Gang, Menachem Begin, notorious for his part in the acts of terrorism against the British in Palestine twenty years before. Friendly neutrality was of course the sentiment most calculated to ensure the success of months and years of Israeli planning. Adroit propaganda guaranteed that friendly neutrality would be available in generous measure at precisely the moment when it was most needed. Goaded beyond endurance, Arab counter-propaganda seemed to be in complete disarray. Not only did it give way to wild emotional threats, but it contradicted itself. It even lost sight of the basic truth of 5 June 1967 when statements were issued wrongly admitting Arab responsibility for the outbreak of war. In the public relations field June 1967 seemed to mark the nadir of Arab fortunes *vis à vis* Israel. Zionism now harvested the fruits of its positive propaganda and of Arab information failures; for example Israel published a collection of the various exaggerated and threatening Arab declarations. Militarily the prospect looked just as bleak. Despite false reports by the Arab command under Field Marshal Amer, the extent of the disaster could not be concealed, and on 9 June President Nasser announced his resignation in a nationwide television broadcast.

(b) Recovery

As the Arab people listened to President Nasser's resignation speech on the evening of 9 June 1967 they could have been forgiven feelings of despair. They seemed to be alone in a disapproving or indifferent world: America's hostility had been obvious even before Egypt broke off diplomatic relations after the Israeli attack; Russia, though concerned, could not risk a major international incident; even the United Nations appeared to have shrugged off the series of Israeli slights to international authority when U Thant precipitately ordered the complete withdrawal of the UNEF. Israel's armed might had all but destroyed the armies and air forces of four Arab nations, her troops were firmly ensconced in Sinai and Gaza, and on Jordan's West Bank, and they commanded Syria's Golan Heights; her government was determined to retain the gains of the past six days. For the Egyptians the immediate task was not so much the recovery of lost territory as the organization of defence against further Israeli advances. The country was in the gravest danger. Even if it could be averted, there remained the longer term problem as to how the armed forces could be restored to normal strength, after the dramatic blows just suffered, and in a situation of near bankruptcy resulting from the loss of the revenues of the now blocked Suez Canal. Underlining the tragedy, the anti-Arab broadcasts from the several clandestine radio stations went on; though, given the prevailing indifference or animosity of much international opinion, the broadcasts amounted to a virtual propaganda over-kill. In the circumstances an uncommitted observer could hardly have quarrelled with Moshe Dayan's confidence in hourly awaiting a call from Cairo offering surrender. To such an observer, defeatism, far from being inadmissible, might have looked like plain common sense.

At this desperate moment a wonderful thing happened. The entire Egyptian nation seemed to act of one accord in demanding the withdrawal of President Nasser's resignation. No sooner was the televised speech over, than, heedless of the risks from possible Israeli air raids, thousands of citizens poured into the streets in unmistakable support of their President. So overwhelming and spontaneous was this demonstration, and so obvious its message, that there can be no question of its having been stage managed. It was the supreme vindication of a leadership built on foundations far more reliable than mere charisma, for, as we saw in our fourth chapter, charismatic leadership as a formative element of public opinion is highly vulnerable to any hint of failure. Gamal Abdel Nasser arguably possessed charisma to a greater degree than any other leader since the Second World War, with the possible exceptions of de Gaulle, Kennedy, Mao and Nehru. But, like them, he possessed more enduring qualities of greatness. His claims to the trust and affection of his people were solidly based on massive and tangible material benefits, as well as on his masterly appeal to their imagination, and on his success in inculcating a sense of pride and purpose in their destiny, both as Egyptians and as Arabs, where these things had barely existed before. His care for public relations now brought its appropriate reward. The people, in whom he had so unstintingly reposed his trust, now returned that trust in full measure at Egypt's hour of need. Miraculous as they may have appeared to outside observers, the events of the evening of 9 June possessed a valid explanation in the context of opinion formation. Accurately sensing the demands of the national will, President Nasser agreed to remain at the helm. Next day to a man the National Assembly endorsed the nation's overwhelming declaration of confidence in their leader.

President Nasser's willingness to change his mind was itself evidence of the fact that at worst the situation was less than hopeless. Had there been no possible chance of a recovery, President Nasser, as the realist that he was, would have insisted on making room for a successor less universally regarded as the champion of Arab unity against the forces of imperialism and Zionism.

Indeed, such thoughts may have been present in his original intention, announced during the course of his televised speech, of handing over to Zacharia Mohieddin, whose mission to the US had been prevented by the outbreak of war on 5 June, and whose diplomatic skill might yet have succeeded in softening hawkish pro-Israeli attitudes among the Americans. The popular manifestation just described showed that all was not necessarily lost. The public had taken the first step in showing that the old morale of 1956 lived on. Here was practical proof of the quality of the government's public relations since 1952.

Thanks to its sure touch in both educating and learning from the people, Egypt's will to defend the gains of the Revolution and the interests of the Arab peoples was unbroken. Despite the imperfections and distractions that had become evident in the handling of the national media since about 1962, and despite the obfuscation and shock resulting from Israel's triumph on the battlefield, the situation was far from hopeless. With the nation solidly behind him, President Nasser could count on a wholehearted response to the fresh efforts and sacrifices demanded by the task that lay ahead, and he knew that his people would make the most of the ultimately promising features inherent in the existing situation.

Although few enough, these features might in the long term be turned to good account. Apart from the basic soundness of the national morale, there was the prospect of outside aid, partly from those Arab states which had not suffered material loss from Israel, partly from the Soviet bloc, which could be relied upon to resist US-Zionist domination of the Eastern Mediterranean by any means short of major international confrontation. Looking further ahead, it was reasonable to anticipate an eventual turning of the tide of Western opinion away from its present admiration for Israel.

The sheer scale of the latter's June War triumph left no doubt that Israel had emerged as a first class military power. By no stretch of the imagination could the Israelis maintain their old image of a small, peaceloving and vulnerable people threatened by the military might of their neighbours. In terms of international public opinion, including opinion in the West, Israel had lost an asset that had served her well in the past, namely the natural and very human feeling of sympathy for the underdog. She might hope to retain some of the pre-existing feelings of admiration for the skill and determination which had made her success possible. But these were wasting assets. They could be preserved only by the most sensitive and adept public relations with the outside world, and by carefully avoiding any hint of self-satisfaction or arrogance by Tel Aviv. On this count Israel failed completely to gauge the sense of international opinion. The comments of her press and the declarations of her leaders left the world in no doubt as to her mood of aggressive over-confidence and to her adamant refusal of any reasonable solution to Palestinian and related problems. For example, on 12 June Radio Israel reported thus:

> "Levy Eshkol declared that Israel, which won the war against the Arabs and now occupies new strategic lands, will never go back to previous frontiers nor the state of insecurity."

A week later on 18 June the London Sunday newspaper *The Observer* revealed Israeli intransigence to a wider audience when it quoted Abba Eban, Israel's foreign minister, as saying that:

> "Israel refuses to submit to any General Assembly resolution on the return of her forces to the pre-war frontiers."

In the euphoria of June 1967 statements of the sort were perhaps understandable. But leaders like Eshkol and Eban set the tone for an attitude that was to persist to the war of 6 October 1973, and which did much to dissipate the fund of Western goodwill available to Israel before, during and immediately after the Six-Day War.

In the pervading gloom of the evening of 9 June 1967, President Nasser was sufficiently prescient to analyse these long-term potential benefits for the Egyptian and Arab struggle. Confirmed in his leadership by the undeniable force of public opinion, he and his government lost no time in seeking to turn the situation to advantage.

From Cairo's point of view the immediate task was defence. Surrender to Israel being out of the question, the Egyptians had to be prepared for a further Israeli onslaught. Even after the UN had managed to impose a cease-fire, there was no guarantee that it would be respected by Israel. As a matter of the greatest urgency, both in her own interests and in those of the Arab World as a whole, Egypt had to repair and restore as much of her military capability as she could. To this end, she looked hopefully to Russia, whose interests also required a rapid correction of the military balance in the area. Complete restoration was for the time being impossible, for it would have required a massive re-training programme such as could not be undertaken in a few weeks or even months. Short of this, it was possible to redress the imbalance in terms of munitions and other defensive hardware, and this the Russians had done by the end of 1967. The UN's cease-fire, coupled with this massive Soviet help, solved Egypt's immediate defence problem and enabled her to resist Israeli pressures for formal and unconditional surrender.

The next task was almost equally pressing, for Arab unity and determination, and the material means to sustain them demanded rehabilitation no less than the Egyptian. In this work the leaders were able to draw on the resources of those states which had not suffered the military blows inflicted on Egypt, Iraq, Jordan and Syria. The suggestion for a new Arab summit conference came from King Hussein of Jordan, and was enthusiastically endorsed by President Nasser. The conference took place in Khartoum in August and September. Thus, within three months of an apparently crushing defeat, the Arab governments demonstrated to their own people and to the world that they too had the will to preserve their unity and their sense of shared destiny, in spite of all that the Zionists could do, and demonstrated also that they had not abandoned the Palestinians.

It was a pity that Syria was not represented at Khartoum. Yet her refusal to attend could not be attributed to any weakening of her resolve, but was rather due to Syrian fears that the conference might result in a sell-out to Israel. Although of course no such solution was contemplated, we may sympathize with the Syrian attitude of resolution, which is especially commendable in view of the barrage of hate and aggression to which she had been subjected by Israel ever since the clashes in the Lake Huleh demilitarized zone.

The decisions taken at Khartoum were of the greatest significance for the future. They marked a new stage in the acceptance of a common cause by all the Arab nations, and did so in a highly practical manner. The wealth of Kuwait, Libya and Saudi Arabia was willingly placed at the disposal of the states that had suffered the most grievous damage in the June war. In the case of Egypt these subventions, made on a continuing basis, amounted to an annual revenue almost equivalent to the income from the Suez Canal dues, which of course had ceased with the blocking of the international waterway during the course of hostilities. This generosity of the richer Arab governments had a value transcending the practical alleviation of pressing financial needs, for it demonstrated to the Arab peoples, to the Israelis and to the world the extent of the new and in some respects greater Arab determination to maintain inalienable rights in face of Zionist intransigence. Properly projected by the Arab information media, this determination had a great impact on opinion in all these areas. And not least in the West, where the new steadiness and resolution of the Arabs contrasted favourably with the arrogant blandishments of the Israelis.

Before the year was out the Arabs had gained a further accession of strength of great value to their continuing efforts against Zionist propaganda. The United Nations became rightly alarmed at the deterioration of a situation which in a way stemmed from U Thant's premature removal of their force in Sinai in May, and which after the June war involved massive increases to the number of Palestinian refugees, and continued fighting across the Suez Canal in defiance of the UN's cease-fire. On 22 November therefore the UN clarified their position through a resolution of the Security Council. This

Resolution 242 of 1967 declared that the Israelis should withdraw "from territories occupied in the recent conflict", that freedom of navigation should be guaranteed in the Suez Canal, that there should be "a just settlement of the refugee problem". The resolution went on to request the UN Secretary-General "to designate a Special Representative to proceed to the Middle East to establish and maintain contacts with the States concerned in order to promote agreement and assist efforts to achieve a peaceful and accepted settlement in accordance with the provisions and principles in this resolution."

In implementation of this request, U Thant charged the Swedish ambassador to the USSR, Gunnar Jarring, with the task of bringing about an accord between Israel on the one side and Egypt and Jordan on the other. While refraining from strident denunciation of any party, Resolution 242, by stressing the Israeli occupation and the refugee problem, could leave no doubt in the mind of impartial observers that the UN regarded Israel as primarily responsible for the continuing Middle Eastern crisis. This clearly expressed view of the international body, coupled with the obstacles subsequently placed by Israel to the implementation of Gunnar Jarring's mission, convinced more and more people in the West of Israel's guilt, thereby much assisted the coming new receptivity of British and French opinion to Arab information, and led to an unwonted suspicion in those countries of the content of Israeli propaganda.

By the end of 1967, therefore, it is fair to say that the Arabs had weathered the particular storms arising from the June war. The prospect was incomparably brighter than that which had faced them on the evening of 9 June. Great challenges remained, and the refugee problem in particular had been cruelly extended by the events of June, but the change was one of degree. Essentially these root problems had existed before the Six-Day War. The important fact was that the major new threats to unity and even to national integrity had been contained, that the Arab defence structure was well on the way to rehabilitation, that the Arab information services, temporarily thrown into confusion, were now again operational and able to develop the outstanding competence which many of them had revealed in earlier years. Looking back to the dark months of 1967, a Cairo Radio broadcast of 19 January 1971 brought out the resilience and determination of the Egyptian people, attitudes derived in great measure from the honest and professional use of the media by the Egyptian authorities over the fifteen years after the Revolution. In this context the following quotation from the January 1971 broadcast is illuminating:

"We will not deny before ourselves, nor before others, that our nation faced a serious setback on 5 June 1967. We lost a battle and had the honour and courage to face the setback and also to face others with reality. We did not deceive or delude, we refused to bury our heads in the sand like ostriches, or pretend that the arrow directed against us did not wound or cause pain. We admitted that we lost a battle, but at the same time we have shown, out of conviction, that we did not lose the war. This was not a pretence on our part, it was the reality concerning the will, the potentialities, the powers and the preparedness of our nation.

"The *fait accompli*, at a certain moment, cannot change the face of the great truth if we can spotlight this truth, and if we possess, in the moment of danger, the strong nerves that can bear the shock and distinguish between what is shallow and casual and what is natural and deep, and has the powers of perseverance and continuity.

"We have lost a battle in the war between us and Israel. This is possible, but we did not lose the whole war because this is contrary to nature, history and progress. The living evidence of this was the stand of the multitudes of our Arab nation behind our immortal leader Gamal Abdel Nasser on 9 and 10 June 1967. This stand was not a passionate outburst, it was a genuine expression of the nature of things. The precise interpretation of this stand was that the Arab multitudes told Gamal Abdel Nasser: never mind a stumble on the road. Let us stand up, start anew and proceed together, believing in God, in ourselves, and in the possibility of achieving victory, ready to bear all its costs and responsibilities.

"Since that day Gamal Abdel Nasser defined our conception of our basic commitments in two points which were accepted by all. The people gave all that they had of money, work and blood in their upholding of these two points, which are as follows:

"*One*—The necessity of restoring all territories occupied since the 1967 aggression and the inevitability of withdrawing all occupation troops from them. These territories as Gamal Abdel Nasser enumerated them before the populace of our nation are Arab

Jerusalem, the West Bank of the Jordan, the Gaza Strip, the Syrian Heights and Sinai. We shall never accept any bargaining concerning our land, for the land of any people represents their national honour, as Gamal Abdel Nasser told us.

"*Two*—The necessity of protecting the Palestinian people's rights. We cannot and it is not in our power to speak on their behalf because we cannot concede or give anything up in their name."

Under the guiding hand of President Nasser, the Egyptian and Arab peoples were by the end of 1967 assured of recovery in all spheres, not least in that of opinion formation at home and abroad. Exactly the right note of confidence and resolution had been struck. The grim realities were admitted, but so too was a measure of cautious optimism, an equally indispensable ingredient for ultimate success.

Gamal Abdel Nasser had another three years of life left to him. These he devoted to the consolidation of the recovery begun on the night of 9 June 1967, to the solution of new problems such as those arising from the clash between the Jordanian army and the Palestinians in September 1970, to the improvement of relations with the outside world. The work was continued, and is still being carried on, by his successors in Egypt and elsewhere in the Arab World. At the present time a measure of success has been achieved, undreamt of in the near despair of June 1967. We must now direct our attention to the manner and extent of this progress, which was secured against mounting international awareness of the Palestinian problem. We shall conclude this chapter by considering the changing situation of the Palestinians themselves.

(c) Some foreign misconceptions removed

The years since the Six-Day War have seen a substantial decline in the impact of Israeli propaganda outside the Middle East. This is the more remarkable when one recalls the West's overwhelmingly favourable reception of the Zionist cause in June 1967. For a variety of reasons, the Arabs were at last granted a hearing by those responsible for the Western media. By this means they succeeded not only in removing much of the misunderstanding bedevilling their interests in the past, but they were also able to reforge old links of friendship with leading Western powers, most notably with Britain and France. This was done without putting at risk the normal good relations with the Soviet bloc and with much of the Third World.

While mutual distrust remained a feature of dealings with the US, relations could hardly deteriorate below the point reached in June 1967, and in some respects even they improved. In endeavouring to assess and account for these changes, we shall see that special reasons applied to particular cases. At the same time, however, certain characteristics of the period made for a relaxation of tension. In general terms conditions were becoming more favourable. Through the information media and in other ways, the Arabs were often able to benefit greatly from their improved opportunities.

For the root cause of this brighter prospect we have to turn our attention once again to Israel. The uncompromising attitude epitomized in the declarations of Levi Eshkol and Abba Eban[1] in mid-June 1967 might at first have been dismissed as little more than expressions of natural euphoria following a great victory. However, so tolerant an interpretation would not stand up for long against the repeated affirmation of a hard line by Israel's leaders. The patience of all but Zionism's most confirmed devotees could not help wearing thin in face of the sustained intransigence of Tel Aviv, and of its lack of co-operation with the Jarring mission established as a result of the Security Council's Resolution 242 of 22 November 1967.

Increasingly, floating opinion in the West gained the impression that the main obstacles to a settlement came from Israel rather than from the Arabs. With this tendency came a growing inclination to place the blame for the continuing crisis on Israel. In a sense, therefore, the onus of proof had been partially removed from the Arabs. The longer the settlement was delayed, the more opinion ceased to regard Israel as an underdog deserving of its sympathy if not its active assistance.

As a reaction to a belligerent refusal of compromise, the new direction of much Western opinion was natural enough. In the conditions of the later sixties, however, it was reinforced by a further element. The period was marked by a relatively new phenomenon of global dimensions, for these were years of protest against established

[1] See page 233 above.

systems and ideas. The reasons for this protest are complex and perhaps not yet completely understood. Nor are they relevant to our present study. What does concern us is the form of the protest. It did not aspire to substitute any carefully elaborated political or social mechanism for the existing arrangements. Rather it sought to draw attention to the shortcomings of those arrangements, with a view either to reforming them, or, as was the case with the more extreme protesters, to destroying them altogether. There was little cohesion. At one level there was peaceful agitation for greater freedom and constructive change. At another the movement assumed violent and even anarchic forms. It confounded the normal political divisions of left and right, for the protesters were as critical of established communism, for example in China or Czechoslovakia, as they were of the more recognizable capitalistic enemy in France and Germany. In their eyes the main target was the *establishment*, irrespective of social or political labels.

Ultimately, of course, the establishments survived. With the defeat of the so-called *New Left* in Paris in May 1968 and of Alexander Dubček's more relaxed form of communism in Prague in August of the same year, the movement gradually lost momentum. But survival is one thing, triumph another. The memory of such a widespread attack on authority, of the doctrines of Che Guevara, of the Chinese Cultural Revolution, of the protests of British, French and Japanese activists, could not be brushed aside. Establishments, or at any rate the more far-sighted of them, heeded the warning and sought to remedy the malaise of which the protest had been a symptom. In other words, they recognized the value of good public relations, the necessity for better communications.

From the point of view of Israel's image, these developments were significant. Although the state was born in 1948 following Zionist agitation against the pre-existing Palestinian arrangements, the Israeli government had long before the Six-Day War become part of the establishment in the contemporary connotation of the term. In the political and ideological climate of the later sixties, therefore, Israel was identified, along with older states and traditional values, as part of an established system in need of drastic reform, if not liquidation. Since the protest movement cut across accepted political, national and regional frontiers, it was only to be expected that the attitudes of Tel Aviv should be questioned by many people in the Western countries which had hitherto been among Israel's staunchest supporters. Put another way, the Arabs could not fail to profit from the self-questioning which has gone on since the mid-sixties among both rulers and ruled in much of the outside world.

In addition to these general reasons for a greater predisposition towards the Arab case, the same period provides special reasons for improved relations with particular Western states. As we have said, these apply especially to the two countries, France and Britain, whose long association with the Arab World had been temporarily embittered by decolonization. In the case of France the process had been the more painful. All the same, it had been completed rather earlier. With the achievement of Algerian independence in 1962, there was no remaining colonialist impediment to a resumption of friendship. Indeed President Nasser had a high regard for President de Gaulle, who had educated his compatriots to an acceptance of the new conditions of international relationships, and whose rejection of over-close military links with the US seemed to echo Egypt's own policy of avoiding excessive ties with either of the Cold War blocs. But solid friendship with France was out of the question so long as that country continued to supply Israel, whose air force was mainly equipped with French Mirages and Mystères. The real turning-point therefore came in June 1967 when, alone of the major Western powers, France condemned the Israeli attack. Since that time France has refused armaments to Israel. Within days of the Israeli attack of 28 December 1968 on Beirut airport the embargo was tightened to include spare parts. It is true that in the following December five fast gunboats, originally constructed in France for Israel but later caught by the embargo, found their way from the French port of Cherbourg to Haifa. But this was done under the guise of a sale to a third party, a company registered in Panama, and in defiance of the intentions of the French government, which took a very serious view of the affair and subsequently instituted a careful enquiry. As a result of the new French policy Franco-Arab relations have become highly cordial. In January 1970, for example, France agreed to conclude a deal with Libya for the sale of over one hundred Mirage aircraft.

With the improvement has come a greater willingness of the

French media and hence of French public opinion to consider the Arab case, and a parallel disinclination to accept Zionist propaganda at face value.

For Britain the process began somewhat later. Decolonization took longer and it was only in November 1967 that Britain removed her forces from Aden. Till then British opinion was influenced by the somewhat romanticized version of the exploits of their troops in Aden provided by television and in the Press. The attitude of Harold Wilson's Labour administration from 1964 to 1970 tended to favour Israel. Resentment at the nationalization of the Suez Canal back in 1956 was not yet forgotten. Yet even in Britain adverse reaction to continuing Israeli intransigence was bound to come.

Already in 1967 the British foreign secretary, George Brown, had denounced Israel's continued occupation of Jerusalem, thereby revealing that the Labour government was less than unanimous in its general sympathy for the Zionists. Again it was Britain, and particularly Lord Caradon, Britain's delegate to the UN, which played the major role in the deliberations leading to the Security Council's Resolution 242 of 22 November 1967. Once Britain had taken the decision to withdraw from Aden, the way was clear for a re-establishment of the formal diplomatic relations which had been broken off in December 1965, and the former ambassador Sir Harold Beeley resumed his commission in Cairo. Since then, and especially since the departure of the military presence from the Arabian Gulf in 1971, cordiality and friendship have developed steadily, a process both illustrated and encouraged in no small measure by the popularity of the Tutenkhamen exhibition held in London in 1972, the fiftieth anniversary of the archaeological discoveries of Howard Carter. The fact that the exhibition took place at all is a measure of the enormous advances which had taken place in Egypto-British understanding since the June war, for it was of course entirely dependent upon the willingness of the Egyptian government to lend Britain some of the Cairo Museum's most treasured possessions. The enormous success of the Tutenkhamen exhibition and its wide coverage in the Press and on television, even the issue of a special British postage stamp to mark the occasion, can have left very few British people unexposed to this particular Egyptian influence.

With exposure came curiosity, a desire to learn more about Egypt and about the Arab World of which she is a part. Given the new interest, it was inevitable that British public opinion had to take some account of Israel as an inseparable feature of the problems of the Arab World. It was equally inevitable that, while still largely motivated by simple curiosity, many British people should have begun either to question the premises on which their previous acceptance of Israel had been based, or to have been encouraged out of their earlier inertia on this topic. To some the very fact of the exhibition may have pointed an instructive contrast between, on the one hand, the civilized relationship between two governments which had brought about this cultural event, and, on the other hand, the rabid vandalism of which Zionism was capable: instances of the latter were provided by the lunatic act of arson at Jerusalem's Al-Aqsa mosque in August 1969, and by the more insidious desecration of that city inflicted by Israeli building developments.

While rightly stressing these improvements and the greater scope for the Arab media which they have brought about, we must avoid the assumption that all sources of misunderstanding have been removed. The roots of Zionism are deep. The plant has been cut back but not destroyed. Given favourable conditions, it could blossom once again as vigorously as ever. In this connection it is probably fair to say that a major threat to a continuing improvement in relations between the Arabs and much of the outside world is today posed by the activities of certain Palestinian guerilla organizations.

The typical Britisher or Frenchman is now basically neutral in the quarrels between the Arabs and Israel. From the Arab point of view the change, and it is a vital one, is that from being largely hostile in the period before June 1967, this neutrality today inclines towards acceptance or at least understanding of the Arab case. But the balance between the two species of neutrality, and hence between acceptance of Arab as opposed to Israeli information, is still delicate. Natural revulsion against the tragic visible effects of some guerilla activity could easily tip the balance once again in Israel's favour. That this has so far not happened is a tribute to the success of Arab information in making public opinion in the West aware of the Palestinian despair, of the root causes of violence, of the calculated terrorism practised by the Zionists. These are key factors in any consideration of the role of the Arab media and of their chances of bringing about a peaceful solution to the present conflict. We shall consider them in more detail at the end of this chapter.

Western public opinion cannot be shaped entirely by the information disseminated from Arab sources, however well intentioned and factually accurate. Even in today's happier circumstances of détente, strategic considerations are still an ingredient of the totality of public opinion in, for example, Federal Germany and France. Contemporary sentiments of benevolent neutrality towards the Arabs could all too readily give way to suspicion and distrust, if it were felt that a major Arab country was prepared to admit the USSR or China to a disproportionate strategic influence. In such circumstances, the West might consider itself obliged to regard Israel, with all its faults, as once again its main defence against undue Soviet interference in the Middle East.

Most Arab countries of course have no intention of allowing strategic advantages of this sort to the USSR or to any other power. But this is not the whole point. Opinion results from appearances as much as from realities, and appearances can be moulded by interested third parties, just as Zionist propaganda has in the past moulded them and created facts to suit its own purposes. Arab information must maintain a ceaseless vigil against the recurrence of such a message from Tel Aviv. Indeed over the past few years it has shown itself aware of the danger. Immediately after the Six-Day War Egypt had no alternative to ready acceptance of generous Russian aid in making up the losses of arms and other material suffered in June 1967. Vital considerations of national defence were at stake, and the Soviet assistance effectively deterred further Israeli advances towards Cairo. But these arms shipments were merely a stop-gap to meet an emergency. In the longer term Egypt and the other Arab countries which fought the June war needed training facilities to make up their losses of manpower and to enable them to use the sophisticated new weapons of war. Given the prevailing coolness in her relations with the West, Egypt again found herself obliged to look to Moscow. Over the next few years, it is true, she much improved her relations with France and Britain. But this did not solve her military problems. In September 1969 President Nixon provided Israel with American Phantoms. Against these powerful jet aircraft no defence system which Britain or France might have been willing to provide would have been adequate for Egypt's purposes. She needed the Russian SAM system of ground-to-air defence missiles. Their installation and the training by the Russians of the military personnel to man them was bound to take time.

Added to the already massive Russian participation in the completion of the Aswan High Dam and in the various industrial projects linked to it, this military involvement was seen as excessive by the Egyptian government. The longer it lasted, the more difficult they realized it would be to limit the effects of Israeli accusations about undue Soviet influence in the Arab World. Such influence was unwelcome to Egypt on two main counts. In the first place, it struck at the guiding principle of true neutrality which President Nasser had followed since the British evacuation of the Canal Zone and the projection of a Third World view at the Bandung Conference. In the second place, its continuation necessarily damaged Arab efforts to promote Western confidence and consequently subserved the aims of Zionist propaganda. Cairo therefore tolerated the presence of large numbers of Russian advisers only for as long as they were genuinely needed. But once this point was passed, President Anwar Sadat in July 1972 insisted that most of them should leave Egypt. This in no way implied ingratitude for the great assistance rendered by the USSR. It was merely the proper removal of a potentially excessive foreign influence, whose continued presence threatened to damage Egypt's essential requirement of friendship with as much of the world as possible. Another possible source of misunderstanding had been removed, and with it another opportunity for continued misrepresentation by the Zionist controlled press in Israel and elsewhere.

Even before the departure of the Russians, the extent of Egypt's success in establishing satisfactory relations with a number of leading powers was indicated by a Cairo Radio broadcast of 23 July 1971 in the following terms:

"The Soviet Union has honestly, and unconditionally, offered us aid without which we could never have withstood the four years in which we have stood fast until today. On the other hand America is giving Israel everything—everything unconditionally. Intelligence reports show that America is producing arms intended exclusively for the coming battle of Israel.

"As for political action, we would also like here to emphasize the role which the Soviet Union played and which is as important politically as it is militarily. Actually, since the aggression it has been standing by our side with the utmost sincerity. We should also like to emphasize the role of the non-aligned countries, and as an example we mention Yugoslavia, India and Ceylon, as well as that of the Islamic countries headed by Pakistan, and the stand taken by Western Europe, particularly France. In fact, we should like, from all our hearts, to greet President Pompidou and the people of France and their government on the stand which France, as a big power, has taken in support of right and justice.

"Britain, too, is definitely taking an improved stand, and as we said once before, there is no doubt that the Conservative·Party has in fact altered its policy from that of the Labour Party, in a truly courageous attitude."

This statement drew attention to impressive successes in international relations since the dark days of June 1967. Events had resoundingly vindicated the reciprocal trusts of the Egyptian people and their leadership. Gamal Abdel Nasser's faith had on that night of 9 June four years before shown a rare intuition and a sure touch. With public opinion solidly behind him, he knew that he could turn to advantage the few potentially promising features which stood out in an otherwise desperate state of affairs. As yet of course relations with the US left almost everything to be desired. But even there patience may have begun to wear thin in face of Israeli intractability.

In 1969–70 the US secretary of state, William Rogers, put forward a plan designed to secure the final cessation of the sporadic hostilities that had gone on across the canal ever since the Six-Day War, and to facilitate Gunnar Jarring's mission and the implementation of Security Council Resolution 242 of 1967. And later still, in August 1973, on replacing Rogers as secretary of state, Henry Kissinger sought to allay misgivings, when in answer to a newsman's question he stated that he would not allow his Jewish origins to interfere with what he saw as America's true foreign policy interests. Admittedly the response was vague enough to cover a multitude of intentions, but the fact that the question was put at all seemed to indicate a greater American awareness of the Arab case.

Moreover, increasing demands for fuel energy were bound before long to bring a greater American dependence on Middle East oil. With dependence would come the obligation to accommodate foreign policy to the just demands of the Arab oil suppliers. At that point American public opinion could not escape the logic that current Israeli intransigence ran directly counter to US interests. The measure of that intransigence was once again displayed in February 1971, when Tel Aviv utterly rejected President Sadat's offer of a settlement to be based on Israel's withdrawal to her pre-June 1967 boundaries, and to provide for the re-opening of the Suez Canal to international shipping.

(d) Further progress by the Arab media

The overwhelming demonstration of support for Gamal Abdel Nasser on the evening of 9 June 1967 showed that Egypt still possessed the prime requisite for success in terms of information. As we saw earlier in this chapter, this basic ingredient of confidence enabled the government to make the most of its few opportunities in an otherwise grim prospect, and within a relatively short time the image of Egypt and of the Arab World was on the way to recovery. Morale was sound, and it was the duty of the media to build on this sure foundation by carefully applying the various principles of effective presentation,[2] and especially that of instilling conviction at home and abroad of the justice of the Arab cause.

In this context it has to be admitted that the Egyptian information machinery continued for some years to fall short of what was expected of it. We have seen how after about 1962 its concentration on home affairs left the international running to the Israeli propagandists; how censorship and the various restrictions imposed on the circulation of Israeli literature denied the people access to important information about their opponents, in partial denial of the principle of presentation which requires a proper exegesis of the enemy's ideology; how exaggerated descriptions of Arab strength were

[2] See Chapter 8, pp. 189–193

substituted for necessary realism; how righteous anger against clever Zionist distortion led the Arabs to utter unintentioned threats and on occasion even to contradict themselves and admit to a belligerence of which they were in fact innocent.

Unfortunately these errors were not corrected as fully or as promptly as they might have been. Part of the explanation lies in the intense pressures which the Israelis and their friends continued to exert. The Egyptian and other Arab governments were faced with a conflict of priorities. Although by and large choosing wisely, and thus achieving the material recovery already described, the effort inevitably slowed down the process of recovery on the information front. But this is not a full explanation. The later sixties saw some disagreement in government circles over certain topics, particularly those relating to home affairs. The argument revolved largely over the impatience of Ali Sabry, chairman of the Arab Socialist Union,[3] at what he considered the government's half-hearted introduction of socialist measures. Gamal Abdel Nasser, with his sure feeling for the innately conservative attitude of much of the population, understood the dangers to national cohesion if too many changes were attempted too quickly. Regrettably this conflict between realism and the more doctrinaire stand of the Ali Sabry group distracted the attention of the information media from the more pressing conflict against Zionist propaganda in all its forms. In 1969, however, Ali Sabry was dismissed from his chairmanship of the ASU, and, though in the following year he became Egypt's Vice-President, his direct influence over the Information Administration was drawing to a close. The way was clear for a drastic overhaul of the machinery of information.

In May 1971 the present author had the privilege to be appointed Deputy Premier for Information, thus resuming his earlier direct association with the national media. On accepting this commission from President Sadat, he was enormously touched by the warmth of the welcome he received from the staff of the information ministry, many of whom had worked with him in the past; and he recalls how in the elation of the moment some of them went so far as to carry the car in which he was seated shoulder high to the entrance of the

[3] The ASU had since the National Charter of May 1962 been Egypt's main political body.

248

ministry building. To his mind, the real significance of this incident lay not so much in a personal triumph as in its evidence of a desire to get back to the true purposes of the information function, in line with the Six Principles of the Revolution, after the lack of proper direction and the obfuscation of the past eight or nine years.

Since then Egypt's information services have striven hard to observe the sound principles which stood the nation in such good stead at the time of the Suez crisis. Along with a renewed sense of direction and with a greater appreciation of the true partnership with the people inseparable from good public relations, there has since 1971 developed a mood at the same time more purposeful and more relaxed.

The latter quality is important. It has encouraged a greater emphasis on logical argument and an acceptance of the truth that the outside world is seldom persuaded by emotional outbursts of the sort that marred the Arab message just before the Six-Day War. Relaxation has also wrought a change in attitudes to censorship. In 1956 the relative freedom accorded to foreign journalists paid high dividends in the form of widespread international sympathy. This contrasted sharply with the misrepresentation suffered by Egypt in 1967, as a result of the paucity of information available to foreign newsmen from Middle Eastern sources outside Israel. No small part of the improvement in the Arab media's impact after 1971 has resulted from a more sparing recourse to censorship by the Egyptian information authorities. The cables of foreign correspondents are now normally free of this inhibition. Egyptians themselves can read Israeli literature, for it is realized that both national morale and the national response to hostile propaganda can only be improved by a sound working knowledge of the ideology and ambition of the enemy. Strict censorship is therefore reserved for circumstances where national security really is at stake. As we shall see in our next chapter, the new policy brought solid advantages during and after the war of 6 October 1973.

The press, the cinema, radio and television have since 1971 concerted their skills in the service of unity and progress. The previous year had been a testing time, for, following the Jordanian army's action against the Palestinian guerillas in September 1970, there was a real threat to Arab cohesion. This of course could only have benefited Israel. Gamal Abdel Nasser's last great service to the Egyptian and Arab causes was rendered at the Arab summit conference held in Cairo that same month, when he prevented the delegates from damaging their common interests through mutual recrimination. Worn out by his tireless exertions, President Nasser died on 28 September 1970 immediately after the conference.

The healing task which he had begun was pursued by the Egyptian media in the years that followed. Nor did they neglect domestic affairs. Just as they had educated public opinion as to the necessity of agrarian and other reforms after the 1952 Revolution, so now they spread information and knowledge about birth control and better farming methods. A plan has been worked out for wide TV ownership through government assisted purchase. Meanwhile public access to radio and TV programmes is ensured through the installation of loudspeakers and television screens in public places. The whole process has of course been much accelerated, and indeed rendered possible, by the Aswan High Dam, which it is hoped will shortly bring electricity to the whole of Egypt.

Egypt's broadcasting capability has kept pace with these plans. In 1971 radio transmissions achieved 5168 kilowatts, of which 2818 were on medium wave and 2350 on short wave, as opposed to a total of 72 kilowatts, on medium wave only, twenty years before. As far as television is concerned, one network transmits programmes on two channels to Cairo, Alexandria and the Delta, while the other network makes the first channel available to Upper Egypt. Nor have the needs of other Arab countries and the world beyond been forgotten. We saw in our seventh chapter[4] that great strides had already been made in the creation of programmes for particular countries, in the installation of broadcasting stations in various parts of the Arab World, in the provision of training facilities. For example, a total of 1,247 people attended the sixty training courses held successively till the end of the June 1971 by Egypt's Radio Corporation. Of these 1,018 worked for Cairo Radio and 229 came from other Arab countries.

An exciting development was the installation in 1972 of a system of broadcasts to Israel. The system cannot be jammed. By this means

[4] See pages 166–167

the peoples of Palestine are apprised of facts which the Israeli authorities have hitherto sought to conceal: the nature of the conflict as essentially between the Arabs and Zionism, not between Arabs and those Jews who were in Palestine before 1948; the expansionist plans of the Tel Aviv government; the defeats in that government's social and economic policies including the depressed conditions of the so-called Oriental Jews; the Israeli leadership's use of the threat of war as a means of covering up these shortcomings; the nature of Israel's Middle Eastern policy as dictated by US strategic needs rather than by the welfare of the Jews themselves; the contradictions of the Israeli leadership; the desecration of Jerusalem.

Recent developments suggest that this comprehensive information service beamed at Israel is beginning to have a considerable impact. Certainly many Israelis are becoming critical of their government. In 1972 for example quite large numbers of Jews showed genuine sympathy for the Arabs by joining them in the demonstrations which took place in Jerusalem over the continued occupation of the two Christian Arab villages of Berem and Ikrit on the Lebanese border, from which the Israeli authorities had expelled the inhabitants—allegedly as a temporary measure—as far back as 1948. Again from 1972 we may cite the address delivered in London on 6 September on the subject of *Civil Rights in Israel Today* by Dr Israel Shahak.[5] From both the Jewish and more particularly the Israeli standpoint, Dr Shahak's reputation would seem to be impeccable. A senior lecturer at Jerusalem's Hebrew University, he suffered under the Nazis, survived the horrors of the Belsen concentration camp, and, both as a Pole and as a Jew, must have welcomed the promise of a new life when he landed in Palestine in 1944. His speech on 6 September 1972 could not therefore fail to bring home to many British people in the large audience the parallels between the attitudes of Israel's existing leadership and those of the Nazis, from whose persecution so many Jews had sought refuge in Palestine. In particular Dr Shahak gave concrete examples, based on individual case studies, of the economic and other forms of harassment practised against the Arabs in Israel, and of the relentless pressure applied against non-

[5] The address was published by The Committee for Justice in the Middle East, London.

orthodox Jews with the object of securing their forcible conversion
to Judaism. A dispassionate observer could hardly fail to conclude
that there must be something seriously amiss with a government and
a philosophy which could antagonize a man of Dr Shahak's standing,
whose past sufferings would seem to make him so representative of
Israel's founding fathers.

Beyond the Middle East, too, opposition to Israel is growing. We
saw earlier in this chapter how French and British benevolent
neutrality towards the Zionists gradually turned to impatience as
those countries developed a better understanding of the Arab case.
Other countries have recently shown themselves even more hostile,
Chad and Uganda, for example, expelling Israelis from their territories. Nor must we forget the anti-Zionist stand of a number of the
most eminent members of world Jewry. Much of this goes back a
long way, for Zionism was from the beginning regarded by some
Jews as a threat rather than a means of salvation; they feared that the
existence of a Jewish state would play into the hands of anti-semitic
groups who would be only too glad of this plausible excuse to expel
Jewish minorities from the countries in which they had settled. Coming down to more recent times, after the establishment of the state of
Israel, the world-famous Jewish scientist Professor Albert Einstein
wrote in 1950:

> "I should much rather see reasonable agreement with the Arabs on
> the basis of living together in peace than the creation of a Jewish
> State . . . Judaism resists the idea of a Jewish State."[6]

An American non-Zionist rabbi, Dr Elmer Berger, described in a
letter to two of his friends what he felt after visiting a few of the
places that harboured the Palestinian refugees in Jordan:

> " . . . I am profoundly, humiliatingly—perhaps unforgettably—
> ashamed of being a Jew . . . Surely—here at least—truth is stranger
> than fiction."[7]

[6] Albert Einstein, *Out of My Later Years*, New York, Philosophical Library, 1950,
p. 263.
[7] Elmer Berger, *Who knows better must say so!*, New York, American Council for
Judaism, p. 65.

Again, in a speech delivered to the Irish-Arab Society in Dublin on 5 February 1970, Dr Elmer Berger said:

" . . . the problem in Palestine is—above all—a problem which the politicians, the power-structure automatons, the bureaucrats, the computers have created by de-humanizing a large segment of mankind. In the Middle East today, this de-humanizing process has produced a geo-political threat to peace of far greater and more frightening portent than in Vietnam. That threat has escalated for more than fifty years because the politicians who run our lives have preferred neat and de-humanizing formulas to the irrepressible spirit of man."

The American Jew, and former Zionist, Moshe Menuhin, says in the preface to his book denouncing Zionism and its leaders:

"I have entitled this book *The Decadence of Judaism in Our Time*, but I almost prefer an earlier title, *Jewish Nationalism—A Monstrous Crime and Curse*. Please take your choice. Both titles mean the same thing to me."[8]

Criticism expressed in such strong terms and coming from such respected sources can hardly fail to stimulate more self-examination by ordinary Israelis, and in time to erode the belligerent confidence of the authorities in Tel Aviv. As it is, the euphoria of June 1967 is a thing of the past in Israel today. Well before the Fourth Arab-Israeli War in October 1973, growing numbers of citizens came to question the premises on which their state was founded, and on which their leaders justified three wars in less than a generation. In time the atmosphere of siege will become intolerable to even more of them, until hopefully a majority will come to accept the inescapable logic of the Arab message, now constantly repeated by means of Cairo Radio's Israel service, to the effect that the Zionists cannot indefinitely ignore the demands of the united Arab peoples for peace and justice. This change is in no small measure due to the way in which the Arab media rose to the challenges posed by the Six-Day War, including the greater effectiveness of the Egyptian Information Administration.

While very properly encouraged and gratified by this success and by the improvement of our relationship with much of the Western

[8] New York, Exposition Press, 1965.

World, we must be on our guard against falling into an insidious sense of security. Israeli propaganda may appear to have run out of steam, but the impression is illusory. It still has ample resources, not least the opportunities for exploiting a natural revulsion against the excess of some Palestinian guerillas, and the continued existence of sympathetic groups and political lobbies in the outside world. While arguably more muted in its espousal of Zionism, the US is still friendly to Israel. Despite the Rogers Plan of 1969–70, despite some dependence on Arab oil, and despite the diplomatic activities of Henry Kissinger after the War of 6 October 1973, the sympathies of much US opinion have probably not changed greatly since, soon after the June war, the American delegate to the UN, Arthur Goldberg, could declare that he was proud of being a Zionist.

Even in Britain, notwithstanding the improved relations of the past few years, the BBC's Arabic transmissions have sometimes betrayed anti-Arab sentiments. As recently as 30 October 1972 one of them could conjecture: "The question now is: for how long will President Sadat remain in the Presidency, for Egypt is heading towards a state of chaos." We must beware of reading into this unfriendly attitude any sinister intention on the part of the British government. Being an independent corporation, the BBC is not the mouthpiece of the British leadership, or for that matter of the British people, and it has on occasion allowed itself to be misled by Zionist information. In responding sharply to misrepresentation, the Arab media intend no disrespect to Britain, but are concerned merely to set the record right, and thus to foster the cordiality and friendship which on the whole have grown so healthily over recent years.

More serious, because intentionally hostile, have been the activities financed by the US and Zionists within the Arab World. These have led to attacks on Egypt by some newspapers in Lebanon and in Kuwait. Egypt's information authorities, however, maintained a close watch on these activities, which threatened her good relations with both Arab countries concerned. This enabled them to warn the Lebanese newspaper in question that, unless the unwarranted attacks ceased, the extent of the CIA's financial contribution would be exposed; as a result the newspaper came out with a headline reading "Long Live Egypt". In the case of the Kuwaiti newspaper, the government of that state co-operated with Egypt to the extent of actually committing the owner, Mr Garalla, for trial towards the end of 1972.

More directly, Israel has maintained her psychological attacks to the present day and has continued to use her sympathizers in other lands as a sort of fifth column against Egypt. For example, Israel, which had for years denounced Egypt as being under Russian influence, took the occasion of the withdrawal of large numbers of Russian advisers in July 1972 as a cue to pose the question as to how long Egypt could maintain its support of the Arabs without Soviet assistance. The intention was to weaken faith in Egypt's prospects by suggesting to interested powers that she had become dependent on the presence of the Russian experts. The truth of the matter was of course quite different. The Russians left not as the result of any rupture in Soviet-Egyptian relations, but simply because they had done their job and in consequence left Egypt stronger rather than weaker. Another form of psychological warfare to which the Israelis have resorted recently is intended to sow religious division by stimulating alarm among the Coptic minority. This has been done by means of private letters. Fortunately the information authorities were alive to the ruse, and were able to set minds at rest by collecting and later publishing the letters in question. The alarm which the Israelis sought to spread among the Copts can readily be seen for the nonsense it was from the following extracts from some of these so-called private letters:

"The Christians who account for 15 per cent of the Egyptian population are excluded from the political activities at the local level as well as at the national level."

and again:

"Paraslavery is practised in some Upper Egypt villages where some poor Christians seek the protection of strong Muslim families. The protector families treat their Christian clients as slaves."

and yet again:

" . . . The objectives are the subjugation of Christians and all non-Muslim minorities in the Middle East, and crushing them, politically, socially and economically, or converting them to Islam . . . We are determined to take many steps until justice and equality are achieved."

While the accusations were ludicrous to anyone in possession of the facts, they may have appeared grimly genuine in the eyes of unsophisticated people. The Israelis are certainly not above playing on the fears of simple men and women in this callous manner.

That they should have considered it worth while to stoop to this level may be a measure of growing desperation among at least some of those responsible for Israeli propaganda. To this extent the episode is one more tribute to the impressive strides made by the Arab media in the years following the Six-Day War. The reissue in 1972 of the Israeli *Book of Jokes* against the Arab leaders seems to provide further evidence of a paucity of constructive ideas on the part of those responsible for Israel's propaganda services.

(e) Spotlight on Palestine

To the extent that prior to 6 October 1973 the Arab struggle continued to held world attention, it did so mainly in the context of Palestine. Attention was maintained largely by the various guerrilla acts, so widely reported and portrayed by the world's media. To understand why this is so, we must go back a few years. With the successful conclusion of the Algerian struggle in 1962, with the proclamation of Aden's independence in 1967, and with the departure of the British military presence from Libya in 1969 and from the Gulf in 1971, the vestiges of old-style British and French imperialism were gone. The Arab struggle had accordingly attained one of its major aims. It could henceforth concentrate on battles yet to be won. They still involved conflict with imperialism of a sort. But it was with an imperialism less readily recognizable, at least to much non-Arab opinion, an imperialism which was implicit in the Palestinian policies of Israel and the United States.

The gradual recovery of Arab strength after the Khartoum summit of August and September 1967, and the improvement of relationships with much of the Western world, meant that powerful day-to-day problems no longer acted to distract Arab attention from the troubles of the Palestinians in the way that they had done in the immediate aftermath of the June war. But arguably the most important reason why attention was focused on Palestine resulted from the changed circumstances and reactions of the Palestinians themselves.

Already, before the June war, the longer term effects of the refugee problem were apparent, at any rate in the Arab World. As we remarked at the beginning of this chapter, a new generation of Palestinians was coming of age.[9] Increasingly fewer of its members would recollect life in pre-1948 Palestine or have any personal reason to take account of Jewish sufferings in a once Nazi-dominated Europe. Their political education had been acquired in the grim surroundings of the refugee camps. Their knowledge of recent history, as of current affairs, was gleaned from the facts presented in the press and over the radio. Cut off from the mainstream of international life they may have been, but the ready availability of these media ensured that they were not left in ignorance of the main truths affecting their lamentable situation. Irrespective of the decline of old-style imperialism and of the recovery of Arab power, the refugees would have demanded a fair hearing from world opinion by one means or another. If when it came this demand seemed to the outside world unduly strident, even intransigent, it has to be recalled that it was perforce made against a background of equally strident Israeli intransigence. The Zionists ensured that there was to be no room for the give and take, the cordiality which had frequently characterized Arab-Jewish relations under the British mandate and before.

The emergence of these new pressures had been recognized by the independent Arab nations when, following the Cairo summit meeting of January 1964, the *Palestine Liberation Organization* (PLO) was set up under Ahmed Shukhairy's chairmanship in May 1964. The PLO was to act in a sense as a government in exile, and to have adequate status to enable it to participate as Palestine's official representative in meetings of Arab ministers and senior officials.

After the June war its obligations towards the Palestinian peoples were enlarged. Up to that point the inhabitants of the non-Israeli parts of Palestine had at least the satisfaction of belonging to an independent Arab sovereign state, the Kingdom of Jordan, which represented their interests, and which in the Six-Day War fought bravely on their behalf. With the Israeli triumph in that war, the

[9] See pp. 222–223 above.

position of the Palestinians was traumatically altered for the worse. They were now a people without a country, either in the narrower Palestinian sense, or in the wider Arab sense. Israel's occupation of the whole of Palestine swelled the total of the Palestinian refugees from around a million to at least one and a half million, about fifty per cent of the entire Palestinian Arab population. The prospect for the one and a half million that remained in the territory controlled by Tel Aviv was precarious, because Israel had in no way abandoned her earlier policy of engineering a massive demographic change through further Jewish immigration, through the refusal of the right of return to the refugees who had left their homes whether in 1948 or in 1967, and through the unrelenting harassment of those Arab Palestinians who remained. The persistence of this policy over the years after the Six-Day War came out in the following reports of statements by leading members of the Israeli establishment. Thus on 19 November 1967 Radio London reported:

> "Yigal Allon stated that new villages must be established in the occupied territories in order to make the Israeli existence a *fait accompli*."

Thus on 10 February 1968 Radio Israel:

> "In a statement made by Zalman Shazar, Head of the State of Israel, to Radio Israel on 10 February 1968, he said that Old Jerusalem will remain in the hands of Israel regardless of any resolution calling for withdrawal from it. Then, he asked for new immigrants to come to Arab Jerusalem and El Mukaber Mountain in order to reinforce the Israeli existence."

Thus on 17 May 1970 Reuter, Tel Aviv:

> "Israeli Minister of State, Shemon Perez, declared that plans are carried out to settle 2,200 immigrants in Jerusalem by the end of 1970. He added that such projects necessitate the establishment of new industries around the city."

Thus on 19 January 1972 AFP Jerusalem:

> "Golda Meir asserted in the Knesset that what concerns Israel most at drawing up the new map of frontiers is that there should not be a great number of Arabs inside the Israeli frontiers."

Thus on 14 July 1972 Israel Broadcasting Station:

"In a lecture given to the Lion's Club in Tel Aviv, Menahem Begin declared that during the five years succeeding the Six-Day War, the Jewish majority in Israel has not decreased; on the contrary it has increased at equal rates. He also expressed his confidence that the Jewish majority will increase in the future due to the expected increase in immigration."

These are no isolated cases but take their place in a continuous succession of declarations. Made in circumstances calculated to secure wide coverage from the Israeli and the international media, they leave no doubt as to the consistency and determination with which Tel Aviv continues to pursue its demographic intent. The reference to Jerusalem in the words of both Zalman Shazar and Shemon Perez, reported above, draws attention to a further impulse towards more active Palestinian activity after 1967, for, to the pre-existing economic and social motives, the Israeli occupation of the historic sector of Jerusalem added a religious dimension of emotional significance to all Palestinian Arabs, whether Muslim or Christian. By their incessant use of the media to publicize their intentions and hopefully to browbeat the Palestinians, the Israelis on the contrary ensured the maximum impact of all these stimuli on Arab determination.

The heightened Palestinian response was not long in making itself felt. Just as the Khartoum summit expressed the refusal of Arab governments to accept a humiliating settlement with Israel, so the PLO expressed its determination by restructuring itself to give the major Palestinian resistance organization *Fatah* a greater voice in its policy making, with Fatah's founder Yasser Arafat as the PLO's new leader in succession to Ahmed Shukhairy. Armed resistance would go on against Israeli oppression in keeping with the continuing state of war. This position of the PLO has often been misunderstood in the West, still to some extent susceptible to the misrepresentations perpetrated by the Zionist media. In attacking the Israelis on Palestinian soil, Fatah and the other resistance groups were doing no more than exercising a patriotic duty, in the same way as the French *maquis* or the Yugoslav *partisans* had done in comparable circumstances during the Second World War. Moreover, the followers of Yasser Arafat were careful to avoid inflicting harm on innocent third parties, and also to formulate a constructive plan for a future peaceful Palestinian state run on democratic lines with equal rights of citizenship for Arab and Jew alike. These facts have generally been lost sight of in the atmosphere of fear and suspicion of the Palestinians generated by Israeli propaganda, even allowing for the growing sympathy for the Arabs which we described earlier in this chapter. We must not forget either that, while these limited, and in the circumstances wholly understandable, operations by the PLO were taking place, the Israeli government was consistently ignoring the fresh succession of UN denunciations of their policy, beginning with the Security Council's Resolution 242 of 22 November 1967.

In the face of Israeli provocation of this magnitude, it was perhaps inevitable that the official PLO policy should appear over-cautious to some Palestinians, and that support should consequently have increased for those resistance groups that favoured militant action against Israeli interests abroad no less than in Palestine itself. Pre-eminent among these hard-liners was the Popular Front for the Liberation of Palestine, started by Dr George Habash after the Six-Day War. The PFLP's activities have brought widespread and perhaps inevitable denunciation from the world's media, and not only from those newspapers and radio stations controlled or influenced by the Zionists. In particular the PFLP acquired notoriety from the succession of plane hijackings, most notably the attack on an El-Al Boeing at Athens airport on 26 December 1968, the attack on another Israeli plane at Zurich on 18 February 1969, the blowing up of three planes, belonging to BOAC, Swissair and TWA, at Dawson's Field in Jordan in September 1970. Inevitably much of the international anger against air piracy on this scale rubbed off on the PLO. The entire future of the resistance was jeopardized too by the rough methods employed by the Israelis against neighbouring states from which they claimed the guerrillas operated. The atmosphere was further charged by some Palestinian fears that the Rogers Plan might presage a sell-out of their interests.

In the bewilderment, confusion and mutual recrimination of September 1970 King Hussein appears to have been genuinely alarmed for the security of Jordan, in face of Israeli threats and the increasingly independent attitude of a section of the guerrillas based in his kingdom whom the official PLO were finding it more than ever difficult to control. The consequence of this explosive situation was the Jordanian army's action against the resistance fighters, resulting in some four thousand deaths. Once again Arab cohesion seemed to be on the brink of disaster just as it had been on 9 June 1967. Now as then it was saved by the promptness, energy and determination of President Nasser, who at the Cairo summit conference just before his death averted the threat of a fatal division in the Arab ranks.

Even so the events of September 1970 introduced a further ingredient of hatred into the Palestinian tragedy. The *Black September* movement was born of a desire to avenge the deaths of the Palestinians who met their deaths at the hands of the Jordanian army in that fateful month. With its appearance, reprisals were no longer confined to Israel, to Israeli property, or to aircraft carrying passengers of Israeli nationality or markedly pro-Zionist proclivities. Foreign countries were no longer exempt, nor was the property of organizations considered to be in any way friendly towards Israel. There has even been a suggestion that the *Black Septembrists* were prepared to ally themselves with anarchist and other extremist groups, such as the Baader-Meinhof group in Federal Germany and the Japanese Red Army in furtherance of a common interest against established organizations.

The first major blow by Black September was on 28 November 1971 with the murder of Jordan's Prime Minister Wasfi Tel at the entrance of the Sheraton Hotel in Cairo. On 15 December an attempt was made on the life of Jordan's ambassador in London, Zaid al-Rifai. The following February brought the murder of five Jordanians near Cologne and damage to oil installations in both Germany and Holland. In May 1972—and this lends credibility to the theory of an international connection—three Japanese terrorists killed twenty-eight people at Israel's Lod Airport. And most memorably of all it was Black September which carried out the September 1972 attack on the Israeli team at the Munich Olympic Games.

From this recital of activities and events pertaining to the Palestinian struggle since the Six-Day War, we can appreciate how the issue has received world attention as never before. Beyond the Arab World, Palestine is no longer the almost exclusive concern of those governments with strategic or economic interests in the area. It has become as much the property of world opinion as, for example, the US involvement in Indo-China. Events like Dawson's Field, Jordan's action against the guerrillas, and the Lord Airport massacre were brought into the homes of millions of television viewers the world over. The impact of the Munich tragedy was greater still. The advance publicity lavished on an international sporting gathering, coupled with the massive appeal of the Olympic Games to audiences in many lands, ensured abnormally widespread public exposure. The spotlight was focused on Palestine as never before. It has hardly been dimmed, let alone averted, since.

Among the *fedayeen*[10] there are some who would claim that this fact alone is sufficient justification for their activities. In their view the main danger is that Palestinian sufferings might be ignored by the international community, which, accepting the specious contentions of Tel Aviv, would come to regard the Israeli occupation of the lands seized in 1967 as representing not only normalcy but also legality. Faced with the overwhelming immorality of Israel's position, the Palestinians cannot afford excessive moral susceptibilities. For decades they had striven by legal means to bring their plight to the attention of world opinion. To a large extent they had quite simply been ignored. Even after the UN took up their cause, the position had hardly improved, because, at little cost to their own image, the Israelis had overridden successive Security Council and General Assembly resolutions. Having been patient too long, and having tried every legal means, some Palestinians decided, in their frustration, that the logical outcome could be nothing less than terror. Feared and despised they might be, but at least the activities of Black September ensured that they were no longer a forgotten people. Thanks to the system of baggage checks introduced by most international airlines, their presence hourly impinged on the attention of travellers the world over.

Of course this view is a dangerous over-simplification. The moral aspect of attacks on innocent third parties are ignored at the Palestinians' peril, for their own demand for justice is essentially an appeal

[10] The fedayeen, already referred to on p. 180 above, are those willing to make the supreme sacrifice for the Arab cause.

to international morality. The fact has been constantly appreciated by Arab governments and by the more responsible Palestinian freedom fighters. Thus, after the Dawson's Field incident, the practice of hijacking was firmly denounced by the PLO, as well as by Egypt, Jordan and other Arab countries. In the end such activities must be counter-productive. International disgust will play straight into the hands of the Israelis. There are signs that the activities of Black September may have prompted the Israelis to settle the internal differences that had begun to appear within their society, and have made it more difficult for moderate Israeli opinion to pressurize government hard-liners into making concessions to the Palestinians.

There seems to be evidence too that the Israeli government appreciates the advantages in these terms to be derived from the more militant fedayeen actions. The longer these go on the more Tel Aviv can hope to confuse world opinion into associating Black September and the PFLP with the PLO, Fatah and other responsible Palestinian groups. Up to the present, therefore, it has probably been in Israel's interests to keep the issue of terrorism to the forefront of attention, though, as we shall explain presently, the situation may be changing. To this end, they have brought to bear their expertise in psychological warfare. Rumours are spread about the possible intentions of the Arab fedayeen and alleged Arab plots are discovered, on the evidence of anonymous phone calls or so-called secret intelligence reports. A favourite device of the Israelis is to try to link Arab embassies with these rumours in such a way as to harm Arab relations with other governments. Writing in the November 1972 issue of *Middle East International*, Tom Little observes:

> "Arab diplomats in London and, I am told, in other European capitals believe the world is witnessing a *tour de force* by Israeli intelligence and propaganda machines, intended primarily to prevent any further strengthening of Egyptian relations with European Economic Community countries."

On balance fedayeen activities have not halted the process of improved Arab relations with the West. That this is so is largely a tribute to the tireless efforts of Arab information media in condemning the death and injury caused to the innocent and in seeking to project the Palestinian issue in truthful terms capable of being understood by the non-specialist. For example, simple non-technical pamphlets have come out on the lines of the one published in January 1972 by the Administration Council of the Egyptian Association of Political Science. Entitled *A Message to Save Peace in the Middle East*, this pamphlet, which was printed in English, French, German, Spanish and Arabic, listed the various UN resolutions on Palestine since the Security Council's Resolution 242 of 22 November 1967, and drew attention to Israel's record of consistent rejection. By such means more and more people outside the immediate area of the confrontation are becoming aware of Israel's lawless conduct. Awareness has brought fuller comprehension of Palestinian frustration, and a readiness to understand, if not to forgive, its more extreme effects. There is a new disinclination in the West and elsewhere to accept Israel's evaluation of her own illegal acts as an admissible response to the PFLP and Black September.

We must of course be on our guard against over-stating this tendency. Israeli propaganda is still resourceful. Any relaxation of Arab vigilance and of Arab care for international relations could set the tide flowing once more in the Zionists' favour. For the moment, however, there is a predisposition to consider the Palestinian case more fully than ever before. The process has recently received encouragement from the War of 6 October 1973 and from the use of the oil weapon, both of which we shall discuss in our next chapter. Given time, a fair chance exists that much of world opinion will become positively aware of the scope of the various UN resolutions against Israeli policy; not merely of those passed since 1967,[11] but also of the succession of resolutions stretching right back to the creation of the Zionist state and equally ignored by Tel Aviv.

Attitudes to Israel hardened also as a result of a series of blatant over-reactions to alleged guerrilla activities. These Israeli acts have received widespread publicity from the international media. A large part of the Western world probably first became aware that terrorism was by no means one-sided when it heard about Israel's attack on Beirut airport on 28 December 1968 in alleged retaliation for the

[11] The text of these and earlier resolutions is reproduced in the appendix to Henry Cattan, *Palestine and International Law* (Longman, London, 1973).

PFLP hijacking of an El Al plane at Athens two days earlier. Other instances of Israeli terrorism and aggression against neighbouring countries to receive much exposure and adverse comment were: the raids on Syria and the virtual temporary occupation of southern Lebanon after the September 1972 Munich tragedy; the shooting down by Israeli Phantoms of a Libyan Boeing over Israeli-occupied territory to the east of the Suez Canal on 21 February 1973 when 105 people died; the Israeli terrorist attack on Beirut in April 1973 in quest of certain Black Septembrists; the interception over Beirut by Israeli planes of an Iraqui Caravelle and its subsequent forcing down on Israeli territory on 10 August 1973 in an endeavour to capture George Habash, whom the Israelis believed to be on board. In its comments on the tragic affair of the Libyan Boeing, the *Sunday Times* of London on 25 February 1973 censured the attitude, still widespread even at that late date, which applied less exacting canons of conduct to Israeli terrorism than it did to the actions of the fedayeen. Referring to the official Israeli statement after the disaster, it went on to say:

" . . . Ministers have expressed formal regrets for the loss of life, but no word of repentance for the catastrophic scale of their pilots' ruthlessness. A hundred totally innocent travellers have been killed. Israel, although belatedly conceding that there was some error of judgement, continues to place the main blame on the airliner's pilot.

"Underlying this, there remains a basic assumption of which Israel and Zionists around the world have long been possessed, namely that for her cause the world must forgive everything. Elsewhere rough codes of morality are recognized, in principle if by no means always in practice. Arabs, in particular, must always be ferociously condemned, and their legitimate interest in, for example, Palestinian refugees disregarded. But whatever Israel does must be exonerated because Israel is fighting for survival. Besides it is a client state of the Western Alliance.

"It is time for Western governments, especially Washington, to make rather more clear than they have been prepared to that this assumption enjoys little popular support. The destruction of the airliner should certainly be followed, as Britain quickly proposed, by an impartial international enquiry. But there should also be a more fundamental review of how much Israeli aggression, at the cost of any prospect of a Middle East peace, the West will continue to underwrite . . . "

The hijackings make for sensational news. In an age where the media provide a surfeit of facts and impressions, they are remembered because of the precautions which governments have found it necessary to introduce and which affect the ever-increasing numbers of ordinary people who have occasion to travel by air. At first it looked as though the activities of the fedayeen could be blamed for the delays and irritations inseparable from the baggage checks and other precautions. But as time goes by the tendency among more and more travellers is to attribute them to the totality of the Palestinian issue. The Israelis are having to share the blame with the PFLP and Black September. More reflectively inclined air passengers are beginning to seek further information about the Zionist terrorists, and hence to discover or recall that the phenomenon is not new. The spectres of the Stern Gang and Irgun are by no means laid.

In this changed climate, there is hope that the international media will be encouraged to give more prominence to the continuing terrorism directed at individual Arabs in circumstances not normally calculated to secure more than a passing reference in the press, acts such as the shooting down of the Fatah member Wael Zuaiter in Rome in October 1972, or the murder by means of a car bomb of Muhammad Boudia, the director of a French theatre, in Paris in July 1973. Once that point has been reached, the Zionists must surely come to appreciate the double-edged characteristic of terrorism. Indeed, even now some of them must have learnt to regret their brazen use of terror, just as many Arabs have always regretted that the Palestinian extremists should have felt it necessary to select drastic means in the pursuance of a just cause. Even before the dramatic events of 6 October 1973 and the succeeding weeks, it had become reasonable to expect majority opinion in the West, whether consciously or not, to echo the sentiments of Sir Colin Crowe, who during the course of a UN Security Council meeting in 1972 made a plea for realism and justice in the following words:

"We must show the hundreds of thousands of refugees in Jordan, Syria, Lebanon, Gaza and elsewhere that the world has not forgotten them. We must take note of, and we must take action on, their legitimate aspirations, which must not be overlooked in any final settlement. In that we must once more give them a reason for living and hope for the future."[12]

By the end of 1973 not only Western but world attention was forced into an acute awareness of the Arab World. The Fourth Arab-Israeli War, which broke out on 6 October, provided the catalyst. We must now consider that conflict and its immediate consequences up to the time of the opening of the Geneva peace conference on 21 December.

[12] Quoted in an article by John Reddaway "What future for the Palestinians?" in *Middle East International* (London, June 1973).

10
Onwards from 6 October 1973

(a) War and diplomacy, October to December 1973

Long before the autumn of 1973 Israel was in a sense in a state of war with her Arab neighbours. She had consistently ignored the Security Council Resolution 242 of 1967, which called for her departure from the lands occupied during the Six-Day War. She had answered that resolution's demands for justice for the Palestinians by encouraging further Jewish settlement in their homeland. She had spurned President Sadat's February 1971 offer of genuine peace based on the pre-June 1967 frontier. She had provoked her neighbours by a succession of warlike acts, as recently as 10 August forcing down an Iraqi Caravelle. In all this she was encouraged by an assumption of American support, for, despite growing US misgivings, especially in the context of the energy crisis, Washington remained a firm ally; less than three months earlier the US had vetoed a draft Security Council resolution which would have castigated Israel's failure to co-operate with the UN quest for a peaceful settlement. The bellicose character of Israel's attitude was further emphasized by Tel Aviv's unrepentant arrogance. For example on 26 July General Arik Sharon claimed for Israel the status of "a military superpower" of unparalleled importance to the US, and he went on to boast:

> "All the forces of European countries are weaker than we are. Israel can conquer in one week the area from Khartoum to Baghdad and Algeria."

If ever a government was manifestly dedicated to belligerence, rejecting all conciliatory moves whether from its opponents or from well-meaning third parties, that government was Israel's. By her provocations and the psychological onslaughts of her propaganda, Israel deliberately prepared the way for the Fourth Arab-Israeli War, which began on 6 October 1973. Hers was the responsibility for its outbreak and for the suffering it was to bring, not least to ordinary Israeli citizens. To all intents and purposes, the only fact which had stood in the way of a state of war in the generally accepted sense was the formal ceasefire ending the hostilities which had begun on 5 June 1967. That ceasefire had as its basis Israel's obligation to carry out the terms of the Security Council Resolution 242 of 22 November 1967. As pointed out by *The Egyptian Gazette* in its editorial of 12 October 1973, Israel had persistently failed to implement this duty and:

> "It follows that if the purpose of the ceasefire was not fulfilled owing to Israel's refusal to comply with requirements the ceasefire became virtually null and void. In any case Israeli violations of the ceasefire had made it ineffective."

These facts are self-evident. But they need to be re-stated, because world opinion has been misled since 6 October by Israeli propaganda, and by Zionist-controlled or influenced media. These information sources have, whether deliberately or inadvertently, sought to place the onus for the outbreak of fighting on the Egyptians and Syrians, and in this way to condemn the victims of prolonged Israeli aggression.

The implications of that aggression had for long been evident to Egypt and Syria. Their leaders therefore bore the responsibility of seeing to it that, when full scale hostilities began, the Arab armies should be prepared, and also, so far as was possible, to make sure that the fighting occurred in conditions favourable to their cause. In this context Arab unity took on a new and pressing importance. Jordan's diplomatic relations with Syria had been broken off in August 1971, in consequence of the measures which Jordan had taken against the Palestinian resistance fighters. Those with Egypt had ended in April 1972, following the announcement of a possible amalgamation of Jordan and the West Bank into a new United Arab Kingdom. On 10 and 11 September 1973 President Sadat of Egypt, President Assad of Syria and King Hussein of Jordan met in Cairo to compose these differences. Full diplomatic relations were restored, and King Hussein on 18 September amnestied about 950 political detainees. In the context of public opinion, it is worth mentioning that the unifying process went beyond the Arab World itself, because, on the day before the Cairo summit, the closing declaration of the fourth conference of non-aligned countries held in Algiers had called upon the seventy-six full member states to lend their aid to Egypt, Syria and Jordan in recovering the lands which Israel had occupied in defiance of the UN.

This is not the place for a detailed account of the Fourth Arab-Israeli War and of the diplomatic activities which led to the opening of the peace conference in Geveva on 21 December. In order that we may appreciate the significance of these events in the context of our subject, however, we believe the reader may at this point welcome a chronological outline of the relevant facts.

On Saturday 6 October Egypt and Syria delivered a massive and co-ordinated response to years of Israeli aggression. Within twenty-four hours the Israeli Bar-Lev line on the east bank of the Suez Canal had been penetrated. Practical expression was given to the concept of Arab unity in the form of prompt and widespread offers of help; over the next few days Iraq on 10 October and Jordan and Saudi Arabia on 13 October entered the war. Having captured Qantara on 8 October, and effected a massive crossing of the Canal against great difficulties, the Egyptian forces, numbering some 100,000 men, launched their attack at the heart of the Sinai peninsula on 14 October. These were resounding military achievements, in no way diminished by the landing of a force of Israelis on the Canal's west bank to form what came to be referred to as the Deversoir Gap. By their skill, determination, and sheer military professionalism, the Egyptian armies had shattered not only the much vaunted Bar-Lev defences but also the illusion of Israeli invincibility, so long propagated by friend and foe alike. On the northern front the campaign proclaimed a similar message. The dogged resistance of the Syrians at Sasa barred the road to Damascus to the Israelis right up to the ceasefire.

So heavy were Israeli losses of material that on 15 October the US admitted that it had put in hand an airlift of replacements. It was therefore clear that the Arabs would not be left free to settle accounts with Israel. Bearing this in mind, and reflecting that their military triumphs at last allowed the Arabs to negotiate from strength,

President Sadat in his speech to the Peoples' Assembly on 16 October raised the possibility of peace proposals, conditional on solid safeguards for legitimate Arab demands, including those of the Palestinians.

Further evidence of the Arabs' new found consciousness of their strength came on 17 October with the decision of the Organization of Arab Petroleum Exporting Countries (OAPEC), meeting in Kuwait, to reduce their oil supplies at the rate of at least 5 per cent a month, although the interests of countries friendly to the Arab cause would be safeguarded. The longer the war went on the greater became the danger of international involvement. Already on 9 October the Israelis had attacked a radar station in the Lebanon. Israeli operations against Syrian ports had caused the destruction of a Greek vessel and on 12 October of the Russian merchant ship *Ilya Machnikov*. Following up the airlift announcement, President Nixon on 19 October asked the US Congress to authorize immediate assistance for Israel of up to $2,200 million.

Nevertheless, the US and the USSR realized the danger of a global confrontation. Jointly they therefore convened an emergency session of the UN Security Council. This led to Security Council Resolution 338 of 22 October, which exhorted the combatants to cease military operations within twelve hours and thereafter immediately to begin carrying out Resolution 242 of 1967. In addition, Resolution 338 declared that negotiations should be promptly initiated with the aim of "establishing a just and desirable peace in the Middle East". Although accepted by both Egypt and Israel, this first ceasefire was promptly violated by the Israelis in an attempt to improve their position in the Deversoir Gap. At the Security Council's 23 October meeting Israel's responsibility in this connection was stated by the Russian representative Yakov Malik, while at his news conference of 25 October, Dr Henry Kissinger was to acknowledge that "certain Israeli territorial gains" had resulted from the violation of the truce. Nevertheless both super-powers were determined to prevent further escalation, and on 23 October they again jointly presented a further resolution at the Security Council. Like that of the previous day, this resolution, Number 339 of 1973, was unanimously accepted by the council's membership, China once again abstaining. Confirming Resolution 338, it called on the combatants to take up the positions existing at the moment of the first ceasefire, and went on to empower the UN Secretary-General, Dr Kurt Wald-heim, to arrange for the proper supervision of the ceasefire by UN observers. This second ceasefire applied to both fronts, being accepted by Syria as well as Egypt and Israel.

The immediate threat to world peace continued for several more days. Israeli violations of the ceasefire were drawn to the attention of international journalists at a briefing in Cairo on 25 October by President Sadat's official press adviser. He specifically mentioned the recurring Israeli air attacks on Port Said and Israeli interference with the work of the UN truce supervisors. Moreover, early that same day, without consulting his allies, President Nixon had placed US forces on a world-wide alert. He later sought to justify this on the grounds that he suspected the Russians of intending to despatch a large expedition to the Middle East. Fortunately, wiser counsels prevailed. Following discussions between Nixon and Brezhnev, this particular crisis passed, and on 31 October the American military alert was cancelled.

Before that date the Security Council on 25 October had accepted a resolution for the creation of a peace-keeping military presence. As devised by Dr Waldheim and approved by the Security Council on 27 October, this United Nations Emergency Force (UNEF) was to operate in the first instance for a period of six months. In addition to overseeing the ceasefire, it was charged with ensuring that the com-batants returned to the positions in which they stood at 16.50 on 22 October. The UNEF was to be built up to a strength of 7,000, and to be drawn from nations other than the five permanent Security Council members: the USA, the USSR, Britain, France and China. A few days later something like 1,000 UN troops from Austria, Fin-land, Ireland and Sweden were taking up their Middle East assign-ment, and over the succeeding weeks further reinforcements arrived from other countries.

Essential emergency steps having been taken, it was time to con-sider longer-term solutions. Already, as we have seen, President Sadat had in his speech of 16 October to the Peoples' Assembly declared his readiness to participate, and to endeavour to obtain

Palestinian participation, in a peace conference under the auspices of
the UN, as well as to re-open the Suez Canal. He referred to these
matters again in his press conference on 31 October.

Early in November diplomatic activity intensified. The Egyptian
foreign minister Ismail Fahmy visited Washington, as did Israeli
prime minister Golda Meir. Israeli foreign minister Abba Eban went
to Bucharest. President Sadat's special adviser Dr Mohammed Zayat
had talks in Paris with President Pompidou and foreign minister
Michel Jobert on 5 November, and in London with prime minister
Edward Heath and foreign secretary Douglas-Home on 6 November.
Continuous high level consultations were maintained between the
Arab nations, as evidenced by the 1 November meeting in Kuwait
between Presidents Sadat and Assad and the Emir of that state, by
President Sadat's flight thence to Riyadh for discussions with King
Feisal, and by his talks on returning to Cairo on 2 November with
President Boumedienne of Algeria, by King Hussein's talks over the
period 5 to 6 November with the Emir of Kuwait, with Sheikh
Zayed of the United Arab Emirates, and with President Assad of
Syria. Between 5 and 9 November US secretary of state Henry
Kissinger visited five Arab countries—Morocco, Tunisia, Egypt,
Jordan and Saudi Arabia. The discussions were on the whole friendly
and fruitful. Those with President Sadat had the constructive result of
restoring Egyptian-US diplomatic relations, in abeyance since the
Six-Day War. They also paved the way for setting the ceasefire on a
more solid footing, a pressing need in view of continuing Israeli
violations.

This formal ceasefire document was signed on 11 November by
the representatives of Egypt and Israel. The formalities were conducted under UN auspices, in the presence of the Finnish general
Siilasvuo, commander of the UNEF, at the UN checkpoint Kilometre
101 on the Cairo-Suez road. Its six points deserve to be quoted:

1. Egypt and Israel agree to observe scrupulously the ceasefire
   called for by the UN Security Council.
2. Both sides agree that discussions between them will begin immediately to settle the question of the return to the October 22
   positions in the framework of agreement on the disengagement
   and separation of forces under the auspices of the United Nations.

3. The town of Suez will receive daily supplies of food, water and medicine. All wounded civilians in Suez will be evacuated.
4. There shall be no impediment to the movement of non-military supplies to the east bank.
5. The Israeli checkpoints on the Cairo-Suez road will be replaced by UN checkpoints. At the Suez end of the road, Israeli officers can participate with the UN to supervise the non-military nature of the cargo at the bank of the canal.
6. As soon as the UN checkpoints are established on the Cairo-Suez road, there will be an exchange of all prisoners of war, including wounded.

Even after the ceasefire arrangements had been spelled out so clearly, and formally accepted by both sides, Israel still made difficulties. The day after the signature some Israeli soldiers tried to resist the UN manning of a checkpoint at Kilometre 119 on the Cairo-Suez road, established under Article 5 of the agreement, and the Israelis only withdrew after a fist fight with Finnish members of the UNEF. On 13 November Israel refused to let a number of international newsmen proceed beyond the Kilometre 101 checkpoint, notwithstanding the newsmen's possession of UNEF permission to visit the town of Suez. On the same day Golda Meir in a speech to the Israeli Knesset claimed that it was not possible to establish the precise location of the positions held by the combatants on 22 October. The argument continued to be employed as an excuse for Israel's failure to carry out Article 2 of the agreement of 11 November. To attempt to break the deadlock, further talks were held at Kilometre 101, but these had to be suspended on 29 November in face of Israeli non-co-operation. Even so a return to full scale military operations was avoided, and progress continued in the quest for a peace conference. This had been proposed by the US to take place probably on 18 December in Geneva, and on 25 November Mrs Meir announced Israel's willingness to attend. Two days later, the Arab leaders at the summit conference in Algiers approved the suggestion that Egypt and Syria should participate at Geneva. Despite further Israeli obstruction, the peace talks opened in Geneva on 21 December between representatives of Egypt, Jordan and Israel, as well as of the UN, the US and the USSR.

From this chronological survey we turn to a consideration of this crucial last quarter of 1973 in the context of our subject of information. We shall discuss the nature of the Arab and Israeli information responses to the challenges of the War and its immediate aftermath. We shall attempt to assess how far events reinforced or modified international attitudes to the Arab struggle, with particular reference to the Arab military achievement and to global energy problems. In drawing this study to a close at 21 December 1973, we do not for a moment mean to suggest that the Arab cause has grown less urgent or important. Patently the reverse is the case. We simply regard the opening of the Geneva conference as a convenient opportunity for taking stock in a continuing crisis, which, while rich in landmarks, is too fast-moving to offer natural pauses.

(b) Arab information vindicated

Israel's rejection of President Sadat's olive branch of February 1971 obliged Egypt to look afresh at every aspect of her defences, and not least at those relevant to the battle for men's minds. In our previous chapter we saw that from May 1971 the present author was once again given the facilities to contribute fully to this area of the struggle. Over the following months and years he was happy to help bring his country's information services back to the sound orientation which had proved its worth in 1956, inspired as it was by the Six Principles of the Revolution.

Priority went to fostering by every justifiable means the national morale and indeed the morale of the entire Arab World. Strict adherence to truth, close communications between government and people, avoidance of strident bombast, all played their part in consolidating a quiet confidence in the essential justness and strength of the cause. National unity was encouraged in positive ways. In July 1972, for example, transport facilities were made available to enable the members of the People's Assembly and of the Arab Socialist Union to witness the military manoeuvres held in the desert to mark the Revolution's twentieth anniversary; in this manner the identity of purpose binding together the army and the nation's civilian leaders was directly and visibly demonstrated to participants and spectators alike.

Good public relations in the maintenance of confidence were not restricted to internal affairs. Throughout the 6 October War, and during the ensuing period of diplomatic activity, President Sadat and his government made a point of keeping the other Arab states fully informed. Thus the high morale of the Egyptians, the Syrians and the other Arab combatants communicated itself to all parts of the Arab World, and in turn the morale of the other Arab countries reacted upon the fighting men, who derived enormous encouragement from it, as well as being materially helped by the generous and widespread forms of assistance so promptly offered after the outbreak of hostilities.

A clear idea of the principles guiding the presentation of news and comment by the Egyptian authorities at this time can be formed from an article appearing in the 19 October issue of the Cairo illustrated weekly *Al-Mossawar*. Entitled *How did we gain the confidence of World Public Opinion?* the article was based on an interview between the present author and the writer Hassan Emam Omar. The present author began by explaining the bases of Egyptian information as:

> "Presenting all facts objectively and truthfully to the people and to the whole world, not exaggerating in speaking about our power and victories, not minimising the power of the enemy, adopting calm methods in giving facts, avoiding emotionalism and depending on deeds and not words—these are the sound lines of our information which made the people trust our military communiqués, follow them closely and turn a deaf ear to hostile propaganda organs and to the lies and falsehoods they disseminated."

He went on to support the superiority of information which appealed to the audience's critical faculties over the sort which relied on a capacity for generating emotion, explaining that:

> "The battle is in reality two-fold: a battle waged by the armed forces on the military front and a battle on the home front. The home front must be calm and act without emotionalism. Everything should be clarified to this front honestly and truthfully. Nobody has the right to hide anything from the people. In this way the two fronts did work together in harmony."

The writer of this article drew attention to the confidence reposed in

Egyptian information by audiences abroad as well as those at home, indicating that the achievement derives from that combination of "science and faith" which President Sadat employed as the foundation of modern Egyptian society. In a further reference to "the confidence and trust of world public opinion", Mr Hassan Emam Omar pointed out that:

> "Scores of world TV and radio stations have paid tribute to the reliability of our statements and communiqués, sending their representatives to Cairo to carry out interviews designed to shed light on the situation."

As in 1956, but in contrast to the heavy censorship which took place in 1967, the Egyptian information administration generously co-operated with representatives of the international media. The present author stressed this policy during the course of an interview which he accorded on 15 October to the BBC's Panorama programme, when he said that one of the aims of his country's information services was to give global public opinion the true facts unadorned by exaggeration and to expose Israeli propaganda for the falsehood that it was. Two days later, he made a point of granting an interview to representatives of French television, at which he explained that Israel's rejection of every opportunity for genuine peace from 1967 onwards had left Egypt with no alternative to the action she took on 6 October for the freeing of her occupied lands.

The paramount importance attached by the Egyptian government to sound public relations, at home and abroad, is brought out by President Sadat's willingness, in the midst of the demands exerted by the military operations, to spare time to address the People's Assembly on 16 October, and on 31 October to speak to the world press, despite the equally intense pressures on his attention arising from ceasefire violations and great diplomatic activity.

In his 16 October address to the People's Assembly, the President paid tribute to the nation's effort, sacrifice, awareness and faith, to the rebuilding of the armed forces after the 1967 setback, to their tremendous achievements on and after 6 October. He congratulated the Syrians on their heroism on the northern front. Turning to the chances of a genuine and just peace, he pointed to past difficulties arising from the vast amount of aid which had flowed, and which unhappily continued to flow, from the US to Israel. Even so the prospect was improving, partly by virtue of the US-Soviet détente and of the economic importance of Arab oil, but very largely from Egypt's new strength and proven military success. On this basis she was in a position to negotiate from strength. At this very moment, when Egypt might in human terms have been forgiven the choice of a hard line based on the exhilaration of her dramatic achievements on the field of battle, President Sadat with rare statesmanship pointed the way to a possible long term solution to the problems of the Middle East, a solution which, by ensuring justice and security to both sides, would also relieve the rest of the world from the inconvenience and danger implicit in the situation as it had existed hitherto. The alternative to such a solution was likely to take the form of a war of attrition, which in the long term the Egyptians were better equipped to win than were the Israelis. In what has come to be referred to as his open letter to Richard Nixon, President Sadat declared that Egypt was ready to accept a ceasefire preparatory to attending a peace conference under the aegis of the United Nations, was ready to use her good offices to attempt to persuade the Palestinians and others concerned to attend such a conference, and was ready to reopen the Suez Canal to international shipping. Egypt's co-operation, however, must be clearly understood to be conditional on the good faith of the Americans. This time "vague promises" were not enough and there must be "clarity of intention and of targets". In particular this meant Israel's withdrawal from lands occupied during the Six-Day War, and the honouring of Palestinian rights as already accepted by the United Nations.

From this account of the address it is clear that the President set out to promote a correct interpretation of Egypt's achievements and aims for the benefit of world opinion. But the first priority remained the maintenance of domestic morale, the essential base for successful image building abroad. In this spirit the Ministry of Education later prepared a booklet for school children, incorporating the text of the speech, along with a simple analysis of its main features and a survey of the events leading up to 6 October, of the war and of its immediate consequences.

Turning now to President Sadat's 31 October speech, we see that he was immediately concerned to provide the world's media with the true facts of Egypt's achievements and her present attitude. This, his first international interview in Cairo since his assumption of the presidency, took place in the presence of 382 international correspondents, as well as of officials of the Egyptian information administration and leading Egyptian publishers. President Sadat's opening remarks covered the military achievements of the recent war, and he pointed out the desperate straits to which the Israelis would have been reduced but for the massive rescue operation mounted by the US. On behalf of Egypt, he accepted the ceasefire jointly proposed by the two super-powers, partly because of the US-Soviet guarantee of the immediate implementation of Security Council Resolution 242 of 1967, and partly because he had no wish to "fight America". To counter exaggerated Zionist claims as to the value of the Israeli position west of the Suez Canal, he placed the Deversoir Gap in its proper military context. The Israelis realized that it was merely a pocket, and for that reason strove to extend their hold by ceasefire violations. They had also used their presence west of Suez to distract world attention from the massive Egyptian achievements, notably the crossing of the canal, the destruction of the Bar-Lev defences, and "the complete tenacity of our forces in the east". Far from jeopardizing the Egyptian Third Army, the Deversoir operation had threatened the Israelis with encirclement. President Sadat indicated that it was this that had prompted Tel Aviv, in a message transmitted through the British prime minister Edward Heath and Leonid Brezhnev, to offer withdrawal from the gap in exchange for Egypt's lifting of the blockade of Bab al-Mandeb and the Red Sea. This matter, like that of the exchange of prisoners of war, could only be tackled after the Israelis had respected the ceasefire. In this connection the Israeli contention that the 22 October positions were indeterminable was a mere delaying tactic, because communiqués had already been issued by both the Egyptians and the Israelis clarifying the matter. In the circumstances President Sadat could reasonably conjecture ". . . is our aim to go on talking about the October 22 lines, the prisoners of war, Bab al-Mandeb, and other issues, or is our aim to achieve peace?" He went on to dispose of another Israeli ruse designed to convince outside opinion that the town of Suez was in their hands, for which purpose they had released a photograph of their prime minister against a background of oil installations:

"For three days they tried to invade the town whose name will go down in history for its heroic tenacity and resistance, the number of tanks it destroyed and its successful defence in preventing the Israelis from occupying a single inch of its land. The Israelis are staying outside in Zeitieh: they brought Mrs Meir and pictured her beside an oil tank in that area."

Turning from military to political aspects, the President went on to mention the various diplomatic exchanges which were taking place, including the steps he had taken to keep his Arab colleagues informed. He paid tribute to the Soviet Union's exertions in the cause of peace and was scrupulously fair in his references to the US in this context. Although the US had supplied arms to Israel, its attitude now appeared to be constructive, and even then President Sadat was awaiting Dr Kissinger's visit.

Looking ahead, the President defined his concept of peace as an arrangement which would not merely provide an acceptable solution to Egypt's territorial rights, but would also satisfy those of the Syrians and the Palestinians. On the oil issue he stressed that the weapon was not "directed at any individual in your countries, nor against the American citizen whose government has supplied Israel with the most up-to-date devices, which have never been used even by America herself." The Arab oil advantage would, on the contrary, be used only to further the right to life of the Arab nations. President Sadat concluded this vitally important speech to the representatives of the world's media with the following words:

"If there is a serious quest for peace, the Security Council Resolution of 22 October must be respected and fully implemented. We are ready to start fulfilling our obligations immediately. The stage we should now head for is the disengagement so that we may seriously march towards peace. I have said that during this stage we would immediately start clearing the Suez Canal and make it ready for international navigation within four months, as I have instructed the Chairman of the Suez Canal Authority. Thus we would help make life more convenient for our brothers in West Europe and elsewhere, and open up the way for world trade and prosperity."

These two speeches of President Sadat's bear eloquent witness to the care for factual accuracy and the dislike of useless polemic which are now characteristic of Arab information. The Arabs have come to realize that, both for relations with the outside world and for the maintenance of national morale, such methods have a long-term value. Properly employed they encourage credence and create a proper impression of steadiness and reliability. Of course after 6 October Egypt could afford to adopt a calm almost relaxed stance, because her information was deployed from the secure base of tremendous military gains. But this fact does not for a moment detract from the solid achievement of her information services. Indeed, against the background of such spectacular and unaccustomed military prowess, the Egyptian media could almost have been forgiven for indulging in the sort of arrogant euphoria displayed by the Zionists after the Six-Day War. Their willingness to resist that temptation reflects great credit on all concerned. As we explained earlier, the art of counter-propaganda involves an ability to profit from the mistakes of one's opponents. The contrast between Israeli use of the media after 5 June 1967 and the Egyptian use of the media after 6 October 1973 shows that the axiom had been taken to heart. The self-restraint it enjoined paid handsome dividends in terms of world attitudes to the Arab cause. The November 1973 issue of *Middle East International* contained the following editorial comment on this aspect of the information struggle:

> "The boasts and the bloodcurdling threats came now from General Dayan and his colleagues—and had often to be revised in the light of events—while more than one unprejudiced correspondent reported finding the Arab communiqués more accurate than those of the Israelis."

The above remarks suggest that for all their professionalism the operators of Israeli media committed grave errors after 6 October. Like much of world opinion, and like the ordinary Israeli, whether soldier or civilian, they were knocked off balance by the unprecedented military successes of the Egyptians and the Syrians. Unlike their opponents, they failed to learn from past mistakes. With the example before them of the ill effects of the emotional bombast which had weakened Arab public relations in 1967, the Israelis proceeded to commit many of the same errors as those of their opponents six years before.

During the June War, as we have seen, the Egyptians clamped down excessively on the activities of foreign newsmen. While not stopping the seepage of essential information to the enemy, this form of censorship meant that the world media were perforce confined to Israeli sources for their supply of news. Now the situation was to a large extent reversed. The limited facilities which the Israelis placed at the disposal of international journalists contrasted strongly with the generally co-operative attitude of the Egyptian information administration. As a result, the Arab successes and the Arab case as a whole were more fully, accurately and sympathetically reported than ever before. Moreover, the sparing use of censorship which made this possible was not at the expense of true security. Again in sharp contrast with June 1967, essential secrets were well guarded, so well in fact that the intelligence departments of leading powers were taken by surprise by the efficacy of the Egyptian and Syrian operations on 6 October. On the other hand, the Israeli attitudes oscillated from merely negative to downright obstructive. They seemed to resent the approaches of outside newsmen, rejecting the attention of media which so short a time before they had cultivated with marked assiduity and on the whole to such good effect in terms of their global image. Psychologically stunned by unimagined military set-backs, they retreated into their shells. The contrast with the healthy, good humoured co-operation between the Egyptians and the international media was manifest. As the official Egyptian spokesman said in a statement of 11 October, Israel deliberately obstructed correspondents from proceeding to the scene of the fighting, whereas Egypt willingly extended such facilities. Egypt did so in the realization that for their credibility newsmen depend on first hand experience. Again the courtesy extended to the foreign media at the time of President Sadat's press conference of 31 October witnessed to the importance he attached to international opinion. And yet, as we noticed in the chronological survey earlier in this chapter,

Israel, with these object lessons of good public relations before her, could still on 13 November permit herself a further outburst of insensitive arrogance, when she refused to let a group of foreign newsmen proceed beyond the Kilometre 101 checkpoint, notwithstanding the latters' possession of a UN entry pass to the town of Suez.

Israel's self-inflicted isolation from much of the world media was matched by her apparent self-inflicted deception. This is of course associated with her policy of manufacturing favourable information for external consumption. Setting out to deceive others with distorted news or downright lies, she ended up, at any rate for a time, by deceiving her own citizens. Attention was drawn to this phenomenon by the official Egyptian spokesman, on 11 October. The following extracts from the State Information Service transcript of this statement are instructive:

> "The official governmental spokesman issued a statement today in which he unveiled the contradictions which characterized the declarations made by the military officials in Israel and which confirmed beyond doubt the extent of the confusion now pervading Israel after the successive defeats it has suffered since the outbreak of hostilities in Sinai and the Golan last Saturday . . .
>
> "The official spokesman added that an Israeli military spokesman had announced yesterday that the Egyptians were still tenaciously maintaining the bridgeheads set up across the Suez Canal. The spokesman pointed out that this contradicts the statement made by an Israeli military commentator, Chaim Hertzog, on October 8, concerning the destruction of most of the Egyptian bridgeheads on the Suez Canal.
>
> "The official spokesman added that Aaron Yariv announced in his press conference that the war in which Israel is now involved will drag on. The spokesman said that the declaration is once again contradictory to the arrogance and conceit which characterized the speech made by Israel's Defence Minister Moshe Dayan on October 6, in which he said that the Israeli forces will put an end to the military hostilities on the eastern bank of the Suez Canal and in the Golan Heights within one day."

Such resounding overconfidence is the more startling when one remembers that the declaration came from Israel's Minister of

Defence. He of all people might have been expected to avoid the contagion of the myth of Israeli invincibility. Propagated by Tel Aviv as a deterrent, this myth had in course of time come to affect the thinking of the leaders themselves. Bearing this in mind, we can begin to comprehend something of the shock felt by ordinary Israeli soldiers and civilians when the truth began to dawn on them. That they were totally unprepared for it was evident from the reactions of people like the captured pilot, who on 9 October told his Syrian captors that his superiors had indicated that his mission—the raid on Damascus—would be "very easy". General Dayan himself revised his initial assessment fairly quickly, and on 17 October warned that "There is no shutting our eyes to the heavy price we are paying." For many of his compatriots the shock was more long lasting, while the Israeli people as a whole sustained a heavy blow to their confidence. In terms of its prime duty of protecting the national morale, the Israeli information service was a failure. Largely discredited at home, it went on to alienate much of world opinion. Even those media which were more or less friendly towards Tel Aviv were now either muted in their support or more abrasive in their criticism. For example the British *Sunday Telegraph*, in its editorial of 14 October, explained that the war had demolished two postulates hitherto widely regarded as central to the Israeli position: the assumption that their army was irresistible, and the assumption that the lands occupied during the Six-Day War would ensure future security.

Their most cherished preconceptions shattered, the controllers of Israel's information services lacked any carefully thought out message or policy. In their place they made do with exaggerated claims, falsehoods or wild imputations, such as that concerning the alleged use of torture by the Egyptians. The latter fabrication was exposed at the November conference of the International Red Cross held in Tehran. Increasingly Israeli information took on something of the character of the Nazi propaganda of World War II. The close parallel between the two was demonstrated in the following Egyptian Information Service transcript of 19 October:

> "The official governmental spokesman announced today that it had become evident to analysts of the techniques of the Israeli mass media that the general aspect of the Israeli information has become

obviously similar—if not identical—to Nazi information during World War II.

"This latter's information concept was mainly based on the persistent reiteration of lies in the hope that these would eventually become credible, and on the reiteration of false reports amidst an atmosphere of false enthusiasm and semi-hysterical slogans.

"The official spokesman went on to say that the reports of the Israeli Corps during the past few days evidently revealed that the Israeli mass media were desperately trying to counter the grave psychological consequences, which bore heavily on the Israelis, resulting from the achievements of the Egyptian armed forces, namely the crossing of the Suez Canal and the storming of the Bar-Lev line.

"In the meantime, the Israelis are trying to cause doubts among the Arabs, through their reiteration of fake victories and their attempt to highlight some limited and conventional military operations as major breakthroughs.

"The official spokesman further said that it was obvious that Israel was motivated in this respect by the ordeal which has befallen it as a result of its conceit. Through adopting such measures, Israel is not only proving to the entire world that the Israelis have not only simulated the Nazis' aggression, terrorism and racist attitudes, but are also adopting the Nazis' media techniques. In doing so, the Israelis seem to have forgotten that the Nazi lies and attempts to mislead the German public opinion had eventually collapsed even before the Nazi military presence itself had crumbled.

"Concluding, the official spokesman said the Israelis had to bear in mind the lessons of history, which lessons have always proved that facts—and facts alone—would eventually survive."

Within the short space of a few weeks then the Israelis had demonstrated their perturbation to the world. Their information services had signally failed to repair the severe damage inflicted on the national confidence as a result of the military setbacks, for which it had been totally unprepared. In face of this challenge the Israeli media provided a spectacle of exaggeration, hysteria and distortion that must have proved to any unprejudiced observer the extent to which Israeli policies had become threadbare and devoid of constructive ideas. The performance was the more lamentable against the background of the enormous information advantages enjoyed by

Israel since the birth of the state in 1948, which we have examined in earlier chapters. It must have been especially embarrassing to Israel's friends and contacts among foreign newsmen, particularly those in the United States.

This hysteria was in spectacular contrast with the general steadiness of the Egyptian and other Arab media. Starting with all the handicaps implicit in Israel's long term advantages, the Arab information services had gradually built up their resources on the solid foundations of respect for truth, avoidance of exaggeration and undue emotion, observance of sound public relations, development of an easy and friendly co-operation with representatives of the international media, in which restrictions should be reduced as far as possible to a minimal censorship necessary for the preservation of state secrets. As a result Arab information now enjoys a widespread reputation for reliability. This fully vindicates the efforts of all the dedicated men and women who, against what must at times have seemed overwhelming odds, struggled for years to obtain a fair hearing for the Arab demands for understanding and justice.

(c) The Arab image

By any standard the new-found reputation for steadiness and reliability is an impressive component of the total Arab image. Respect for truth and the ability to conduct one's affairs in a calm and purposeful manner are valuable attributes anyway. The confidence which they radiate among those possessed of such virtues habitually impresses itself upon the beholder. In the context of the Arab-Israeli information struggle, the favourable opinions earned by the Arabs have encouraged the media of even hostile nations and groups to re-appraise hitherto entrenched attitudes, while the effect upon the less partisan has been almost universally beneficial.

We shall now endeavour to identify what we regard as significant examples of these trends, both at the level of the widest international groupings and at that of individual regions or countries. First, and at the risk of repetition, it seems appropriate to comment on the massive vindication of Arab unity which, based as it now is on the real achievements and heightened confidence of the past few months, has emerged as a key factor in the global situation. It has received practical expression from a series of events, beginning with the Cairo summit of President Sadat, President Assad and King Hussein on 10 and 11 September 1973. That meeting rehabilitated Jordan's diplomatic relations with Egypt and Syria, and led also to the amnesty for the Palestinian guerrillas granted by King Hussein on 18 September. On and immediately after 6 October came the many offers of support and the practical aid to Egypt and Syria, whether in the form of actual participation as in the case of Iraq, Jordan and Saudi Arabia, or in the form of medical and other assistance contributed by Algeria, Kuwait, Lebanon, Libya, Morocco, North Yemen, Sudan and Tunisia, and of the threat to supplies to countries friendly to Israel from the Arab oil states. In terms of military operations solidarity was evident. Even the Israelis admitted it. Thus on 9 October in Tel Aviv a military spokesman conceded that the Arabs "are fighting in an orderly manner. There is no indication of a break in their psychological or military make-up." From more friendly quarters the message was the same. On 11 October the British *Daily Mail* noted the speed and efficiency of the Egyptian crossing of the Suez Canal. The same day the British *Financial Times* noted the vigour shown by the Arab soldiers, while defence experts in London, commenting on earlier incorrect judgments about the Arab-Israeli balance, expressed admiration for Arab handling of the SAM ground-to-air missiles, and for Arab ability to maintain the greater part of their airpower intact.

The Arab summit conference in Algiers between 26 and 28 November showed the Arabs to be as impressively united in the diplomatic struggle as they were in the military, their number being now increased by the admission of Mauritania as the nineteenth member of the Arab League. The mood was well expressed in President Sadat's warning of the real danger of a resumption of the fighting, and in President Assad's reminder of Israel's expansionist aims. Yet, while determined to preserve unity in face of an uncertain future, the leaders at Algiers wished to encourage every opportunity for a just peace, and, to this end, they supported the suggestion that Egypt and Syria should attend the projected Geneva conference in the following month.

In our sixth chapter we saw the correlation between the identity perceptions of any given group and the standing which that group possesses in the eyes of others. The more the peoples of the Arab world came to regard themselves as a unity, the more outsiders were disposed to think of them as a single Arab nation. Opinion became receptive to the concept of Arab rights and to Arab claims on first the attention and later the support of international justice. More than ever before, the spectacular demonstration of Arab unity after 6 October predisposed the world body to look favourably on the Arab cause. The same can be said for a mounting tally of national governments, regional units, specialized groups and inviduals, not a few of whom are able to influence the direction of public opinion. Arab unity then works to encourage acceptance of the confident and steady message projected by the information media of particular Arab governments.

The Organization of World Journalists speaks for over one hundred press syndicates. In the early days of the October war this body denounced Israel as an aggressor. As the fighting went on more and more foreign journalists used the opportunities granted by Egypt and her allies to visit the battle fronts. Consequently they were able to reveal the extent of Arab success and of Israeli falsehood. International opinion was moved too by the UN Truce Supervision Organization's 10 October statement about Israeli napalm attacks on Syria. Other Israeli contraventions of civilized behaviour included: the 9 October air attack on Damascus, when a Norwegian UN observer and his family perished; the air attack on a Lebanese radar station; and the sinking of a Greek freighter and of the Soviet merchant ship *Ilya Machnikov*. World opinion was stirred further by the facts of Israel's cease-fire violations presented at a briefing on 25 October. Conducted by President Sadat's press adviser, the briefing covered the persistent Israeli air attacks on the town of Suez, and Israel's obstructive attitude towards the UN observers. The adviser pointed to the continuing Israeli onslaught against the Egyptians on the western side of the canal as giving the lie to General Dayan's assertion the previous day that the Egyptian forces in that sector had already surrendered.

Actions of this sort consolidated support for the UN, which, as we saw, had for years censured Israel's neglect of a succession of Security

Council declarations long before the famous Resolution 242 of 1967. Israel's indifference to peace and justice was again evident when, having in principle accepted the idea of a conference, she said that the discussions would have to be adjourned till after the Israeli government had secured a mandate following a general election. As *The Egyptian Gazette* put it in its aptly entitled editorial *Trying to Buy Time* on 5 December:

> "For the past few years, however, the Israeli government has been demanding 'negotiations' with the Arabs. Would a general election have had to be called in Israel had the Arabs suddenly agreed to negotiations at any time prior to 6 October? If Mrs Meir had a mandate then, why does she suddenly not have one now? What mandate, moreover, is required when Israel is under UN orders to make peace? And what are the negotiations she wants, when the terms of the peace are already contained in Resolution No. 242 of 22 November 1967?"

Given heightened international awareness of the Middle East crisis, the Israeli attitude over the timing of the Geneva talks appeared to many as the prevarication that it was. The logic of the situation was not lost on world opinion. Israel's isolation from the mainstream of international thinking and of international sympathy became still more marked.

If we turn from world opinion in its wider connotation to the views of regional groups, we see the same process at work, to the advantage of the Arab image. The spirit of Bandung is still a factor of importance as far as the outlook of the Third World is concerned. For present purposes we can perhaps consider together the views of the Third World and of the non-aligned nations, for these two groupings are substantially coextensive. The fourth conference of non-aligned states took place in Algiers between 5 and 9 September. In addition to its seventy-six full members, its proceedings were attended by the Palestine Liberation Organization among other liberation movements, by nine observers mainly from Latin America, and by Austria, Finland and Sweden as guests. The political declaration issued on the last day of the conference showed unequivocal disapproval for Israel's disregard of UN resolutions, and for the support which she had received from the US in the pursuit of this policy; it also confirmed the members' promise to do all they could to assist Egypt, Jordan and Syria in the recovery of the territories illegally held by Israel. In response to a separate resolution for a boycott of Israel, Cuba on 9 September and Togo on 21 September severed diplomatic relations with her. Other declarations against Israel were made by individual non-aligned leaders, including Sheikh Mujibur Rahman of Bangladesh, Prince Norodom Sihanouk of Cambodia, Emperor Haile Selassie of Ethiopia, Mrs Indira Gandhi of India, President Yakubu Gowon of Nigeria, and Marshal Josef Tito of Yugoslavia.

The reference to President Gowon reminds us of the importance of the African states in the Arab-Israeli struggle to gain the sympathy of outside opinion, for in 1973 he was the President of the Organization for African Unity. Most of the OAU countries are to be counted among the members of the non-aligned group. During the course of 1972 and the earlier part of 1973, and increasingly after the outbreak of the War of 6 October, one after another of the African states broke off diplomatic relations with Israel. This solidarity on behalf of the Arab cause appears the more impressive when one recalls the assistance which Tel Aviv had in the past furnished to a number of African governments, in an effort to win influence and good repute.

Similar tendencies operate in the modification of the views of another grouping, the European Economic Community. Early in November the EEC issued a statement to the effect that no settlement of the problems of the Middle East could be expected until Israel had disgorged the occupied lands. The EEC's declining links with Israel were noted with approval in a declaration of the Algiers summit conference later that month, which read:

> "We look forward with greater concern to the signs of understanding of our position which have begun to appear in the States of Western Europe."[1]

Individual countries within the EEC, and elsewhere, went a good deal further.

As we have already seen, France had for several years past evinced

[1] Quoted from an article entitled "Sadat wins himself strategy mandate" which appeared in the British *Guardian*, 29 November 1973.

much sympathy for the Arab cause, being the only leading Western power to condemn Israel's attack of June 1967, and imposing a strict embargo on military supplies to Israel. France subsequently supplied Mirage jets to Libya. On 8 October 1973, during the course of an interview, the French foreign minister Michel Jobert said, in reply to a questioner:

> "Can an attempt by someone to return to his own home from which he was forcibly ejected be termed an unexpected aggression?"

At the Security Council session of 8 and 9 October the French representative Louis de Guiringaud saw Israel's illegal possession of Arab lands as the chief impediment to a negotiated solution based on Resolution 242 of 1967. Again on 9 October Radio Paris referred to the way Israeli information had forfeited the confidence of European opinion, for, contrary to what the Israelis claimed, their soldiers were not invincible, neither had there been any Egyptian or Syrian collapse. France was critical of US operations in support of Tel Aviv, on 29 October pointing out that Washington had not even approached Paris for the right to use French air space, and that President Nixon had failed to consult President Pompidou in the matter of the world-wide alert of American forces which might have entailed the gravest consequences for France and Western Europe. On 5 November President Sadat's special adviser, Dr Mohammed Zayat, had cordial talks in Paris with both President Pompidou and foreign minister Jobert. Following the latter's two day visit to Tunisia, a joint Franco-Tunisian communiqué was published on 17 November stressing the need for Israeli withdrawal from the lands occupied since June 1967 and for respecting legitimate Palestinian rights. Later Michel Jobert urged the powers to think again about the composition of the proposed Geneva peace conference, which he felt could not be fully effective unless it included all the parties closely involved in the Middle East crisis, notably the entire Arab World and certain European states. As he observed in the French assembly:

> "How can one believe that the search for a lasting solution can be successful without the participation of the Arab World, which has just shown its determination at the Algiers summit?"

In Britain a parallel process was at work. To the annoyance of the Israelis and their sympathizers, the British government after the outbreak of the October war stopped the supply of spare parts for Israel's Centurion tanks. Much of the British press showed an improved understanding of the current military situation and of the longer term political and strategical factors. The London *Times* of 11 October called on Israel to consider peace with the Arabs,

> "based on a recognition that they too have strength, and strength that is likely to grow, and they have fears for their security, just as Israel has for hers."

America's world-wide nuclear alert produced grave misgivings in Britain, where it brought home to many people just how vulnerable the country was as the result of the presence on British soil of US military installations, over whose use apparently neither the British Parliament nor the British people possessed effective control. Nor were the changing accents of British public opinion attributable only to this fear or to the possible difficulties arising from the Arabs' use of their oil weapon. As the British foreign secretary, Sir Alec Douglas-Home, now pointed out in a speech to his Scottish constituents, he had over three years earlier—long before the threat to British oil supplies—made it clear that true Israeli security was not to be had from the continued occupation of Arab land.

The West German response to the war of 6 October reproduced some of the features of the French and British, inasmuch as there was resentment over the use of national facilities for the furtherance of Zionist or American policy. This came to a head when it was learnt that military supplies had been despatched from Bremerhaven in Israeli vessels without the consent of the appropriate German authorities. Thereupon the government placed an embargo on American shipments for Israel.

In the case of Japan a dominant consideration was the country's enormous reliance on Arab petroleum, for it is reckoned that Japan depends on imported oil to the extent of nearly three-quarters of its total energy requirements. We may therefore appreciate the economic imperatives prompting prime minister Tanaka's warning to Dr Kissinger on 15 November that for the future Japan's policy would be conducted independently of that of the US. At the same time Japan's minister of trade urged upon the American secretary of state, currently on a visit to Tokyo, the necessity for promptly carrying out the terms of Resolution 242. Seven days later a measure of Japan's policy reappraisal became visible through the government's exhortation to Israel to give up the areas seized as a result of the Six-Day War.

In keeping with her identification with the countries of the Third World, China had long opposed Israeli pretensions. Her abstention from Security Council voting on the two ceasefire resolutions of 22 and 23 October, and on the 25 October resolution covering the formation of the UNEF, did not in any sense imply reluctance to bring pressure to bear on Israel. Rather it was meant as an expression of China's view that the measures did not go far enough. Already on 11 October prime minister Chou En-Lai had promised his country's wholehearted support to Egypt and Syria.

Of the two superpowers, the USSR remained a firm friend. Assurances on this score were published on the morrow of the outbreak of the Fourth Arab-Israeli War, the moment when they were most needed in the context of a necessary display of world solidarity against Tel Aviv, for on 7 October *Pravda* squarely placed the blame for the fighting on Israel, while the news agency *Tass* repeated earlier demands that Israel abandon her expansionist policies and respect legitimate Palestinian rights. During the Security Council's 23 October discussions preparatory to the acceptance of Resolution 339, the Russian representative Yakov Malik denounced Israel for the manner in which she had broken the ceasefire of the previous day for the sake of military advantage. The value of the Soviet attitude during the 6 October War was acknowledged by President Sadat in his press conference of 31 October.

Before concluding our survey of the attitudes of individual countries, we must say something of American opinion, as expressed both by formal government actions and policies, and by the press and other organs of opinion. In some ways the trends visible in the totality of American opinion are among the most interesting features of the information battle waged by the Arabs and the Israelis on the world stage. Enough has been said in earlier chapters about the extent of Israel's propaganda advantage in the US to render repetition superfluous. To avoid premature assumptions then, all we need say here on the score of continuing Zionist influence is that it was too deeply embedded to subside rapidly in face of the countervailing pressures now being exerted more strongly than ever before. That the Zionist cause is still powerful in the United States is evident from the US veto on 26 July of the Security Council's draft censure of Israel for her continued presence in Arab lands, from the volume of American aid made available to Israel before the 22 October ceasefire, from President Nixon's 19 October request for Congress approval of further military assistance to the value of $2,200 million.

Nevertheless, forces working in the opposite direction, while still far from decisive, received an important impetus from the 6 October War and its aftermath. The dictates of America's global strategy and global diplomacy had already suffered from the excesses of Israeli intransigence. In the past this had threatened to advance Soviet Middle Eastern influence resulting from Russia's championship of the Arabs, and more recently it clearly endangered the US-Soviet détente. American endeavours to moderate Zionist ambition had been wrecked by the Lavon affair[2] as far back as 1954, while more recently the Israelis had thwarted the long-term aims of the Rogers Plan of 1969–70. To these irritations suffered by American policy makers at the hands of Israel has been added growing criticism in Western Europe, especially after the high-handed use of European facilities to rush supplies to Israel, and after the world-wide nuclear alert of late October. In addition there are the pressures of current US energy requirements. In the past virtually independent of Middle Eastern oil, America's petroleum consumption is increasing at such a rate that as time goes on the US must expect to obtain a large part of her additional requirements from Arab suppliers. She will therefore become increasingly dependent on Arab goodwill, and to that extent can no longer tolerate Zionist pressures. Tel Aviv knows this, and is seeking to halt a trend in American policy that could become irresistible before very long. For example, on her visit to Washington on 7 November, Mrs Meir maintained her hard line in face of US pressure on the Israelis to withdraw to the positions occupied at the time of the 22 October ceasefire. Nevertheless, the US government

[2] See p. 162.

are now inclined to resist the more uncompromising Israeli attitudes. Already on 15 August the US had supported the Security Council's censure of Israel over the forcing down five days earlier of an Iraqi Caravelle on its flight between Beirut and Baghdad. America's improved flexibility in dealing with the Arab World seems to have been encouraged by the appointment of Dr Henry Kissinger as secretary of state. From the beginning of his new assignment he has stressed his intention of not allowing his own Jewish origins to deflect him from acting strictly in accordance with what he regarded as America's true interests. It was the US which, jointly with the USSR, presented the form of the ceasefire resolutions adopted by the Security Council on 22 and 23 October. At his 25 October news conference Kissinger underlined the need for "peace with justice", and acknowledged the territorial advantages which Israel had obtained from the breach of the ceasefire. During the course of his speech of 31 October President Sadat referred to America's recent helpful attitude. This was maintained early in November, when Kissinger conducted a generally cordial series of talks with Arab leaders in Morocco, Tunisia, Egypt, Jordan, and Saudi Arabia, a mission which among its contributions to easier relations restored full diplomatic contact between Cairo and Washington.

As regards American public opinion, while avoiding excessive optimism in a situation where much of the media remains Zionist orientated, we are justified in pointing to significant improvements. These were noted on 5 November by Egypt's foreign minister Ismail Fahmy, when, on his return from Washington, he drew attention to the effects of Arab unity on the views of average Americans. Already, a few days before, the New York magazine *Newsweek* had explained Israel's acceptance of the ceasefire as attributable to the fact that she was "groggy from appalling losses", the Pentagon's preliminary assessment of casualties being "about 10,000 Israeli soldiers killed or wounded." Developing this theme, *Newsweek* in its issue a fortnight later pointed to the enormous material price which Israel had had to pay for the 6 October War, which cost her more than her budget for the whole of 1973, and which severely damaged her industry, including her tourist trade. For these reasons *Newsweek* concluded that she must seek a successful settlement.

Our survey of world reactions to the events of the autumn of 1973 reveals an enormous improvement in the state of the Arab image. The Arabs have come a long way since 1948, and even since 1967. The change results from an amalgam of different factors, and perhaps most notably from the great advance in the Arabs' handling of opinion-forming techniques, from their steadiness and reasonable demeanour in the novel situation arising out of military success and hysterical Israeli psychological warfare, from the solidarity of the Arabs, from their generous co-operation with the representatives of the international media, from their judicious employment of the oil weapon at a time of awakening realization of world energy problems.

While acclaiming the extent of this Arab achievement, as spectacular as it is well deserved, we must avoid complacency. So long as the basic conditions of the present Middle Eastern conflict endure, the information battle can never attain definitive victory. Confidence resolutely achieved must be as resolutely defended. Although temporarily disorientated, the Zionist media are still resourceful and can look to powerful external allies. Israel will be quick to exploit signs of irritation among the peoples of industrialized nations in face of discomforts inflicted by the oil shortage. Anticipating this, the Arab oil states have tried to distinguish between their customers in such a way that, as far as possible, countries friendly to their cause are not exposed to excessive hardship. In practice the mitigation cannot be complete, because friendly states may be dependent on others less friendly. For example, much of Western Europe uses refineries in Holland, a state whose pro-Israeli sympathies have earned Arab hostility. And it has to be remembered that a large proportion of the world's oil is distributed by American concerns. Moreover, shortages directly attributable to the OAPEC cutback cannot easily be separated in the public mind from a development which, while strictly speaking unrelated, is understandably seen as another difficulty emanating from the same Arab source. We refer to the increased oil prices, necessary to safeguard the value of oil revenues from global inflationary tendencies. The complexity of the oil question as a whole offers ample scope for Zionist misrepresentation.

Similar dangers threaten from some guerrilla activities. An instructive recent example was the outrage at Rome airport on 17 December, when a group of terrorists hurled bombs into a Pan Am Boeing, killing over thirty people including two Moroccan government officials, and then went on to hijack a Lufthansa Boeing. This madness was promptly condemned by Arab governments and by the PLO. But, in the emotionally charged atmosphere arising from incidents of this sort, public opinion is only too likely to ignore the proper stand of the Arab states, or simply not to be informed about it. The Zionist-influenced media may well seize on the chance for such over-simplification, distortion and concealment, so that the opprobrium attaching to criminal acts may rub off on to individual Arab governments, legitimate Palestinian agencies, and the Arab people as a whole. If the Arab cause is to retain its better world image, and to improve it, then it will need every grain of the cool-headedness, patience, respect for truth and professionalism that have served it so well during the past years and especially since 6 October 1973.

11
Peace in the Making

In their struggle for recognition and justice the Arabs have come a long way since the beginning of the century, surmounting first their own limited identity perceptions, and then the failure of others to recognize them as a single people with distinct traditions, interests and aspirations. Hand in hand with the fight for recognition went the fight against imperialism. This too has been won, as far as it related to straightforward colonialism. But it must still be waged against the more insidious imperialism of the Zionists.

At first the odds against Arab success looked overwhelming. But the Arabs rose to the challenge through their determination, their high morale, their conviction in a just cause, their steadily improving handling of the media, and their good leadership. The mistakes of the Israelis also helped, mistakes bred of arrogant over-confidence. Palestine is at last a focal point of world attention and likely to remain so. Predictable nausea at the effects of some guerrilla actions has not destroyed the Arab gains, for the world has understood that this extremist weapon is far from being an exclusive Palestinian preserve. It is realizing that terror was employed by the Zionists, coldly and with cynical calculation, many years before the appearance of the PFLP and of Black September. For practical purposes, the world's attitude may now be said to correspond with the sentiments expressed in July 1973 by the PLO's London representative, Said Hammami. Recalling how, after the British withdrawal in 1948, the Israelis had blown up his parents' home in Jaffa, he declared:

"We condemn everything that Black September has done. But we understand it. We are not criminals, but we have a duty to fight for our homeland, and we must."[1]

The widespread acceptance of this view outside the US and Israel speaks highly for the effectiveness of the Arab information services in counteracting Israeli propaganda. These services are now beginning to reap the reward of decades of devoted work, which took the form of information for truth, information for the national morale, information for the fight against colonialism, information for a better relationship with the outside world.

But impressive as they are, the reader is entitled to ask whether these achievements of the Arab media have brought the prospect of a lasting settlement any closer. To outward appearances, right up to the opening of the Geneva conference on 21 December 1973, peace still appeared to be a singularly elusive commodity in the affairs of the Middle East. Whatever their other merits, can the labours of the Arab press, radio and television, the policies and declarations of the Arab leaders, the work of official Arab spokesmen and of Arab Information Offices really be judged in the context of information for peace? Has there not perhaps been too exclusive an emphasis on the qualities of self-sacrifice, courage and military resistance? Does one really prepare for peace with constant talk of war and defiance?

Such misgivings are understandable. But they betray a limited appreciation. In the situation in which the Arabs found themselves, there were no short cuts to a settlement that would be both permanently peaceful and permanently acceptable to all parties. The interests of peace could only be served by thinking in long terms. In place of Tel Aviv's adamant refusal properly to consider the various conciliatory Arab efforts, the only sure hope was so to educate the outside world to the true facts that in due course global pressures for a more amenable Israeli attitude would become irresistible. Information for peace in the narrower sense, therefore, had to be preceded by information for truth and justice. This educative task was inevitably long, and it suffered reverses along the way, especially at the time of the Suez crisis and of the Six-Day War. To the extent that the dissemination of the truth is an essential ingredient in the struggle for lasting peace, the efforts of the Arab media have certainly been of the essence of information for peace. A similar interpretation applies

[1] Quoted in an article by Christopher Dobson in the *Sunday Telegraph*, London 15 July 1973.

to the assistance rendered by the Arab press and radio to the efforts of individual countries, in the Arab World and elsewhere, to free themselves from alien rule, because, as we saw in our introductory remarks, there can be no lasting peace while colonialism survives. Again, by their expression of solidarity with the Third World in the spirit of Bandung, the media of several Arab countries declared their refusal to be drawn into the cold war alignments of the great powers. Recognizing the perils inherent in this confrontation, they bore the pejorative overtones which attached to neutralism for much of the 1950s, and eventually had the satisfaction of seeing their stand accepted by both the leading world powers. By refusing to be drawn into quarrels which did not directly concern them, they prevented the further polarization of military power, and in that way made their contribution to the encouragement of the present détente.

Having at last begun to obtain a reasonable world hearing, the Arab media possessed one of the prerequisites for the dissemination of positive information for justice and peace. To be effective, the message must enlighten not only foreign governments, but also foreign peoples. Justice and peace can be permanently guaranteed only when world opinion is genuinely convinced of the rightness of the Arab cause, because, in these days of mass opinion, government policy, however well disposed, succeeds in proportion to its ability to *communicate* with peoples, educating opinion and reacting to it, in line with good public relations principles. What is true of individual national governments applies equally to world bodies. The guidelines suggested in our second chapter for the definition of public opinion apply just as much to world opinion as to any other kind. Thus world opinion must be formed voluntarily and not imposed by authority, even the authority of the United Nations, must take account of minority opinion, must relate to identifiable controversial issues, must be conspicuously expressed. In their approach to world opinion, the Arab media have to recognize the two-way process of good public relations. Arab information authorities have to be able accurately to gauge the prevailing world sentiments on relevant issues, and at the same time so to frame their message that it can perform its educative role in sustaining sentiments conducive to justice and peace, and in encouraging the abandonment of sentiments of the opposite tendency. Like all good public relations, the process must be conducted in a manner calculated to diffuse the maximum harmony between those responsible for the media and their audience. The process has constantly to be repeated in connection with every relevant controversial issue as it arises, so that eventually the succession of world opinions formed may develop into deep rooted international convictions.

By these means we may hope that Israel will be brought to realize the extent of her isolation from the mainstream of the world's public opinion, as well as from the majority view at the United Nations which she has hitherto ignored so flagrantly. There are grounds to hope that the process may already have begun. In the past Israel attempted to justify her uncompromising stance and territorial expansionism on the grounds of strategic necessity and the protection of vital security interests. The 6 October War showed the barrenness of this thesis, which was tenable for only so long as Israel could be tolerably sure of quickly eliminating any likely combination of Arab forces. Arab achievements in October 1973 destroyed the grounds for any confidence which Israel may have cherished on that score. *The Times* of London on 16 October carried an article by Louis Heren entitled *Israel must think again now myth of might is shattered.* Referring to recent Arab military successes, it went on to observe:

"To that extent, they have questioned the very foundation of Israeli defence thinking, the assumption that Arab troops are inferior, and always will be inferior. Given that assumption, Israel could afford to take a strong diplomatic line and hold the occupied territories with a small permanent force.

"If it no longer holds, the consequences are likely to be more serious than the losses incurred in the fighting. An Israel unwilling or unable to come to terms with her neighbours might have to become a garrison state, a modern Sparta, to ensure survival. This would be self-defeating, if history is any guide."

Israel must face up to the likelihood that, in any future trial of strength, her favourite strategy of *blitzkrieg* would give way to a war of attrition. As President Sadat pointed out when speaking on 16 October to the Peoples' Assembly, the Arabs are far better equipped than the Israelis to win such a war. A war of attrition would drain Israel's life blood, for she could hardly count on indefinite supplies from the US, in the face of a world consensus, and in a situation where America's oil and diplomatic interests argued for cordial relationships with the Arab World. Moreover, the Arabs have made it clear that they do not aim to destroy the Israelis, but only to recover lands illegally retained after the Six-Day War, and to secure the just rights of the Palestinians as accepted by Security Council Resolution 242 of 1967. Israel's true security lies in the attainment of a settlement on this basis, rather than in a policy of continual aggrandisement, which has already brought the problems and mighty expense inseparable from extended lines of communication, without providing protection against possible attack from long range missiles aimed at the Israeli heartland.

Coupled with the consciousness of isolation, the logic of the crippling economic price of the 6 October War and of improving US-Arab relations can hardly fail in time to demonstrate, to all but the most unregenerate hard-liners, the folly of the policy pursued for a generation in the name of Israel's imagined security. At that point it is surely not too much to hope that Tel Aviv may at last modify its conduct in ways conducive to a peaceful settlement. We must, however, expect the process to be slow and arduous, and to test further those qualities of patience and resolution which the Arabs have already so admirably displayed. But it seems to be the only sure way to the sort of peace worthy of the struggle, a peace both just and permanent.

In working towards this goal, the Arabs need every refinement and skill in the pursuit of good public relations and every sophisticated technique of the modern mass media. Nor can they ignore the legitimate weapons of propaganda. So long as Zionist propaganda continues to misrepresent and over-simplify key issues, and as the Zionists, notwithstanding their diminished credibility after 6 October 1973, continue to enjoy access to some of the principal international media, so long must the Arabs, in self-defence, deploy an adequate response by counter-propaganda. We saw in our third chapter that public relations and propaganda part company over the way in which the views to be disseminated are in fact formulated: public relations normally require that doctrines should first be tested by argument and discussion, whereas propaganda tends to release them in predetermined form. This short-circuiting process is not necessarily harmful, provided the message is put together honestly and with strict adherence to the whole truth. And, as we saw in the same chapter, there is an area in which public relations and propaganda tend to merge. Where the issues are either urgent, or, as is more than ever the case in our technological age, where they are highly complex, the government may have to propagate instant solutions in discharge of its overall responsibilities to the people, and not infrequently to prevent a wrong choice that would be as harmful to the national interest as it would be disastrous to public relations.

In justifying the use of propaganda, we do not appeal solely to the obvious necessity of self-defence against Zionist distortion. There may be times in the future, as there have been in the past, when governments for their own internal purposes, unrelated to the Arab–Israeli confrontation, may wish to attack individual Arab states; for example they may decide to arouse populist sentiments of aggression or xenophobia as a means of distracting national opinion away from domestic shortcomings. In such circumstances any nation so attacked has the right to resort to counter-propaganda, if only to set the record straight.

Again, propaganda may be needed to focus attention on particular issues. We touch here on what threatens to become a growing problem. With the spread of education and the accessibility of the principal media of information, it is becoming extremely difficult to hold public attention for any issue, however important in itself, which either lacks the capacity for almost continuous sensationalism, or which does not obviously impinge on the public's material interests. Public systems of education may be more comprehensive than ever before, but the quality of mass education is not yet such that publics can always be expected to distinguish between the relatively trivial and the truly important. The 1973 Watergate investigations in the US are a case in point, for, while much of the American nation appeared to be mesmerized by the revelations of the committee charged with the consideration of improper practices in high places, it largely ignored the contemporaneous visit of the Soviet leader Leonid Brezhnev in June 1973 and the latter's declaration that the Cold War was at an end. While not for a moment seeking to depreciate the importance of Watergate, which was far from being a trivial issue, one cannot help feeling that the almost exclusive popular interest which it claimed in the US may have betrayed some lack of balance. It has to be admitted too that those responsible for the US media seem to have done little enough to induce a sense of proportion. One is inclined even to question whether American thinking was conditioned by the media, or whether perhaps the media took their cue from their own market research findings in deciding what their readers, listeners and viewers wanted to know.

If ever they were faced with a comparable situation in relation to the affairs of the Middle East, the Arab media would have a duty to keep the key issues before world attention by means of strenuous propaganda. Otherwise their case would be in danger of going by default, and to that extent world opinion would receive a distorted impression of the facts. Of course, in terms of our remarks about the possibility of maintaining interest in topics with an obvious bearing on public well-being, the Arabs can expect to feature continuously in the thoughts of the typical citizen of many industrialized countries. Power cuts, talk of petrol rationing, and calls for economy in the use of heating and electric light combine to keep the Middle East well to the fore of international concern. On the one hand, this promises to guarantee the Arab cause from the sort of neglect it has suffered in the past. On the other hand, the change involves risk. As we observed in the previous chapter, Zionist propaganda will have opportunities for exploiting world attention by falsely laying on the Arabs the blame for inconveniences and shortages. That the Arabs are aware of this danger is evident from their highly responsible use of the oil weapon, and from their care in emphasising and indeed practically demonstrating that it will not be used frivolously or indiscriminately. All the same, this battle, like the battle for confidence, has to be waged incessantly. Vigilance and imagination are called for from all those in any way concerned with the projection of the global Arab image.

In addition to the efforts of the Arab media to hold and educate world opinion, other factors may be expected to subserve the cause of peace. The Rogers Plan of 1969–70 raised hopes of a less uncritical

American support of Israel. A new American susceptibility to Arab attitudes concerning Palestine seems likely to develop in proportion to American realization of the future need for Arab oil. Dr Henry Kissinger's diplomatic activities following the 6 October War indicate a timely accession of realism by the US. Israel's occupation of Jerusalem evokes western misgivings of another sort, particularly in view of the threat to the historic parts of the old city at the hands of insensitive Israeli building developers. Alarm on this score is not confined to practising Christians. It became deeper after the destruction of Jerusalem's Al-Aqsa Mosque on 21 August 1969. The criticism of Israel by Christian leaders has gone beyond matters relating to Jerusalem. The Pope, for example, condemned the Israeli raid of 28 December 1968 on Beirut. Something of a rift between the Israeli leaders and much Catholic opinion is suggested by the following report from AFP Milan dated 3 July 1971:

> "In an interview with the Italian newspaper *Corriere della Sera*, Eban stressed that this country considers the Judaization and unification of Jerusalem a fact that everyone must accept with joy, and that the question of partitioning it as was the case prior to the June war is not subject to discussion at all. He also refused the idea of internationalizing Jerusalem, and expressed his regret to the criticism directed by the Vatican and Jordan concerning the process of the Judaization of Jerusalem."

The influence of the Vatican extends far beyond members of the Catholic Church. Although it has avoided strident denunciation of Israel, its measured criticism undoubtedly fulfils some of the functions of leadership in the formulation of world opinion. It is not unreasonable to expect similar acts of leadership from other sources in intensifying international pressures on behalf of eventual peace, and of its prerequisite of a just settlement of the Palestinian issue. The career of Gamal Abdel Nasser illustrates the incalculable contribution of which dedicated and honest leadership is capable. The career of Charles de Gaulle during the Algerian war shows how far one man can sometimes transform the views of an entire nation. Where the leader enjoys a reputation for probity, and already inspires widespread trust—the case with Pope Paul VI, President Nasser, and

General de Gaulle—uncommitted opinion is at least predisposed to listen to what he has to say. Hopefully this tendency may in the future encourage a more discriminatory attitude among those sections of world opinion which at present have to try to make sense of a veritable surfeit of news and views.

Even so, the brunt of the struggle for peace continues to fall on the Arab media. They have shown care and imagination in explaining the reasons for change, for instance in the matter of Egypt's agrarian reforms, and thereby have given proof of their understanding of the conservatism which operates in the processes through which opinion is formed. For this reason, they are unlikely to give way to undue disappointment, much less despair, if at times the pace of international support seems slower than circumstances warrant. Old attitudes die hard. Even in countries generally favourable to the Arabs, the findings of public opinion polls do not always accurately reflect the direction of official policy. This fact reminds us of the public relations duty which all governments have to enlighten their peoples in the matter of unfamiliar and often complicated components of their foreign policy. We must also avoid placing too literal an interpretation on the findings of public opinion polls. Their message is subject to distortion from the manner in which the questions are worded, while the answers need to be related to earlier opinion diagnoses on the same issues. Public opinion polls are often more useful in illuminating trends rather than as an indicator of the exact state of opinion on a given issue at a particular moment in time. Nonetheless, some of the polls conducted over the period of the 6 October War are significant. They contained the salutary warning that, although the Arabs possess a much better image as far as governments and official bodies are concerned, at the grass roots level the Arabs still encounter hostility or cold neutrality. For example 47 per cent of Americans came out in support of Israel, as against 6 per cent in support of the Arabs, in response to the Gallup Poll Institute's question on the Fourth Arab-Israeli War: "Do you feel inclined in this crisis to sympathize more with the Israelis or with the Arabs?" Before hazarding any conclusions about the significance of this poll, we must note that the questions dealt in inclinations to sympathize with one side or the other, rather than in definitive opinions. Also that a high proportion of those questioned either declined to express a view (22 per cent) or were undecided (25 per cent). Allowing for these qualifications, the fact remains that getting on for half the views canvassed revealed an inclination in favour of Israel. As the Egyptian newspaper *Al-Ahram* put it, the above figures

" . . . reveal to us how the Zionist propaganda is still deep rooted in the outside world. Thus we see many western governments, being more aware of the facts and of their interests, change their attitudes towards the Arabs faster than the ordinary citizen does, the latter being still influenced for twenty-five years now by the vestiges of the Zionist propaganda.

"The poll also reveals to us, as Arab countries and as a League of Arab nations, that a considerable activity still lies ahead."

Al-Ahram's comment is a good example of the realism characteristic of much contemporary Arab information. Among those responsible for the Arab media there is now widespread recognition of the fact that personal conviction in the justness of the cause, itself utterly indispensable to success, is not enough when it comes to projecting the message abroad in terms capable of enlisting sympathy, good repute and active support. Proper allowance must be made for the various components of outside opinion, for the well nigh automatic tendency found among all peoples to react to new situations in the context of pre-existing attitudes, assumptions, fears and prejudices.

The first major achievement of the Arab media was to instil a deep conviction among the Arab nations as to their common identity and the rightness of their claims. This conviction gradually communicated itself to the outside world, at first largely in terms of the struggle against colonialism, and later in terms of the new imperialism of Zionist Israel. Given a predictable maintenance of watchful dedication, there is now a good prospect for consolidating and extending the improved global Arab image. The Arabs can do this by building on their hard won expertise in the presentation of their case, by preserving their reputation for reliability, by continuing to radiate a quiet confidence and unity founded on real achievements particularly during and after the 6 October War. It is upon these facts, and also on the proven failure of Israel's past aggressions to safeguard Israel's security interests, that we justify our cautious optimism that the Middle East may look forward eventually to the just peace which has too long eluded it. Such a peace will surely point the way to that genuine international accord on which the hopes of mankind depend.

Index

Index